Baudelaire · Rimbaud · Verlaine

SELECTED VERSE AND PROSE POEMS

BAUDELAIRE
RIMBAUD
VERLAINE

Selected Verse and Prose Poems

EDITED, WITH AN INTRODUCTION, BY

Joseph M. Bernstein

A CITADEL PRESS BOOK
Published by Carol Publishing Group

Acknowledgements

This collection is made possible by the generous prermissions extended by the holders of copyright listed below.

ALBERT BONI. The Arthur Symons translations of *FLOWERS OF EVIL* and *Prose Poems* by Charles Baudelaire.

GERTRUDE HALL. The Gertrude Hall translations of *Selected Verse* by Paul Verlaine.

THE HOGARTH PRESS. LONDON. The J. Norman Cameron translation of *Illuminations* by Arthur Rimbaud.

NEW DIRECTIONS. The Louise Varèse translations of *A Season in Hell* and *Prose Poems* from "Illuminations" by Arthur Rimbaud.

SAMUEL ROTH. The Arthur Symons translation of poems from "In Parallel Fashion" by Paul Verlaine.

Carol Publishing Group Edition - 1993

A Citadel Press Book
Published by Carol Publishing Group
Citadel Press is a registered trademark of Carol Communications, Inc.
Editorial Offices: 600 Madison Avenue, New York, NY 10022
Sales & Distribution Offices: 120 Enterprise Avenue, Secaucus, NJ 07094
In Canada: Canadian Manda Group, P.O. Box 920, Station U, Toronto, Ontario, M8Z 5P9, Canada

Queries regarding rights and permissions should be addressed to:
Carol Publishing Group, 600 Madison Avenue, New York, NY 10022

Manufactured in the United States of America
ISBN 0-8065-0196-0

15   14   13   12   11   10   9   8

Carol Publishing Group books are available at special discounts for bulk purchases, for sales promotions, fund raising, or educational purposes. Special editions can also be created to specifications. For details contact: Special Sales Department, Carol Publishing Group, 120 Enterprise Ave., Secaucus, NJ 07094

Contents

Prose Poems

ARTHUR RIMBAUD

A Season In Hell

Prose Poems from "Illuminations"

Illuminations

PAUL VERLAINE

Selected Verse

Introduction

IF WE WERE TO ASK AN ENGLISHMAN to name the single greatest poet in English literature, his answer would unquestionably be: Shakespeare. Similarly, a German upon questioning would reply: Goethe; an Italian, Dante. And an American could surely make a good case for Walt Whitman. These men are more than national poets—they are universal figures, expressing the genius of their age, their country, their language, and their culture.

But who is the greatest poet in French literature? Here we get a variety of answers, for there is no one French poet who towers so high above his fellows as to leave no doubt about his unique pre-eminence. There are many great French poets: François Villon, Pierre Ronsard, Jean Racine, Alfred de Vigny, Victor Hugo, to cite but a few across the centuries. Some years ago the contemporary French writer, André Gide, was asked who, in his opinion, was *the* outstanding poet of France. He answered: "Victor Hugo, alas!" Admiring the powerful sweep and indefatigable eloquence of Victor Hugo, "the sonorous echo" of the 19th century in prose and verse, we cannot share Gide's "precious" aesthetic dismay. Nevertheless, we have in mind not Hugo but one of his contemporaries, Charles Baudelaire, as our candidate for the first poet in the republic of French letters.

Increasingly of late, lovers of literature have come to recognize the true stature of Baudelaire. In the eighty years since his death, his reputation both in France and abroad has grown apace. His life spanned the years 1821 to 1867; yet he is strikingly "modern" in every sense of the term. Stendhal, the French novelist, predicted around 1830 that his novels would be understood in fifty years; and as he had foretold, his fame grew after 1880. In the case of Baudelaire, no such prediction was forthcoming; yet it is a fact that in his own time he was little understood or completely misunderstood. Writing to his mother in July, 1857, he declared: "This book, *Flowers of Evil*, . . . is clothed in cold and sinister beauty, and was created with rage and patience. Besides, the proof of its positive value lies in all the evil that has been said of it. The book infuriates people. . . . People refuse me everything: power of invention and even a knowledge of French. I despise all those imbeciles, for I know that this volume, with its defects and its qualities, will make its way in the minds of the literary public beside the best work of Victor Hugo, of Théophile Gautier, and even of Byron." In our own day we have begun to make up for the neglect and hostility which Baudelaire suffered among most of his contemporaries.

Now it is true that Baudelaire is not a world poet, a *summum*, in the same sense as Shakespeare, Dante, or Goethe. He is not on their lofty, all-encompassing level, "out-topping knowledge." To assert that would be to push one's admiration to the edge of idolatry. Yet as a poet of love, a master in depth, a craftsman in the sensuous and the sensual, a devotee of the Cult of Beauty, a practitioner in what has been aptly called the Alchemy of the Word, an inexorable self-analyst and explorer of the sub-conscious in poetry, a creator of images that fire the senses, quicken the heart, and illumine the mind, Baudelaire has few if any peers in the entire roll-call of modern poets. Not to know him is to deprive oneself of a pleasure as rare as it is indispensable to any real understanding of the aims and direction of modern literature.

Wherein lies his greatness? Why do we insist on stressing his modernity, his direct and unusually vibrant appeal to modern man? There are many reasons: here let us state the most important ones.

In the first half of the 19th century, the leading poets of Europe were Romantics. Romanticism placed emphasis on sentimentality and wayward inspiration, on meetings in the moonlight, disappointed love, solitary walks in the woods, and nostalgic trysts by the shores of lonely lakes. There was in the poems of Romanticism a certain softness, a tendency to histrionics, self-pity, self-dramatization, and emotional over-indulgence. As a result, rhetoric was often substituted for emotional truth, tearfulness for tragedy. The idea of escape, escape either in time or space—"anywhere out of the world"—prevailed. Baudelaire, whose *Flowers of Evil* appeared in 1857, travelled a different road from these practitioners of Romanticism. Where they sentimentalized, he was disciplined, rigorous, and astringent in his self-analysis. Where they dissolved into soft, loose, vaporous tears, he cut through to the hard core of things—the "tragic sense of life," which great artists of all times have expressed. All through his *Flowers of Evil,* his prose-poems, and his *Intimate Journals,* this constant self-scrutiny and self-dissection have a "modern" ring. They throw light on the central problem of the artist in our time. At one point in his diaries, for example, Baudelaire confesses his purpose: "To be a great man and a saint every day for oneself." On another occasion he invokes the aid of "souls of those I have loved, souls of those I have sung, fortify me, sustain me, banish from me the lies and obscuring mists of the world; and you, Lord God, grant me the grace to compose a few beautiful verses which will prove to me that I am not the lowliest of men and that I am not inferior to those I despise." In his poem, *A Journey to Cythera,* he suddenly cries out at the end:

> In thine isle, O Venus, I found only upthrust
> A Calvary symbol whereon mine Image hung.
> —Give me, Lord God! to look upon that dung,
> My body and my heart, without disgust!

This mixture of love and hate, of attraction and repulsion; this antithesis of the sublime and mean, the radiant and banal; this intermingling and interpenetration of good and evil, heaven and hell, mark Baudelaire out as a *homo duplex,* a divided man often at odds with himself and with life but always striving to fuse these conflicting elements into a poetic synthesis. This ambivalence is one of the familiar hallmarks of the poet in our century.

This dualism is strikingly evident in his Cult of Beauty. As he asks in his *Hymn to Beauty:* "Do you come from high heaven or from the abyss, O beauty? . . ." Always a conscious artist, polishing and re-polishing his verses, a superb master of the prose poem and an art-critic of rare insight and understanding, Baudelaire never wavered in his devotion to the ideal of beauty. He described himself as an "Icarus burned by his love of the beautiful"; and in a letter written to the notary, Ancelle, on whom he depended for funds, he asserted: "Literature must come before everything else, before my hunger, before my pleasure, before my mother," and he underlined these words in heavy ink. To Baudelaire, "the study of the Beautiful is a duel in which the artist cries out with fear before he is vanquished."

In his notes for the preface of the second edition of *Flowers of Evil,* he jotted down some of the stages in the conscious process by which he sought to achieve beauty in his art:

"How, by a determined series of efforts, the artist can achieve proportionate originality;

"How poetry borders on music by a prosody the roots of which go deeper into the human soul than is indicated by any classical theory;

"That French poetry possesses a mysterious and misunderstood prosody, as do the Latin and English languages;

"Why any poet who does not know exactly how many rhymes there are for each word is incapable of expressing any idea whatever . . ." Proceeding thus, he aimed at a combination of the senses: sight, touch, hearing, and smell, and succeeded in creating what might be called plastic harmonies. In this, he was the great precursor of Symbolism in art; and in his famous sonnet *Correspondences,* he formulated and summed up this aesthetic creed:

> Nature is a Temple where we live ironically
> In the midst of forests filled with dire confusions;
> Man, hearing confused words, passes symbolically
> Under the eyes of the birds watching his illusions.
>
> Like distant echoes in some tenebrous unity,
> Perfumes and colors are mixed in strange profusions,

Vast as the night they mix inextricably
With seas unsounded and with dawn's delusions.

And there are the perfect perfumes of the Flesh,
That are as green as the sins in the Serpent's mesh,
And others as corrupt as our own senses,
Having the strange expansion of things infinite,
Such as amber, musk, benzoin and sweet incenses,
That seize the spirit and the senses exquisite.

Baudelaire, in the words of the American critic, James Huneker, is "a master of harmonic undertones. He carved rather than sang; the plastic arts spoke to his soul." But his plasticity is resonant and alive, not remote and lifeless like a marble monument. His poems fill us with their passion and their immediacy.

Sensuality in Baudelaire's poetry is complex and evocative, extending in depth and forging images that suddenly light up the reader's mind. He is a master in kindling associations: one sense calls to mind a host of other sensory reactions, and the reader is carried along as the poet plunges into "the depths of the unknown in order to find the *New!*" It is like a chain-reaction in which one sense gives rise to and merges with another. Here too the characteristic dualism is at work. You will not find in his poems sensuality for the sake of sensuality, cheap vulgarity, mere lubricity, or an itching desire to invite a lascivious leer. On the contrary, Baudelaire explores the voluptuous in order to attain the spiritual. He roams through the entire luxuriant world of the senses in order to know himself better and to analyze more completely his own shortcomings. The sense of solitude is ever with him—but not in the blurred, misty manner so characteristic of the Romantics. As he notes in his *Intimate Journals:* "After every debauchery one feels lonelier and more abandoned."

This was particularly true of his love-affair with Jeanne Duval, "the brown-skinned Enchantress." The tall "dark Venus" was not remarkable for her beauty, intelligence, or even kindness. Yet she had a hold over Baudelaire throughout most of his adult life despite her infidelities and the excessive demands for money and attention she made on him. His letters to his mother are pathetically revealing in this respect. On several occasions he declares that he has finally broken with Jeanne. Thus in March 1852, he writes: "I am most anxious to buy some linen, in which I am almost totally lacking, and to send some money to Jeanne . . . I shall keep twenty francs for myself, and I shall send her twenty francs, imploring her to try and hold on. I have forbidden her to come and see me here; an odious sense of pride made me do so. I do not want them [i.e. his friends] to see a woman who was once mine, beautiful, healthy and elegant, in *poverty, ill and badly dressed.*" Four years later he wrote, again to his mother: "My liaison, my liaison of fourteen years with Jeanne, is broken. I did all that was humanly possible to prevent the rupture. This tearing apart, this struggle, has lasted fifteen days. Jeanne replies imperturbably that nothing can be done with my character, and that anyhow I shall myself some day thank her for her resolution. There you see the gross bourgeois wisdom of women. For myself, I know that, whatever agreeable happening comes to me, joy, money or vanity, I shall always regret this woman." Nevertheless, the liaison continued for years after this letter was written. What did he see in her? By what alchemy of the imagination did Baudelaire transmute his Jeanne Duval into a paragon of beauty, a goddess of sensuality beyond compare? In himself was the unsatisfied desire, the unassuaged voluptuousness, the quest for satiety which he futilely sought in Jeanne Duval. One has only to read such poems as *The Jewels, Thee I Adore, Exotic Perfume,* and *Sed Non Satiata* to see how Baudelaire was in the grip of an ambivalent passion of love and hate.

Baudelaire's sensuality was the very opposite of lustful sensation-mongering. It was the avenue along which he travelled in his difficult search for moral integration and equilibrium. Thus when his *Flowers of Evil* was condemned by a French court and several individual poems in the collection banned, he protested vigorously against the ban, writing to the judge who tried the case: "No one, any more than I, could imagine that a book characterized by such ardent and eloquent spirituality as *Les Fleurs du Mal* could be the object of proceedings, or rather the cause of a misunderstanding." Indeed, Baudelaire wrote to the Secretary of State at that time: *"I do not feel guilty at all.* I am, on the contrary, very proud of having written a book that inspires only fear and horror of evil."

One of the poems specifically condemned was *Femmes Damnées* (Damned Women). This study of Lesbian love ends, however, on an outspokenly moral note. Having painted a dramatic picture of the two lovers, Hippolyte and Delphine, the poet concludes:

> Descend, descend, Lesbians lamentable
> Descend the way that leads to hell infernal;
> Plunge in a deep gulf where crime's inevitable,
> Flagellated by a wind driven from the skies eternal,
>
> Where all your torments, and for all the ages,
> Mad shadows, never at the end of your desires,
> Shall never satisfy your furious rages,
> And your chastisement be born of loveless fires.
>
>   .   .   .
>
> Far from the living world, in condemnation,
> Wander as wolves after a ghostly vanity;
> Make of your destiny, souls disordered, your damnation,
> And escape the duplicity of your insanity!

Literally translated, the final verse is even more explicit: "Flee the Infinite that you bear within yourselves!" The two women are damned because they flee the Infinite they bear within themselves. It was this Infinite for which Baudelaire ceaselessly strove as he sought with artistic conscience to fuse the spiritual with the sensual.

II

The bare facts of Baudelaire's life shed at least some light on the intense "duel with the Beautiful" in which he engaged throughout his existence, a duel which ended grimly with the poet a helpless paralytic, victim of a long-developing syphilis, barely able to stammer a few words like a child in early infancy. He was born in Paris on April 9, 1821, the son of a father aged 60 and a mother aged 26. His father, a man of artistic tastes and broad learning, introduced him at an early age to the various museums and cultural monuments of Paris. But he died in 1827; and Baudelaire's mother hastened to re-marry in 1828, her husband a rising young officer named Aupick, destined later under Napoleon III to become a general, a senator, and ambassador of France in Madrid.

Those who have studied problems of heredity may find matter for reflection in the disparity in age between Baudelaire's father and mother; those more concerned with problems of environment will note that while a young boy Baudelaire reacted violently against his stepfather. Like Hamlet, he felt doubly wounded that his mother, whom he loved, should have re-married with what seemed to him to be unseemly haste. Hence when he graduated from the *lycée*, he refused to heed his stepfather's injunction that he prepare himself for a career, preferably in the diplomatic service. He resolved instead to devote himself exclusively to literature. Already restless, he lived a carefree, dissolute life and soon squandered away much of the money inherited from his father. Alarmed and not a little incensed, General Aupick prevailed upon him to take a long sea-voyage. Leaving France in June 1841, Baudelaire journeyed around Cape Horn and went as far as the Isle of Mauritius in the Indian Ocean, where he spent some three weeks. This small island, with its tropical fauna and flora, its exotic and languorous perfumes, its palm-trees and sun-drenched landscapes, left a deep impression on the young poet. Many pieces that appeared years later in *Flowers of Evil* attest to the vividness of these impressions. It is also probable that his brief stay brought him in contact with attractive native women of color, thus foreshadowing his later liaison with the octoroon Jeanne Duval.

Baudelaire returned to Paris in 1842. Having reached the age of 21, he came into possession of the bulk of his inherited fortune. Living extravagantly in a circle of artists and writers, many of them out-and-out Bohemians, he soon ran through most of the money. His family thereupon sought to curb his spendthrift mode of living by placing him under the legal tutelage of a plodding, unimaginative notary.

But despite the outward frivolousness of his life, despite his dandyism, Baudelaire never forsook his first and overpowering passion: literature. He labored painstakingly to perfect his style. He made his literary début in 1845 as an art-critic: his critical evaluation of such diverse painters as Delacroix, Daumier, Constantin Guys, Manet, Courbet, and others reveal him as a critic of the first magnitude. At about this time, too, he began his translation of the works of Edgar Allan Poe, a task that occupied him intermittently for seventeen years and is a model in the field. As early as 1850, he announced the forthcoming publication of a volume of poems. It bore several titles before it finally saw the light of day: first *Limbos*, then *The Lesbians*, and finally *The Flowers of Evil*.

Baudelaire continued to write: translations of Thomas de Quincey, art-criticism, another corrected edition of *Flowers of Evil* in 1861, prose-poems, and his prose-work, *Artificial Paradises*. But in 1860 he suffered an initial stroke. His body was beginning to disintegrate: long years of reckless living, excessive use of alcohol and other artificial stimulants, including even a go at hashish and opium, had ravaged his body. He had early contracted a venereal disease for which there was then no medical cure, and so he was doomed to a long-drawn-out physical agony. He began to suffer mental crises, passing from deep depression to exaltation. The idea of suicide occurred to him on several occasions. As he confessed, he felt pass over him "the wind of the wing of madness." At forty, he was a physical wreck of a man, on the verge of insanity and paralysis. His letters to his mother during this period are heart-rending: incessant pleas for money, an almost feverish desire to write more poetry and more books, and foreknowledge of his impending paralysis. In a desperate endeavor to earn some money, he went in 1864 to Belgium where he delivered a number of lectures. They were all failures, the Belgian public receiving him with hostility and disdain. Instead of fleeing such a decidedly unfriendly environment, he stayed on and on, unable any longer to make any firm decisions for himself. In 1864, he suffered a second stroke at Namur; and in July 1866 he was finally brought back to Paris, hopelessly paralyzed. He lived on for another year in this tragic twilight zone of mental obscurity and complete physical helplessness. Then on August 31, 1867, death came to him as a release.

So died a man who in his devotion to literature, in his unswerving probity as a writer, in his constant self-analysis, in his awareness of the "tragic sense of life" was a precursor and a shaper of the modern spirit in literature. Most of the important currents and tendencies in the poetry of our time find their roots and inspiration in Baudelaire. He gave French poetry, just emerging from the sentimental effusions and prolixities of some poets in the Romantic school, a stamp and a direction that are still in evidence among the best of the contemporary French poets. Beyond national boundaries, Baudelaire has become a world poet, profoundly influencing such diverse trends as Parnassianism, Symbolism, Impressionism, Imagism, and Surrealism. Like the great artists he evokes in his poem *The Beacons,* Baudelaire too is

> . . . a lighthouse lit with sacred fire for the perilous
> Sailors that shed in the storms for their sins their blood!

And like them too he is one of the

> . . . Spirits of all our Sages
> That give us signs of our own dignity.

III

Late in 1865, a "little" magazine, *L'Art,* carried in three numbers a critical article praising the poetry of Baudelaire. The author of the article was a young poet named Paul Verlaine. Baudelaire read the essay and on March 5, 1866 wrote about it to his mother in the following vein:

> There is talent among the younger men, but how much folly; and what exaggerations and youthful fatuity. For some years I have surprised, here and there, imitations and tendencies which alarmed me. I know nothing more compromising than imitators, and I love nothing so well as being alone. But that is not possible, and it seems that there is now a *school of Baudelaire.*

There was a *school of Baudelaire*, but not in the precise or somewhat critical sense that Baudelaire indicated in this letter.

Two of the outstanding French poets of the latter half of the 19th century, Verlaine (1844–1896) and Arthur Rimbaud (1854–1891), were not only deeply influenced by their predecessor but by a striking coincidence rich in overtones their two lives were intimately and violently intertwined. Perhaps it may be said of Verlaine and Rimbaud that each carries forward a different latent aspect of Baudelaire. Despite varying temperaments and genius, all three have marked affinities.

Rimbaud carries to its logical conclusion the Baudelairian preoccupation with the world of the Unconscious and with the concept of the poet as a magician or alchemist in words. This remarkably brilliant boy burst forth in French letters at the age of 16—at a moment of national humiliation and despair for his country, decisively defeated in 1870 by the Prussia of Bismarck and torn by civil strife. Three years later, at 19, he brusquely turned his back on literature, never to write another book. Then he embarked on a series of amazing adventures that took him to various places in Europe, Asia, and Africa, including remote spots in Abyssinia where often he was the first European white man the inhabitants had ever seen. He tried his hand at a dozen or more occupations and professions: indeed the only calling he seemed to neglect was literature, the field in which he had already demonstrated his prodigious talents. How can we explain this disavowal? What accounts for this abdication from the literary life for a life of raw, undiluted, almost naked action? The young man who, in the words of one of his biographers "lived in three years the literary evolution of modern times," later became a gun-runner, an explorer, and a rubber-trader, and wrote that his one ambition was "to have at least one son whom I could spend the rest of my life bringing up according to my own ideas, cultivating and arming him with the completest education that one can get in this age, and whom I could see become a famous engineer, powerful and rich through science." Is this flight from literature something unique, simply one man's solution of his personal predicament?

Or is it rather a symbol, a portentous symbol perhaps, of the predicament of the modern poet? Flight from literature, flight from Christianity, flight from France, flight from Western civilization. Not a flight to evade or escape reality but rather to confront and master it. This was a gesture of resolute will not of cowardice or instability. As Rimbaud himself, in a letter to his sister, wrote: "I could not go on, I would have gone insane—and then . . . it was bad."

Arthur Rimbaud was born in 1854 in Charleville, a French town near the Belgian border. His father was an army officer who later deserted his wife and children; his mother was a strict disciplinarian who found in her stubborn, self-willed son a temperament not unlike her own. At the age of 8, Rimbaud was writing verse: he combined an amazing precocity for literature with a wild and headstrong taste for adventure. On several occasions he violently quarrelled with his mother, after which he left home and wandered like a vagabond through the streets of Paris, Brussels and other cities in France and Belgium.

Like Baudelaire, Rimbaud throughout his writings manifested a deep humanitarian sympathy with the poor and downtrodden. Moreover, it is interesting to note that the younger poet first became acquainted with *The Flowers of Evil* during this period of restlessness. In a letter written in May 1871 to a friend, Rimbaud exclaimed: "Baudelaire is the first seer, king of poets, a *real God!*"

His inner turmoil found political expression in the midst of the Franco-Prussian War. After the crushing defeat of France, revolutionary sentiments rose among the common people. Rimbaud on his own went from his native town of Charleville to Paris, where he served briefly with the people's army during the popular uprising known as the Paris Commune. He left Paris abruptly, however, when the fighting was still in progress and returned to his mother's house. The motives for his departure are obscure. His revolt against bourgeois morality, which for a short-lived period had expressed itself in his participation in the Paris Commune, now found expression on the one hand in his concentrated, almost apocalyptic writing and on the other in a fitful personal life, during which he completely neglected his appearance and at times almost starved to death.

In 1871, he wrote his now-famous poem, *The Drunken Boat:*

> I, trembling at the mutter, fifty leagues from me
> Of rutting Behemoths, the turbid Maelstrom's threats,
> Spinning a motionless and blue eternity
> I long for Europe, land of ancient parapets. . .

He sent a copy of it to Paul Verlaine who, not knowing that the author was a youth of seventeen, urged him to return to Paris. He did so; and thus began a friendship with the older poet which was not without sordid, even melodramatic qualities. Their joint *sortie*, with its feverish homosexual passion, its escapades, and its emotional abnormalities, lasted for some thirteen months: it ended in Brussels in 1873 when Verlaine tried—he made two attempts—to kill Rimbaud who had grown disgusted with the former's drunken orgies interspersed with accesses of religious fervor. That same year, returning to his mother's house in Charleville, he published his *Season in Hell*, a unique and daring contribution to world literature. It was the first and last volume he personally published.

As we have noted, Rimbaud abandoned literature at 19 for a life of action. He studied foreign-languages and mastered a number of them. He became a language-teacher in Stuttgart, Germany; then a circus-attendant; and, making his way on foot to Italy, a dockworker in Leghorn. In 1875, Verlaine, just released from prison, had come to visit him in Stuttgart. Of this meeting, their last, Rimbaud wrote to an old friend: "Verlaine arrived here the other day pawing a rosary . . . Three hours later he had denied his God and started the 98 wounds of Our Lord bleeding again."

Enlisting in the Dutch Army in 1876, Rimbaud was sent to Indonesia. He soon deserted and made his way back to Europe. Then he found work in the quarries on the island of Cyprus; and finally he came to Africa, where he was to spend some eleven years of his life as a trader, smuggler, geographer, explorer, and dealer in gold, ivory, coffee, perfumes, and rice. Living among the native tribes in the Ogaden region of Abyssinia, he wrote detailed reports of his travels for the sober publications of the French Geographical Society. He even became a kind of unofficial white chieftain and represented France in negotiations with the Abyssinian King Menelik. He occupied a large house in Harrar with the native-girl, Djami, and led a relatively prosperous existence. But his physique was already undermined: he had contracted syphilis in Africa and the effects were beginning to tell on him. Finally, early in 1891, a leg-injury he had incurred became aggravated and he was forced to leave Abyssinia for Europe to undergo a surgical operation. But it was too late: he landed later in 1891 at Marseilles where his right leg was amputated; and that same year he died in a hospital there.

At his death on November 10, 1891, Rimbaud was already a legendary figure, particularly among the young school of Symbolist writers. In 1886, Verlaine had published what he thought was a posthumous edition of Rimbaud's poetry, *Illuminations.* These poems attracted widespread interest, especially *The Drunken Boat* and the sonnet, *Vowels,* which became one of the "sacred texts" of Symbolism.

In the preface to his *Prose-Poems,* Baudelaire wrote that he had dreamt of the "miracle of a poetic prose, musical without rhythm and rhyme, flexible enough and harsh enough to take the mould of the lyric impulses of the soul, the variations in mood and dreams of the poetic temperament, the agitations of the conscience." In his *Season in Hell,* a veiled allegory of his tragic adventure with Verlaine yet much more than autobiography, Rimbaud sought to achieve this "miracle." He wanted to give words a new intensity, a new imagery; he was looking for a new insight into the heart of things. One of the sections is entitled "Alchemy of the Word" and in it Rimbaud, "finding sacred the disorder of his mind," seeks to make himself the Seer, the Visionary. "I say that one must be a *visionary*—that one must make oneself a

VISIONARY. The poet makes himself a *visionary* through a long, immense and reasoned *derangement of all the senses."*
Thirsting to "possess truth in a body and a soul" he wrote:

> I dreamed crusades, unrecorded voyages of discovery, republics without a history, religious wars hushed up, revolutions of customs, the displacements of races and continents: I believed in sorcery of every sort.
>
> I invented the color of vowels—A black, E white, I red, O blue, U green.—I regulated the form and the movement of every consonant, and with instinctive rhythms I prided myself on inventing a poetic language accessible some day to all the senses. I reserved all rights of translation.
>
> At first it was an experiment. I wrote silences. I wrote the night. I recorded the inexpressible. I fixed frenzies in their flight.

In our own day, the Surrealists, consciously cultivating the world of dreams and exploring the uncharted depths of the Unconscious in their hunt for new images and new thrills, look upon Arthur Rimbaud as their spiritual begetter. In this they are right —he is their master. But they offer no satisfactory answer to the enigma posed by Rimbaud's abrupt exit from literature at the age of 19. Self-intoxicated, they have substituted for Rimbaud's pure tragicness and verbal alchemy a pattern of posturings, an ingrown cult of the outlandish, a snobbish disdain for life which ends up in the quicksands of frivolousness and sterility. There is something else: their own literary forebear may have sought the answer which they themselves are so eager to shun. The latest evidence about Rimbaud's life between 1873 and 1880, the year in which he left Europe for good, indicates that he stopped writing because he felt that he was on the wrong road. He tried to retrace his steps and, turning his back on the precipices of the unreal, confront and describe the real world. If this be true, and the English critic, Cyril Connolly, has furnished interesting evidence in this connection, it offers at least a partial answer to Rimbaud's sudden abandonment of literature.

IV

Paul Verlaine represents in his poetry another and quite different projection of Baudelaire. In Verlaine, everything is acute sensitivity; lyric effusion; clear and subtly nuanced sensation and emotion; momentary transport of the senses, then contrition; indulgence and exaltation, then repentance and strongly avowed Catholic faith. Here there is no delving into the Unconscious, no soundings in depth but lucidity, surface brilliance, and immediacy. It is no accident that most of Verlaine's poems are short, evanescent, almost fugitive pieces, emotions caught on the wing and then soaring into space again. Modern musicians, especially such French composers as Debussy, Ravel, Fauré, and Reynaldo Hahn, have set many of Verlaine's lyrics to music. Verlaine is, if anything, a Symbolist in poetry. Baudelaire in his sonnet, *Correspondences*, provided a theory for this school in poetry; but Verlaine has given perhaps the best definition of Symbolism in his poem, *Art Poétique*. Here he asks for "music above all else" and writes:

> For we seek the nuance,
> Not color, just the nuance
> Oh! the nuance alone
> Joins dream with dream and flute with horn.

In this poem too is the line that became the battle-cry of the Symbolist poets: "Take rhetoric and wring its neck!"

Verlaine's life was a storm-tossed one in which this gifted creator of short, almost short-winded, lyrics alternated between drunken excesses and religious pleas for forgiveness and absolution. Two symbols seem to dominate his life: absinthe, the "green fairy" as he called it, and the confessional of the Catholic Church. Sin and the consciousness of sin; guilt and the washing away of guilt. In his own words:

> What have you done, O you that weep
> In the glad sun—
> Say, with your youth, you man that weep,
> What have you done?

He was born in Metz in 1844, the son of an army officer who had fought under Napoleon. Educated in Paris, he began to work in the office of an insurance company but soon left to devote himself exclusively to literature. His first volume of poems—he published 18 in all—was *Poèmes Saturniens* (1866), in which he showed the influence of Baudelaire but more immediately that of the Parnassian School of Leconte de Lisle. During the troubled war years of 1870–1871, his personal behavior involved him in difficulties with the authorities and he was forced to leave France. He was already an addict of the potent *liqueur*, absinthe. Although married, he brought the young Rimbaud into his household and began with him a period of dissolute wandering in many cities in France, England, and Belgium. Their lurid relationship almost ended in tragedy in Belgium when, as we have seen, Verlaine fired a shot at his young friend but missed. This marked a rupture between the two poets and Verlaine spent two years in prison at Mons for his attempt on Rimbaud's life. His confinement made him profoundly religious—at least for a time—, and upon leaving prison he published *Sagesse* (1881), a collection of religious poems in which he ardently proclaimed his Catholicism. Meanwhile, his wife had divorced him, one of the reasons having been her husband's intimacy with Rimbaud. The rest of his years Verlaine, despite his religious faith, lived a Bohemian life of dissipation and poverty that earned him the condemnation of the "right-minded" in French society. He was a pathetic figure as he flitted from one café to another, from one drinking-session to another, a helpless and hapless individual who nevertheless continued to write one volume of verse after another. Although hailed in certain literary circles as an outstanding poet, he died in Paris in 1894 almost penniless and in relative obscurity.

Verlaine's poetry has been well characterized by his friend, François Coppée who, a companion of Verlaine in his stormy youth, settled down to become a conservative member of the French Academy: "Verlaine created poetry that was unique, of an inspiration both naive and subtle, made up of nuances, evoking the most delicate vibrations of the nerves and the most fugitive echoes of the heart; yet it was a natural poetry, at times even rooted in folk-poetry; a poetry in which the rhythms preserve a delightful harmony, in which the stanzas recur and sing as if in a children's roundelay, and the verses—some of them exquisite—merge with music." Perhaps the most colorful portrait in fiction of Verlaine is in Anatole France's novel *The Red Lily,* in the leading character Choulette.

V

There is of course a marked difference in the specific gravity, so to speak, of these three poets: Baudelaire, Rimbaud, and Verlaine. Yet they have certain underlying attributes in common. Important poets in their own right and worth reading for the inimitable music of their poetry, they speak directly to us. Both Rimbaud and Verlaine learned much from Baudelaire and each in his way projected aspects of the latter's genius. But in another sense beyond the purely literary—we may call it the *social* sense—all three are closely bound together, products of the same epoch. All three were gifted poets of the French middle class but in *rebellion* against their class. Born in families of bourgeois respectability, they revolted against this respectability and assailed the philistinism surrounding them.

This rebellion took many forms. In the generation just before Baudelaire published his *Flowers of Evil,* the Romantic writers had done their best to "shock the bourgeoisie": Victor Hugo defied the strict traditional canons of classical French verse; Théophile Gautier donned a red waistcoat and appeared at the head of a noisy enthusiastic claque at opening nights of plays, such as the memorable première of Hugo's *Hernani;* Berlioz, "Hector of the flaming locks," cultivated Byronic moods in music.

Baudelaire's revolt was less flamboyant, less melodramatic, more complex. Most critics skim lightly over the fact that he "mounted the barricades" in the June Revolution of 1848; and it is true that his avowed reason for joining the revolutionaries on the streets of Paris was: "We must shoot General Aupick!" Aupick, his hated stepfather, was not merely the object of his personal wrath; Aupick personified all the bourgeois attributes he detested: careerism, opportunism, smugness, vulgar materialism, and toadying to the great. Moreover, throughout his writings, particularly in his vivid realistic descriptions of Paris and his insight into the wonder and beauty of big city life, Baudelaire never failed to manifest a profound humanitarian sympathy for the poor and lowly. For a brief period he collaborated with a people's poet, Pierre Dupont, on a revolutionary periodical, *Salut Public*. He was a friend and admirer of Honoré Daumier, a critic in art of the existing order of society, and of the painter of realism, Gustave Courbet. True, the failure of the 1848 Revolution, the rise of Louis Napoleon and the latter's successful *coup d'état* in 1852 leading to the repressive dictatorship of the Second Empire, filled Baudelaire with disillusionment. Thereafter, he turned away from politics in disgust. Embittered, he questioned all social progress and toyed with a theory of original sin to rationalize his pessimism and lack of faith in democracy. But in his way—in his writings—he continued his revolt against the sordid money-grubbing of the Second Empire epitomized in the phrase of Guizot: *Enrichissez-vous!* (Get rich!) His hatred of the stifling, vainglorious, imperial regime of "Napoleon the Little" did not abate. Nor did the judge's condemnation in 1857 of his *Flowers of Evil* increase his respect for the judiciary of Napoleon III.

A great contemporary of Baudelaire, Gustave Flaubert, similarly poured out his hatred and scorn of the *parvenus* of the Second Empire in his novels: *A Sentimental Education* and the unfinished *Bouvard and Pécuchet*. Victor Hugo, displaying astonishing vitality despite his advancing years, challenged the regime in his savagely satirical, Jacobin-minded poems, *Les Châtiments*. Baudelaire's reaction was neither satire nor republicanism: he concentrated even more intensely on fashioning great verse and prose—"to be a great man and a saint every day for oneself." Artistic conscience was his answer to bourgeois philistinism.

Historically, middle-class values and standards still dominated in the field of the arts as well as in expanding industry and on the

Stock Exchange. Nor had the common people—the masses—developed a cultural, artistic and literary life in which men like Baudelaire, Flaubert and their literary contemporaries could feel at home. Hence the best, the most sensitive, and the most creatively endowed sons and daughters of the bourgeoisie rejected the ideals of their own class as false and shabby and vulgar; or else they turned artistic handsprings, or wrote with biting satire in order to shock the middle-classes into a recognition of their philistinism.

Unable to accept the modes of thought and action of the smug prospering bourgeoisie, the creative artist was not yet ready or able to "go to the people" and find in them a congenial and stimulating audience. Hence tortured consciences, divided souls, the hunt for new thrills, and defiance of bourgeois moral and artistic standards. In many of the rebels, this revolt was at best picturesque or amusing—a Bohemian tempest in a teapot. But in a Baudelaire as in a Flaubert, the challenge assumed major proportions. Indeed Rimbaud, "the marvellous boy," who fought with the Paris Communards in the bloody days of 1871 and then turned his back on literature and European civilization, carried this defiance a giant step forward by foreswearing literature altogether. As for Verlaine, never a strong-willed character, he sought refuge periodically in the bosom of the Catholic Church. That was his solution—a solution by religious faith—of the conflicts in his life.

All of these 19th century writers felt themselves, in Matthew Arnold's words,

> Wandering between two worlds, one dead,
> The other powerless to be born.

They were not always conscious of their position. In fact, their expression of the dilemma is perhaps purest and most revealing when they are most unconscious of it. The dilemma has not yet been fully resolved, as any close study of the trends and currents in contemporary European and American literature will show. But flight from reality—in whatever seductive guise or under the impulse of whatever artificial stimulant—is certainly not the answer. The proper study of mankind is not flight from man; nor is it a nihilist rejection of human society. So in this sense, Rimbaud emerges as the boldest, but Baudelaire as the most consistent, the most thoroughgoing, and the most enduring searcher after reality in modern French poetry. Almost a century removed from us in time, Baudelaire is nevertheless the nearest to us in his artistic integrity, his discovery of new aesthetic horizons, and his creative sense of the whole.

VI

A few words are in order about the translations used in this volume. It is almost a truism to point out that these three poets, like the great French poet-dramatist of the 17th century, Jean Racine, and like the giant of Russian poetry, Pushkin, offer almost unsurmountable difficulties for the translator. So much is locked up in the inner rhymes and rhythms, the assonances, the overtones, and the evocative quality of the words themselves that the task of rendering them in English is ungrateful even for one extremely gifted in English poetry. It is unfortunate that there does not exist in English a translation of *The Flowers of Evil* comparable to the magnificent German rendition of Stefan George. Of the available translations, the most complete single version and the one, in our opinion, nearest the original in spirit is that of Arthur Symons. There is much of the decadent and many purple passages in this British poet of the mauve decade, contemporary of Oscar Wilde, Aubrey Beardsley, and Ernest Dowson. Yet we believe that Symons has best caught the spirit of Baudelaire. And it must not be forgotten that he lived through the period in which English poets first discovered Baudelaire. It was Algernon Charles Swinburne who introduced him to the reading public in England; and it was Swinburne who paid him a most beautiful tribute in his poem:

AVE ATQUE VALE
(*In Memory of Charles Baudelaire*)
Thou sawest, in thine old singing season, brother,
Secrets and sorrows unbeheld of us:

Fierce loves, and lovely leaf-buds poisonous,
Bare to thy subtler eye, but for none other
Blowing by night in some unbreathed-in clime.

Symons did perhaps more than any other English writer of his time to make the French poet known in Britain and the United States.

As for Rimbaud, his *Season in Hell* and *Prose Poems* from *Illuminations* were recently published in splendid translations by Louise Varèse, which we are privileged to use. For the poems from *Illuminations,* we have availed ourselves of the best extant translation by J. Norman Cameron. In the case of Verlaine, author of eighteen volumes of verse, we have chosen a translation of selected poems by Gertrude Hall. We have also seen fit to include several poems from the volume, *Parallèlement* (In Parallel Fashion), translated by Arthur Symons.

JOSEPH M. BERNSTEIN
January, 1947

Charles Baudelaire

Flowers of Evil

To the Reader

STINGINESS, SIN, STUPIDITY, shall determine
Our spirits' fashion and travail our body's forces,
And we shall feed on the corpses of our remorses
Like the beggars who nourish their own vermin.

Our sins are strenuous, cowardly our repentances;
Abominably we pay for our nights and days,
As we return gaily along the miry ways,
Thinking by vile tears to cleanse our cruel sentences.

On the pillow of Evil sits Satan, Hell's Creator,
Who lulls our Spirits with his mad Sorcery;
So that the metal of our will is melted magically
And vaporised by this learned Prevaricator.

The Devil pulls the strings where we sway shrinking!
In repugnant things we find forms formidable;
Day by day we descend to the uttermost Hell;
Where, in the night, we smell the darkness stinking.

As a lewd libertine who bites and who smutches
The martyred breasts of an abominable Whore,
We steal our pleasures inside a Brothel's door
Insidious as the orange-skin one touches.

In our miserable brains, like the seven damnations,
Swarm, riot, surge, swirl the Demons of the Deep,
And, when we breathe, that Death who gives us sleep,
Plunges itself into obscure lamentations.

If ravishment, poison, poignard and conflagration
Have not with their intolerable designs repainted
The banal canvas of our Destinies, sin-tainted,
It is that our Soul, alas! lacks violation.

But amidst the jackals, panthers, all hell's devices,
The scorpions and the vultures, serpents, apes,
Monsters howling, growling, prowling, yelping shapes,
In the infamous menagerie of our Vices,

There is one more ugly, more foul, than hell's first dawning!
And though he makes no great gestures nor great cries,
He would willingly make of the Earth a ruin of Lies
And swallow the World in one tremendous yawning.

He is Ennui!—more malevolent than his Mother,
He dreams of scaffolds as he smokes his houka.
You know him, this delicate monster, in his felucca,
—Hypocritical Reader—my co-equal—no, my Brother!

Benediction

WHEN, BY A SUPREME DECREE of Evil's Expiation,
The Poet appears in the World, this worn-out City,
His terrified mother cries in exasperation
With shrivelled hands toward God, who takes her in pity:

"Ah! that I had not a knot of vipers in reversed revulsion
Begotten rather than this infamous derision!
Cursed be forever the midnight of convulsion
When my womb conceived my expiation and my vision!

Since you have chosen me among curious women, Shame's
Centre I am, to be thrust out by one man's disgust,
Because I have not cast into the furious flames,
Like a love-letter, this stunted monster of Lust.

I shall cast back the hate that overcomes me
On the infernal instrument of your perversity,
Fixed in a fever that infamously benumbs me
Like a plague-stricken tree that shakes incessantly!"

She swallows the foam of hate under her henna,
Unaware of the infinite divine designs,
Herself preparing in the depth of her Gehenna
A hell on earth that uttermost hell maligns.

The Child that is from heredity disinherited
Endures the sun's implacable intoxication,
Knowing by all that he eats that his sins are unmerited,
And that in wine resides his exasperation.

He plays with the wind of the wide world that covers
His enchantment as he sings the Ways of the Cross,
He knows that the Spirits who follow him are his Lovers,
So are the Birds, and the Seas in the Storms that toss.

Those he would love fear him, with consternation
They wonder at his intense audacity,
Seeking for their sakes to draw from him a lamentation
As they make a trial of him with fierce ferocity.

With the red wine and with the warm bread he clutches,
They mixed shaken ashes with their impure spittle,
With hypocrisy they cast back at him all that he touches,
And accused themselves of breaking things too brittle.

His wife goes crying in the public places:
"Since he has found me fair and that he can adore me,
I shall trade on the ancient idols and their grimaces
That he must paint until they bow down before me.

With nard and incense and benzoin I shall be sated,
And with crucifixions and with foods and with wines,
To know if I can find in the heart of some snarer baited
An admiration my ardent spirit divines!

When I am tired of the fiercer forces of the hell-rats
I shall raise my hand in the absolute act of slaying;
And my nails, sharper than the nails of all the hell-cats,
Shall seize on his heart and choke him while he is praying.

As a young bird pants in his tremulous trepidation
I shall tear out his red heart, satiate not its pain,
And, to assuage my favourite beast in exasperation,
I shall hurl him this heart with the fury of disdain."

Towards the sky where only the High God's Throne is,
The Poet with his amorous passionate eyes
Lifted, shall wonder if the Spirit in him alone is,
That hides from him the vast fury of the people's cries:

"Blessed, O my God, who gives me the quintessence
As a divine healing of our impurities,
And as the infinitely finer and purer essence
Which adds savour to our sensualities!

I know that you shall keep a place for the Poet in Heaven,
A place with the Legions and with the Nominations,
And that you shall invite him to the feast that shall be given
By the Thrones, by the Virtues and by the Dominations.

I know there is a sorrow in the Soul's confessing
That shall never bite the hateful hollow Hells,
That, so as to weave my mystical crown by God's own blessing
The Universe and Time must render up their spells.

But in the land of buried jewels and of the treasures
Of the unknown metals and of the furious Sea
There shall be made out of many marvellous measures
A diadem by your hand woven wonderfully.

For this shall be created only by pure vision,
Taken from the mirrors of the primitive lights,
And from the flaming fires of the soul's division
Out of the veritable hearts of the ancient nights!"

The Balcony

MOTHER OF MEMORIES, mother of mistresses,
O thou, in whom my pleasure bites and smites!—
Thou givest me the beauty of divine caresses,
The heart's fire at the midnight of the nights,
Mother of memories, mother of mistresses!

The nights ignited by the fire's fierce fashions,
The shadow of the unveiled Invisible,
How sweet thy breast, thy heart and all its passions!
We have often said strange things imperishable,
On the nights ignited by the fire's fierce fashions.

Scents and heats of Hell's Hallucinations!
Space, and the heart's beating and our changing mood.
Thou canst give me, O queen of my Adorations,
The very perfume of thy most precious blood.
Scents and heats of Hell's Hallucinations!

Night and the absolute horror of a Vision,
Mine eyes on thine in the dark one's sense depresses,
When I drank thy blood, thy breath, poison, derision!
When thy feet slept, when slept thy dishevelled tresses!
Night and the absolute horror of a Vision.

I know the art of evoking invocation,
And I have dreamed deep hidden between thy knees
Of languorous beauties, of thy fascination,
Thy body's beauty, the savage wind-swept Seas!
I know the art of evoking invocation!

These oaths, these perfumes, these kisses, mad, ferocious,
Shall these arise from a great gulf interdicted?
Some deep abyss, sombre, sunless, atrocious,
The depths of the illimitable seas by our Sins predicted?
—O oaths! O perfume! O kisses, mad, ferocious!

The Sun

ALONG THE OUTSKIRTS, where the Venetian blinds from ruins
Hang, shelter of secret luxuries and of new inns,
Where the ferocious sun strikes with his rage redoubled
The city and the fields and leaves one troubled,
I go to fence fantastically where men's crimes are,
Scenting the corners where my capricious rhymes are,
Stumbling over certain words and on the pavement,
Striking on verses, wondering what the grave meant.

This nourishing father, hating the wench who dozes,
Wakens in the fields the worms that hate the roses;
He makes one's fears evaporate, tosses one's money
And fills our imagination with the bee's best honey.
He rejuvenates those who are fated to use crutches,
And makes them gay and sweet as the girl one touches,
And makes the harvest ripen as he cherishes
The immortal heart before the whole world perishes!

When, like a Poet, he descends into the City,
He makes vile things seem good, makes base men witty,
And, as a King, who hates his soul's perdition,
He enters the hospitals where he finds sedition.

Elevation

ABOVE THE POOLS, above the valley of fears,
Above the woods, the clouds, the hills, the trees,
Beyond the sun's and the moon's mad mysteries,
Beyond the confines of the starry spheres,

My spirit, you move with a pure ardency,
And, as one who swoons in the senses of sound,

You furrow furiously the immensity profound
With an indicable and male sensuality.

Fly from those morbid miasmas and their mire;
Purify your own self in the mid air malign,
And there drink, as a delicious and rare wine,
The enormity and the intensity of fire.

Beyond the universe and the vast chagrins
Which load the smoky air with their existence,
Joyous is he who can with a bird's persistence
Rush toward the heavens not fashioned by our sins!

He whose thoughts, like the lark that sings and wings
Its way at dawn toward the sky in a higher flight,
Wandering over the immensity of the night,
Knows the flowers' speech and the speech of silent things!

Exotic Perfume

WHEN WITH EYES CLOSED as in an opium dream
I breathe the odour of thy passionate breast,
I see in vision hell's infernal stream
And the sunset fires that have no instant's rest:
An idle island where the unnatural scheme
Of Nature is by savourous fruits oppressed,
And where men's bodies are their women's guest
And women's bodies are not what they seem.

Guided by thine odour towards the heat of veils,
I see a harbour filled with masts and sails,
Wearied by the sea wind that wearies me,

And in the perfume of the tamarind there clings
I know not what of marvellous luxury
Mixed in my soul with the song the mariner sings.

Gypsies on the March

THE TRIBE PROPHETIC with their ardent eyes
Wander along the roads unendingly,
With appetites that rend them furiously
As their imagination that never dies.
Their women, Oriental merchandise,
Beside the chariots that roll heavily,
Gaze furtively on skies that passionately
Desire the Chimeras of the absent skies.

From their deep holes, the sullen grasshoppers,
Hearing them pass, repeat their double whirrs;
Cybele who loves them as she loves her Kings
Shows them in vision her swift charioteers
Who fling wide open before these Travellers
The tenebrous Empire of imperishable things.

The Beacons

RUBENS, RIVER OF OBLIVION, garden of idleness,
Pillow of fresh flesh in love's anxiety,
Where life grows strong and wild in wantonness,
Like the air in the air and the sea in the sea.

Leonardo da Vinci—somber mirror of sorcerous terror,
Wherein sexless creatures that are made magical
Out of the night's mystery appear in the shadow of terror,
Like souls in Circe's snares made tragical!

Rembrandt—sad hospital filled full with rottenness,
Decorated only by an immense Crucifix,
Where prayers exhale with odours of men's filthiness,
Traversed by the under worlds beyond the Styx.

Michelangelo—vague void in enormous infinite spaces,
Whose Christs turn Pagan, and in the night there lingers
Ghost after famished ghost with anguished faces,
That tear their shrouds asunder with exhausted fingers.

Wraths of a boxer, a Faun's impudence, Donatello's,
You who only painted the beauty of the knavish,
Melancholy as the mere colours of your yellows,
Puget, King of the criminals, convict's slavish.

Watteau—mad Carnival where madder hearts are winging
In their butterfly fashion, than these more jolly
That wander in the shadows subtly swinging
And floating over this Ball of whirling Folly.

Goya—enormous nightmare filled with things inhuman,
Of foetuses, of Sabbats and of the Spirit's mockings,
Where Spanish children are stript stark naked by naked women
That tempt the Demons as they adjust their stockings.

Delacroix—lake of blood by Evil Angels haunted,
Shadowed by a green wood's mad mysteries,
Where, under an angry sky in the night undaunted,
Pass stifled shadows, Weber's, to their destinies.

These blasphemies, these maledictions, these lamentations,
These cries, these ecstasies our *Te Deum* divines,
Are as labyrinthine as our exasperations
That demand a divine opium after the wines.

This is the cry of the infinitely amorous,
Hurled by an enormous wind across the flood:
This is a lighthouse lit with sacred fire for the perilous
Sailors that shed in the storms for their sins their blood!

These, Lord, are for the Spirits of all our Sages
That give us signs of our own dignity,
This intolerable howling of the inevitable ages
That merge and surge and emerge in Eternity!

The Cat

COME ON MY HEART, my amorous cat,
And keep away from me your claws.
Are you more amorous than that
Of metal for agate, passion's pause?
When my hands take on them to caress
Your supple back and splendid head,
And with intoxicatedness
My fingers fasten on you with dread,
I see in my spirit my one mistress,
Her eyes like yours, not that nor this tress,
But eyes that penetrate my heart,
And her fair feet that make me start
As her brown body in my room
Exhales a dangerous Perfume.

Correspondences

NATURE IS A TEMPLE where we live ironically
In the midst of forests filled with dire confusions;
Man, hearing confused words, passes symbolically
Under the eyes of the birds watching his illusions.

Like distant echoes in some tenebrous unity,
Perfumes and colours are mixed in strange profusions,
Vast as the night they mix inextricably
With seas unsounded and with the dawn's delusions.

And there are the perfect perfumes of the Flesh,
That are as green as the sins in the Serpent's mesh,
And others as corrupt as our own senses,
Having the strange expansion of things infinite,
Such as amber, musk, benzoin and sweet incenses,
That seize the spirit and the senses exquisite.

I Love the Memory

I LOVE THE MEMORY of those naked ages
When the sun shines on wise men's and fool's pages.
Then the man and woman in their agility
Exulted and lied not in their anxiety,
And, the amorous sun caressing their spine, unseen,
Made far more wonderful their mad machine.
Cybele, then, in all her products fertile,
Not finding in her sons the weight of a myrtle,
Like a warm-hearted she-wolf in the hot noon
Intoxicated both the Universe and the Moon.
Man, being robust, had certainly the right
To be proud of his beauty, mirroring the night,
Pure fruits of outrages and of virginless night
When the skin's fevered and the senses bite!

The Poet now, when he desires to conceive
These native grandeurs, and when he is fain to believe
In men's and women's shameless nudity,
Feels in his soul a tenebrous cold, a crudity,
At the mere aspect of those vestments venomous
That clothe the bodies of monsters poisonous;
Of withered virgins, uglier than their masks;
Of these poor bodies, thin, swollen like wine-flasks,
That the God of the awful, vast, implacable,
Shrouded in iron shrouds as hot as Hell,
Of these women, alas! pale as the moths, who emerge in
The infamous horror of a shrieking virgin,
Of the maternal vice trailing the heredity
And all the hideousness of their fecundity!

We have, for certain, many corrupt nations,
Whose unknown beauties were their tribulations:
Visages graven by all the diseases of the heart
Whose beauty languishes for lack of art:

But these inventions of our modern Muses
Could never hinder in sick races the abuses
Which gave to youth the aspect of a stranger,
—Nor from Saintly graces, nor from the wind's danger,
Youth whose clear eyes were simple as water flowing,
That flows forever over all things, knowing
The way the wind blows and the planet's visions,
The heats, the perfumes and the sun's derisions!

Sed Non Satiata

BIZARRE DEITY, dark as infernal nights,
Whose perfume mixes with musk Arabian,
Work of some Obi, Faustus, that learned man,
Sorceress with ebony thighs, child of midnights
I prefer to all things, opium and the nights,
Thy mouth's elixir, strange as a Pavane;
When toward thee my desires in caravan
Pass, thine eyes assuage mine appetites.
By those black eyes, vent-holes of thy soul's shame.
O pitiless Demon, pour on me less flame;
I am not the Styx to embrace thee nine times, nay,
Alas! I cannot, Maegera of the Sorrows nine,
To break thy courage and to set thee at bay
In the hell of thy bed, become thy Proserpine!

The Evil Monk

THE ANCIENT CLOISTERS on the altar-rails
Exposed huge pictures of Saint Verity,
Whose effect, warming their infamous entrails,
Was to assuage their cold austerity.

When Christ's seeds flourished, what then else avails,
When illustrious Monks, famed for futurity,
Painting graveyards, before which the spirit quails,
Glorified Death's inevitable Irony?

My soul is a Tomb that, evil Cenobite,
Since Eternity inhabits day and night;
The walls of this cloister are odious as the skies.

O, idle monk! God! When shall I ever have finished
This image of my soul's misery undiminished,
The travail of my hands and the love of mine eyes?

Allegory

SHE IS A WOMAN rich in her caresses
Who lets her wine fall in her dishevelled tresses,
The claws of love, poisons of the Evil Houses,
Glide on her skin as her warm passion drowses.
She laughs at Death and jests at one that writhes,
Monster whose hands are sharper than the scythes,
In her destructive games she is respected,
In her rude majesty nothing is neglected.
She has her way of walking and of repose,
And only Mahomet for her sins she knows,
And in her arms and in her heaving breasts
She calls men's eyes to be her servile guests.
She imagines, this virgin pregnant, that she has curled
Voluptuously around the serpent world,
That body's beauty is God's gift in the garden,
And that all infamy can be consoled by pardon;
Purgatory she ignores as she ignores Hell,
When the hour comes she enters the dark cell
Of Death, and as a phantom of frail Breath
Re-born she, hateless, gazes upon Death.

Ill Luck

To LIFT A LOAD so heavy and crazy
One must have your courage, Sisyphus!
If the heart of Tantalus is lazy,
Art's long, Time's short, for Tantalus.

Far from graves where vermin are feeding
On bodies in miasmic marshes,
My heart, my passionate heart is bleeding,
The very sense within me parches.

—Many a jewel sleeps enshrouded
In the darkness which is overclouded
Where the great heart of the midnight broods;

Many a flower in many a room
Exhales the odour of its perfume,
Some wanton's scent, the scent of the blood's.

The Jewels

KNOWING MY HEART, the dear thing was quite naked,
And she was wearing one resplendent jewel,
And even her nakedness, when one could slake it,
Had the exotic charm of being cruel.

When this world dances most luxuriously,
This metal world one's imagination transfixes,
It gives me ecstasy, and I love furiously
Things thoughtless where the sound with colour mixes

So she was lying, and she let me love her,
And from the height of the divan, she in her fashion
Smiled at the depth of my love the seas swirl over,
In the infinite immensity of their passion.

Her tigerish eyes, fixed on mine with curiosity,
Gave her a dream-like air one's sleep uncloses,
And all this adding to her lubricity
Transmuted her incredible metamorphoses.

And her arms and legs, her reins and her thighs' spices,
Undulated, and nothing more divine is
Than, in mine eyes, visions of her separate vices;
Her breasts and her belly, grapes of my vine where wine is,

More caressing than all the Angels of Evil,
To trouble my soul's repose, not to awake it,
But to excite in me my Satanic revel:
For there my mistress lay, superbly naked.

I thought I saw by a new design united,
Antiope's haunches: how her flesh seemed to wake up!
From her waist to the most secret places ignited.
Superb on her tawny skin the rouge of her make-up!

—And the lamplight dying and that midnight tearing
The very firelight as it were in sunder,
Always when the lamplight was least flaring
It bathed with blood her olive skin, a wonder!

The Sick Muse

MY POOR MUSE, why is your aspect so ominous?
Your hollow eyes are filled with nocturnal visions,
And I see change in your complexion, furious
Folly and horror, taciturn as derisions.

The green-eyed Succubus and the rose goblin luxurious
Have they poured fear and love from their urn's divisions?
Has the nightmare, with his wrist despotic and mutinous,
Drowned you between two fabulous elisions?

I would that exhaling the odour of scents demented,
Your breast with visions were forever frequented,
And that your blood flowed always rhythmically,
Like the sounds of the ancient syllables articulately,
Where reigned the father of songs, Phoebus, and of rhymes,
Pan, the great God, the Lord of the Harvest times.

The Venal Muse

O MUSE OF MY HEART, lover of palaces where meet
The extremes of heat when the winds of January,
During the dark hours of winter's misery,
Howl, had you a firebrand to warm your violet-veined feet?

Did not your shoulders shudder for lack of heat
When the night's rays fell on you furiously?
Finding your purse was dry and high the sky,
Did you find the gold of the vaults in some sinister street?

You must, so as to gain your bread day after day,
Like a young chorister make the censer sway,
Chant the *Te Deums* wherein no God was seen,

Or, fasting mountebank, expose your charms and after,
Hide your soaked tears that do not hide your laughter
From the common herd's exclamatory spleen.

The Enemy

MY YOUTH WAS NOTHING BUT A STORM, tenebrous, savage,
Traversed by brilliant suns that our hearts harden;
The thunder and the rain had made such ravage
That few of the fruits were left in my ruined garden.

Now that I have touched the autumn of Ideas,
One must use the spade before the whole earth consumes
Itself like the strangled sons that were Medea's,
Where the water digs deep holes as damp as tombs.

But who knows if the flowers I dream of and adore
Shall find in this soil, naked as any shore,
The mystic nourishment of the magician's art?

—O Sorrow! Time eats our life and mortifies himself,
And the obscure Enemy who gnaws our heart
From the blood we lose increases and fortifies himself!

Punishment of Pride

IN THESE MARVELLOUS AGES when Theology
Flourished with most of sap and of energy,
It has been said that a Doctor of great parts
—After having forced the most indifferent hearts,
And having stirred them, fathomed these hearts' stories,
After having rushed toward the celestial glories,
And found these singular ways to himself unknown,
Where the pure spirits by the wild winds were blown,
—Like a man risen too high, being seized with panic,
He howled aloud, then transported by a pride Satanic:
—"I have lifted thee up too high, Jesus, little Jesus!
But, if I had desired, being emulous of Croesus,
To find in default thy shame, since our sins cheat us,
Thou hadst been no more than a derisory foetus!"

Immediately there went from him his reason.
The shining of this sun vanished like treason;
Dark chaos rolled into this intelligence,
A living temple, once full of opulence,
Under those heavens which were as pomp to him.

Silence and night installed themselves in the dim
Brain as in a cavern of which the key is lost.
He wandered with the wild beasts, the city's ghost,
Nothing he saw, no more than certain mummers,
Of the changes of the winters into the summers;
Foul, unclean, ugly, like a cast-off toy,
He was the children's derision and their joy.

Don Juan in Hell

WHEN DON JUAN DESCENDED to the Underworld
And had given Charon his obolus supreme,
A sombre beggar, prouder than the Thunderworld,
Seized both oars as if to avenge his dream.

Showing their open robes and heaving bosoms,
Women writhed under the dark firmament,
And, as a crowd of creatures decked with blossoms,
Behind them a long bellowing came and went.

Demanding his wages, Sganarelle, with laughter,
Showed Don Luis, in the void where void is none,
And to the wandering dead, under hell's rafter,
Seville's famed Jester, his audacious son.

Under her mourning chaste Elvira, shivering,
Turned to the perfidious serpent, her last lover,
In one intense and intolerable quivering
In all her limbs his secret to discover.

Upright in armour, a man of stone from the Ghetto
Stood at the helm, furrowing the sunless flood;
But the great Spaniard, fingering his stiletto,
Gazed on the foam and felt the heat in his blood.

My Former Life

I HAVE DWELT under the reign of Dynasties,
Where the seas cast under the sunsets flames and fires,
I have seen the Nile yellowing its moods and mires,
And, under the Pyramids, Idolatries.

The surges, mirroring the images of the Skies,
Mixed in a fashion mystical with the choirs
Of the powerful accents of music richer than lyres,
The sunset colours reflected in mine eyes.

It is there that I have lived in Sensuality,
In the midst of the waves and the splendours and the events
Of the naked slave-girls, impregnated with strong scents,

Who refreshed with their waving fans my Luxury,
And whose only trouble was to investigate
The sorrowful secret of my languishing Fate.

Thee I Adore

THEE I ADORE as the vault of night's pure madness,
O silent and taciturn, O thou source of pure sadness,
I love thee more, O fair, when thou fliest from me,
And when thou seemest, night's sister, the slyest from me,
Before league upon league the Sea's insanity
Shall sever us from the immense light's vanity.

I advance to the attack, I climb to the assaults, whose storms are
As it were beside a corpse where a crowd of worms are,
And I cherish thee, O Beast implacable and cruel,
Because thou art more wonderful than a jewel!

Man and the Sea

MAN, YOU MUST ALWAYS LOVE THE SEA with all your passion!
You see your soul in the infinity of the sea's surges,
And in your mirror a phantom self emerges,
Your spirit is a bitter gulf whose sinister fashion

Excites you to plunge into your image which can ravage
Your very senses, and your heart, that in your breast hammers,
Hears in its deepest depths the intolerable clamours
And the lamentations of the sea, unconquerable and savage.

You and the Sea are tenebrous and of an intensity;
Man, none has sounded the depths of your abysses;
O Sea, you only know your most intimate riches,
So jealous you are of your secrets and your immensity!

And yet during all these centuries innumerable
You fight together pitiless as the swirling water,
So enormously do you love death and death's infamous slaughter,
O fighters eternal, O brothers implacable!

Reversibility

ANGEL FULL OF GAIETY, have you known anguish,
Sobs, sorrows, miseries, remorse, the shame that blushes?
And the vague terrors of those awful nights when we languish,
And that hurt the heart like the paper that one crushes?
Angel full of gaiety, have you known anguish?

Angel full of goodness, have you known hate the eternal,
The witch tricked in shadow and the tears of malice,
When we hear beat to arms Vengeance the Infernal,
That seizes our faculties, makes us drink sin's chalice?
Angel full of goodness, have you known hate the eternal?

Angel full of health, have you known the Fevers,
That along the walls of hospitals go sagging,
Like exiles who seek the sun, find hell's retrievers,
Who move their lips, foot after tired foot dragging?
Angel full of health, have you known the Fevers?

Angel full of beauty, have you known the Wrinkles,
And the fear of ageing, and this hideous commotion
In the eyes our greedy eyes drank, and in one who sprinkles
Holy Water, and the mad horror of devotion?
Angel full of beauty, have you known the Wrinkles?

Angel full of joy, and of light unwonted,
David dying and desiring health in what adoration
Of the emanations of thy divine body enchanted?
But of thee, angel, I implore thy prayers, my sin's salvation,
Angel full of joy, and of light unwonted!

Remorse After Death

WHEN THOU SHALT SLEEP, my fair Tenebrous,
In the depth of a monument eternally,
And when thou shalt have for alcove certainly
A wind-swept cave and a deep grave ruinous;
When the stone, oppressing thy breasts amorous
And thy sides made supple by their melancholy,
Shall hinder thy heart from beating violently
And thy feet from escaping their ways adventurous:

The tomb, confidant of my dream infinite—
For the tomb always understands the Poet—
During sleepless nights when the dire demons flit,

Shall say to thee: "Imperfect harlot, shalt thou know it,
Know what it is that makes all the damned dead weep?"
And the vermin shall gnaw thy flesh, destroy thy sleep.

Beauty

I AM BEAUTIFUL AS A DREAM OF STONE, but not maternal;
And my breast, where men are slain, none for his learning,
Is made to inspire in the Poet passions that, burning,
Are mute and carnal as matter and as eternal.

I throne in the azure with Satan, a Sphinx, sound sleeping;
This frigid and furtive heart of mine no man divines;
I hate the movement that displaces the rigid lines:
Satan has never seen me laughing nor even weeping.

The Poets, before the strange attitudes of my gloom,
That I assume in my moods of alienation,
In austere studies all their days and nights consume:

Always, when I draw my lovers with my fascination,
There are pure mirrors, wonderful as the nights:
Mine eyes, mine eyes immense—Satan's delights!

Couldst Thou Not Hurl the Universe

COULDST THOU NOT HURL THE UNIVERSE into a jewel,
O impure woman? Thine own can make thee more cruel
When, biting with thy teeth in thy singular game,
Thou seemest to cast from thee thy utmost shame.
Thy glowing eyes that shine like furious beasts
Are like the flames that lick up furious feasts,
Using indolently a power beyond their duty
Of never knowing anything but their beauty.

Blind and deaf machines poignant in cruelties! sinking,
O salutary instrument, to capture world's blood, drinking
Shame after shame. Now hast thou not seen thine errors,
Seeing thy pallid visage before thy mirrors?

The grandeur of this evil thou art but learning,
Has it not made thee recoil with the fear of burning
Nature herself, for all her delights are hidden,
Which makes thee, O woman, queen of sins unforbidden,
—Thou evil animal—a genius engender?
O sublime ignominy, filthy panderess, and no surrender!

The Ideal

THERE NEVER SHALL BE the strange beauties of Vignettes,
Prurient products born of a century malign,
These feet with buskins shod, these hands with castanets,
That shall not satisfy a heart like mine.

I leave to Gavarni, the Poet of Sexual Poses,
His twittering beauties of an hospital too real,
For never shall I find among these pale faded roses
A flower that can inflame my red ideal.

What a passionate heart needs for an Abyss sublime.
It is yours, Lady Macbeth, spirit terrible in crime,
Or some magnificent dream of Æschylus;

Or you, great Night, Michelangelo's delight,
That writhes against the shadow of that Light,
That night of fever fierce and calamitous!

The Serpent That Dances

I LOVE TO SEE, snake fascinating,
In thy frame so thin
Like a rare stuff vacillating
Shine thy satin skin!

On the depths of thy dark tresses
With bitter perfumes
Where the floods of the sun's caresses
Shine on the odorous wombs

Of the seas, as a ship awaking
With the wind of morn,
My soul as a dream forsaking
Life, of life outworn.

In thine eyes where nothing cruel
Shines in their desires,
As a jewel mixed with jewel
These shoot fires.

As I see thy slow advancing
In abandonment
One would say a serpent dancing
In a tent of scent.

Under the weight of thine own passion
Thine head fair
Nods as an elephant's whose fashion
Is rare as air.

So thy body reels and revels
As a lovely ship
That rolls and plunges on its levels
Where sea-waves drip.

As a flood the sun surprises
Under a cloud-wreath,
When thine exquisite saliva rises
To the edge of thy teeth,

I drink Bohemian wine that shatters
Mine own taste
As a liquid sky that scatters
Stars that haste to waste!

The Giantess

FROM THE TIME when Nature in her furious fancy
Conceived each day monstrosities obscene,
I had loved to live near a young Giantess of Necromancy,
Like a voluptuous cat before the knees of a Queen.

I had loved to see her body mix with her Soul's shame
And greaten in these terrible games of Vice,
And to divine if in her heart brooded a sombre flame,
Before the moist sea-mists which swarm in her great eyes;

To wander over her huge forms—nature deforms us—
And to crawl over the slopes of her knees enormous,
And in summer when the unwholesome suns from the West's

Winds, weary, made her slumber hard by a fountain,
To sleep listlessly in the shadow of her superb breasts,
Like an hamlet that slumbers at the foot of a mountain.

With Her Vestments Iridescent

WITH HER VESTMENTS IRIDESCENT and undulating,
Even when she walks it seems as if she dances,
Like those sly snakes the jugglers, strange signs creating,
Make coil in cadences and then fall in trances.

Like the dull sand and the deserts and men's fretwork,
Insensible to suffering and to mere indolence,
As in the swish and the swell of the waves the network
Rises, she develops herself with indifference.

In her eyes one sees the refractions of a jewel,
And in this symbolical nature mixes and drinks
The inviolate Angel with the inevitable Sphinx,

Where all is diamond, light, gold, steel, more cruel
Than these, the cold majesty of the woman sterile
Shines everlastingly like a star in peril.

De Profundis Clamavi

I IMPLORE THY PITY, Thou, the unique, I adore,
From the depth of the deep gulf where my heart lies dead.
It is an universal universe of lead,
Where horror swims in the night's far-reaching shore;
A sunless heat that has the heat of the blood's,
For half the year, there the night hides the earth;
This naked land gives naked toads their birth:
Besides, no beasts nor birds nor herbs nor woods!

There is no horror in the world that surpasses
The cold cruelty of the frozen sun that masses
The immense nights into chaos chaotic;
I envy the fate of the wild wolves, erotic,
Who plunge into stupid sleep. What hides itself
When the skein of Time slowly divides itself?

Confession

ONCE ONLY, ONLY ONCE, O woman amorous,
It was no ancient history,
We walked (in the deep depth of my soul tenebrous
This memory is no mystery);

It was late; in the heavy sky above us we saw quiver
The full moon, her watch keeping;
And the solemnity of the night like a rapid river
Shone over Paris sleeping.

Along the houses—were these only waking?—
Some cats passed us furtively,
All on the prowl for prey, like shadows shaking,
With their insatiable curiosity.

All at once—am I right in my recollection?—
As it were out of a girl's bosom,
There came your voice, instrument of mine own delection,
Just as if a flower might blossom,

From you, as a sonorous and exuberant fanfare
Before the bright dawn saw crumbling
One cloud, a plaintive note, a note bizarre
Escaped from you, as if stumbling,

A fearful child, horrible, sombre, hideous
As any beaten slave
Who, for the world's sake had been thrust, perfidious
Into a hollow cave.

Poor angel, she sang, your shrill voice itself fainting:
"That nothing here is certain,
And that always, when one has finished one's own painting,
On one's own self comes down the curtain;

That it is a hard trade to be a fair woman, acquainting
Herself with the banal passion
Of a mad dancing-girl whom one sees suddenly fainting
In a mere mechanical fashion;

That to build our hearts is stupid as a closed casket,
That all cracks, beauty, Insanity,
Until Oblivion hurls them into her basket
To give them back to Eternity!"

I have evoked this enchanted moon and our vision,
And this silence, quintessential,
And this horrible confidence whispered on a note of derision,
At the hurt Heart's Confessional!

One Night

ONE NIGHT when I lay beside a Jewess I had hired,
As if a corpse were more than corpse-like cold,
I began to dream beside this body sold
Of the sad beauty my desire desired.
Her flesh was not in nakedness attired,
Only her tragic eyes that a thirst consumed,
Only her tresses by their own scent perfumed,
Stung me, and all the shame in me retired.

I might have kissed with fervour thy naked body
All over from the roots of thy black tresses,
Dishevelled as the savagery of thy caresses,
If on one night, when all the stars were bloody,
Thou hadst, too cruel to be crucified
On my Sin's Crucifix, thrice lived, thrice died!

A Carcass

THERE ARE SOME SOULS that are most amorous
That know not when the Spirit moans.
Saw we not, soul, at a corner an infamous
Carcass strewn on a bed of stones,

Lewd legs in the air, like a lewd woman's passion
Burning with odious revelations,
Showing in a sad and cynical and cruel fashion
Its belly full of exhalations?

The sun shone hotly on all this rottenness
As if it were in some sense boiling,
As when Nature in her absolute nothingness
Cares nothing for her creature's spoiling.

This superb carcass was not even blinking
Under the aching moon;
The stench was really beyond all possible stinking
And on the grass you seemed to swoon.

The hideous flies upon this belly rotten
Were buzzing like obnoxious hags,
Black larvae in lurid regions misbegotten
Were crawling along these living rags.

And all that rose, and all that descended,
As in a wind of dislocation;
The body, swollen, might have perhaps offended
The sense of my exasperation.

And all this world like some strange music burning
As with the wind wrestles a man,
As the winnowed grain rhythmically turning
A winnower of the wind shifts in his van.

And these forms vanished as in some upheavement
As when an artist violently
Leaves to the world his last and best achievement,
Not caring for futurity.

Around the rocks a restless bitch was eyeing
Us with a look of one forsaken,
As if from the living skeleton she were spying
The flesh that from it had been taken.

—Yet you were like that filth and rottenness
Even in its horrible infection,
Star of mine eyes, sinister of nothingness,
Passion of mine and my delection!

Yes, such shall serve you, O Queen of all the graces,
After the ultimate sacraments,
When you shall wander in the shadowy places
With the white bones and the elements,

O my Beauty, say to the vermin's quintessence
That with kisses foul shall bite you,
That I have kept the form and the divine essence
Of my lost loves that spite and bite you!

The Vampire

THOU WHO, like death's deceiving stroke,
Knocks at my heart's deep melancholy;
Thou who, like a troupe of hideous folk
Of Demons, wines and maddened Folly,

Of mine own my Spirit humiliated
Makes thine own bed and thy domain,
Infamous, by whom I am vitiated
Like the convict fastened to his chain,

Like to the Gambler with his game reversed,
Like to the drunkard with his wine-bottle,
Like to the vermin that the carrion throttle,
—Be thou for ever and ever accursed!

I have said to the sword perfidious
To lavish on me Liberty,
I have said to the poison insidious
To shake me from my lethargy.

Alas! The poison and the sword that crave thee
Said in disdainful knavery:
"Thou are not worthy that we should save thee
From thine accursed slavery,

Fool! from his empire base and bloody,
If we deliver thee by our hate,
Thy kisses shall resuscitate
Thy Vampire and his buried Body!"

I Give Thee These Verses

I GIVE THEE THESE VERSES so that, if my name
Shall become as famous in the aftertimes
As a ship driven hellward by the north wind's flame
That makes men think of how the spirit climbs

The heights of our Parnassus, fabulous game
Enough to weary a reader who begrimes
His face as an Actor's; these shall waft my Fame
On the mystic chains of all my haughty rhymes;

Accursed being to whom from hell's fell track
To highest heaven I only answer back!
O thou, who like a shadow wan as the moon's wane,

Treadest underfoot, as any angel-devil,
Those stupid slumberers who have sinned and slain
The beasts they prey on, seize these rhymes, and revel!

Lethe

COME ON MY HEART, soul too cruel,
Adored tiger with cold caresses:
I will plunge into that jewel
Crowning thy too heavy tresses;

Swathe my head in thy skirts swirling
Perfumes that one never borrows,
Perfumes of some flower unfurling
Leaves like loves that hate their morrows.

Sleep were better far than living!
In a sleep, one fears its waking;
Bodies' kisses unforgiving,
All my passions in thee slaking.

All thy sobbings I shall squander
In thy bed's abyss, beneath thee,
Drink thy mouth where lost loves wander
In the shadowy halls of Lethe.

To my destiny obeying,
One predestined to his evil
Limbs of mine they may be flaying,
Yet, if all's not worth the Devil,

I shall seek, as one anointed,
Hemlock and a drug liquescent
From thy breasts, where they are pointed
Where the moon is not senescent.

Altogether

THE DEMON into my haunted room
Flew up from his infernal vault,
And said to me: "What of her perfume,
If I might judge you in default,

That as the Evil spirit dozes
On her fair body's sorcery,
Among the red and the black roses
That give to her her harmony,

Which is the sweetest?"—O my Soul's shame,
Thou wouldst reply to the Abhorred:
"Since all in her is fire and flame,
I prefer nothing, O my Lord."

When all things ravish me, I ignore if
There is a more seductive passion
Than the dear Dawn's that I adore if
Night were more sinister in her fashion.

The harmony is too exquisite
That governs that strange body of hers,
For the ineffable analysis of it
To note the accords of Idolators.

O most mystical transfiguration
Of all my senses that swoon in the room!
Her breath makes music her creation,
Her voice creates its own perfume.

To Her Who Is Too Gay

THINE AIR, thy head, thy gesture,
Nothing to call thee after
But, in thine own investure,
A being made of laughter.

The colour to thy pale cheek rushing
Dazzles all beholders.
This passes into blushing
Of naked arms and shoulders.

That shifting colour, know it's
A serpent's in a valley,
That in the mind of Poets
Evokes a flowerless Ballet.

These mad clothes, they are jolly,
Thy spirit seems to await thee;
Thou fool to mine own folly,
I love thee as I hate thee.

And sometimes in a garden
When I am slowly dragging
Mine own self, I ask pardon
Of the sun that's lagging;

And what all surpasses
In my heart's derision
Is my hate of grasses,
Nature's insolent vision.

So on a night I owe man,
When the glow-worm's calling,
Towards thy treasures as no man
Thou shalt see me crawling,

Thy flesh to admonish,
Thy breast pardoned follow,
And in thy breast astonish
Flesh with a wound that's hollow,

Vertiginous divining!
Through thy new lips' aversion
To infuse in twining
Venom-stung aspersion!

The Gambling Room

IN FADED ARMCHAIRS ancient whores are wrangling
—Heads heavily painted, eyelashes that shock,—
Who in their meagre ears hear the loud jangling
And the cruel and criminal tick-tack of the clock;

Around green tables in ominous revulsions,
Colourless lips, the colour of sin's guests,
With their infernal fingers in convulsions,
Fumbling an empty purse or the heaving breasts;

Wonderful ceilings making their grimaces
Where enormous lamps hurl their atrocious lights,
Now on this tenebrous Poet, on other faces,
On all who squander the sad sweats of their nights.

Behold the black picture of a dream nocturnal,
Flashed on the passion of my visionary eyes;
Myself, in one corner of this lair infernal,
I see myself seated, silent, envious of the skies,

Envying in some of these the tenacious passion
Turned in these whores to a damnable gaiety
That traffic in my face in an infamous fashion,
One of her beauty, one of her lost virginity!

And my heart was afraid of envying some poor man sunken,
In the abysmal depths of his damnation,
Preferring, having of his own blood heavily drunken,
Sorrow to Death and Hell to annihilation!

Evening Harmony

THE SEASONS make shake in violent vibration
Flowers that evaporate in a sacred room;
In the air of the night turn sound and perfume;
—Waltz vertiginous in intoxication!

Flowers that evaporate in a sacred room;
The Violin shivers like a heart in agitation;
—Waltz vertiginous in intoxication!
The sky is sad as a shrine that the flames consume.

The Violin shivers like a heart in agitation,
A heart that hates annihilation like the Tomb!
—The sky is sad as a shrine that the flames consume;
The Sun is drowned in his blood's coagulation.

A heart that hates annihilation like the Tomb
Gathers the Past into an Hallucination;
—The Sun is drowned in his blood's coagulation;
Thy memory haunts me like an aching Womb!

What Would You Say To-night

WHAT WOULD YOU SAY TO-NIGHT, poor soul, after what fashion,
What would you say, my heart, heart withered and malign,
To the most dear, most fair, most good, except that her passion
Must be a sudden silence and a regard divine?

—We shall be proud in singing all her praises,
Nothing is worth the sweetness of her vanity;
Her spiritual flesh has the angel's perfume, which amazes
Those that assume the guise of Insanity.

Whether it be in the night or in the solitude,
Whether it be on the street or in the multitude,
Her ghost in the air dances like a torch lit with wine.

Sometimes it speaks and says: "I am fair as Belladonna,
For the love of me you must love only the Divine;
I am the Guardian Angel, the Muse and the Madonna!"

The Living Torch

THEY WAVER BEFORE ME, those Eyes full of lights,
That a most learned Angel has inspired with desires;
They wake, those divine brothers, brothers of the nights,
That fascinate mine eyes with their myriad fires.

Escaping from all snare and from all sin that's grave,
They lead me toward Beauty's vain Virginity;
They are my servants and I am their only slave;
My entire being obeys this torch's Divinity.

Eyes I adore, you shine with shadows orgiastic
Like the candles that burn at noon; the Sun with his hot breath
Reddens, never extinguishing their flames fantastic;

These sing the Awakening, you celebrate our Death;
You advance in singing my soul's eternal shame,
Stars of which no Sun can ever wither the flame!

Overcast Sky

ONE MIGHT SAY your regard was covered with a vapour:
Your green mysterious eyes that like a taper
Alternatively tender, drowsy, cruel,
Reflect the pallid indolence of a jewel.

You recall those days moist, under which the witches
Betray girls' hearts and steal from them their riches,
When, agitated by an unknown evil that twists them,
The awakened nerves scorn the spirit that resists them.

You have the likeness of these tragic treasons
That excite the suns in their most magic seasons.
—How you shone, in an enormous interfusion,
Inflaming the rays that fell from the sky's confusion!

O dangerous woman, O seductive regions!
Shall I adore your frosts and snows and the legions
Of locusts and from the pitiless winter environ
More bitter pleasures from frozen ice and from iron?

The Poison

WINE KNOWS HOW TO DECORATE the Evil Houses
With a luxury miraculous,
And to make surge from a sunset fabulous
The red gold, where the hot sun drowses
Before he falls into the Ocean perilous.

Opium heightens our unlimited Illusions
Beyond Eternity,
Deepens Time, hollows Sensuality,
And, with the pleasures of our Delusions,
Fills the soul beyond its own captivity.

All that is not worth the poison that is distilling
From thy green eyes, to clash on
Clouds when my soul trembles in an inverse passion;
My dreams as visions stilling
Their thirst in the bitter gulfs of furious fashion.

Nothing is worth the horrible projection
Of thy saliva, thy breath is
About to plunge my soul where Hades' wraith is,
And, *charioting* the creation,
Hurls it hideously where its ultimate Death is!

The Cats

THE WISE MEN LOVE THE CATS for their perversity;
They love them passionately in their sensual seasons;
Sweet subtle cats, so traitorous in their treasons
That, as they, shiver in their dire adversity.

Lovers of strange science and of sensuality,
They seek the intense horror that makes them furious;
They had been seized as his ghastly slaves by Erebus,
Had they inclined to him their sombre savagery.

They assume in dreaming the ancient attitudes
Of the great Sphinxes in the depths of their solitudes
That seem always to sleep in their virginity;
Their pregnant reins are full of the Signs of Magic,
Strange sparks of gold, like fine dust, magically
Shine like stars in their regards, tenebrous, tragic.

The Cat

IN MY BRAIN wanders in vain,
As in his own appointed room,
A cat luxurious in perfume
Who, when he mews, excites my brain,

So sweet and tender is his note;
But when his voice greatens and thunders,
His voice is made of several wonders,
Which is the charm that haunts his throat.

This voice which in its passion hates me;
And in my tenebrous depth's reverses
Satiates me as my nervous verses,
Just as a poison penetrates me.

It sends asleep most cruel evils,
It contains all the ecstasies;
But for the sensual harmonies
It needs no words—not even the Devil's.

No, there is no bow more biting
On my heart, a perfect instrument
With strings as if in vision rent
From chords that vibrate, that are smiting,

Save thy voice, cat mysterious,
Seraphic cat, cat cynical,
In whom all is diabolical,
As subtle, as harmonious!

—From his fur, soft as satin for the nonce,
Exhales a perfume so that, one night,
I was embalmed in his delight,
For having caressed him, only once.

He is the familiar spirit of the place;
He judges, he inspires, presides

All things in his empire, and, besides,
Is he not a god before God's face?

When towards this loved cat turn mine eyes,
Drawn by a something that in it burns,
Suddenly upon himself he turns,
And as I regard my Destinies,

I see, I see astonishingly,
The fire of his eyes on fire,
The shining opals of my Desire
That stare upon me fixedly.

St. Peter's Denial

WHAT HAS GOD DONE with all this flood of sacrifices
Which rises to his Seraphim divine?
As a tyrant intoxicated with his wine
His fearful sleep is haunted by his vices.

The sobs of martyrs slain, hallucinated,
Are an enormous monstrous Symphony,
Since, despite the rich blood of their sensuality,
The eternal Skies are never satiated.

—Ah! Jesus, dost thou remember the olive-garden?
Didst thou not kneel and pray—where none avails—
To him who in heaven laughed at the sound of the nails
Planted in thy living sides without God's pardon;

When thou sawest spit on thy Divinity
The filth of the kitchens where guards drank the wines,
And didst feel driven deep the execrable spines
On thy skull where lived immense Humanity;

When from the horrible weight of thy broken Body
Stretched thy distended hands, and when thy blood

And thy sweat poured from thee as a ravening flood,
When thou wast almost naked, almost bloody,

Didst thou dream of these immaculate visions
When the eternal promise had come to pass,
When thou dost trample, seated on a gentle ass,
On the narrow ways of the world and their derisions,

Where, with hearts' hope and hatred of the advances
Of the vile merchants thou didst scourge with rods,
Being Master then? Had not the thought of God's
Remorse penetrated thy sides before the Lances?

I shall leave Life satisfied, after the trial
Of the world where dream and action are absurd:
Might I use the sword and perish by the sword!
Saint Peter has denied Jesus? God's denial?

Spiritual Dawn

WHEN IN AN EVIL HOUSE the dawns awaken
Creatures more sodden than their Destiny,
By the sudden vision of its mystery,
In these drunken brutes an angel is suddenly shaken

From the huge height of the spiritual skies,
For the stricken man who hates his own submersion,
Dragged into the gulf in hideous immersion:
So, dear Goddess of Lucid Destinies,

On the smoking ruins of these stupid revels,
Shine to me from the very dawn of memory
Where in mine eyes fascination flies incessantly.

The sun has blackened the flames. By all the Devils
That haunt my Hell and damn me for my Obsession,
Save not my Soul save by its own Confession!

Invitation to the Journey

My CHILD and my star,
Let us wander afar,
None can resist her,
In the desire of living together;
—To live there at leisure,
To die there for pleasure
Under this wonderful weather!
The suns that have sunken
From these skies drunken
For my spirit have charms and have fears,
Like the mysteries that rise
From your treacherous eyes
That dazzle me over their tears.

There all is beauty, ardency,
Passion, rest and luxury.

The shapes that are shining
For our divining
Shall decorate our chamber;
The flowers in their flavour
Shall mix with the savour
So vaguely voluptuous of amber,
All these for the sleeper,
The mirrors are deeper,
In Oriental splendour
All these shall be token
Of the words I have spoken
In the spirit's sudden surrender.

There all is beauty, ardency,
Passion, rest and luxury.

See how on these Lagoons
Sleep sinister moons,

Vagabond and everywhere hurled;
It is to respire
Your most passionate desire
That they come from the ends of the world.
The suns that are setting,
All things else forgetting,
Over the city without pity,
Are hyacinths for one's keeping;
—The entire city is sleeping
In the luminous light of the city.

There all is beauty, ardency,
Passion, rest and luxury.

The Irreparable

WE HATE REMORSE: only can we stifle him?
Who lives in hideous damnation,
And feeds on us, like death's worm, none can rifle him,
In many a devious evasion?
We hate Remorse: only can we stifle him?

In what phial, in what wine, in what infusion,
Can we drown this old enemy,
Destructive and greedy as whores in their confusion,
Who live and die impatiently?
In what phial? In what wine? In what infusion?

Tell me, dost thou say it, O fair Sorceress,
To this spirit filled with anguish,
Like the dying, the wounded hurt in the battle's press,
And that in dying, languish,
—Tell me, dost thou say it, O fair Sorceress,

To this dying man that the wolf is flairing
And who is watched over by the Crows,

—To this broken soldier, if he is despairing
Of having his cross amidst his woes,
To this dying man that the wolf is flairing?

Can one destroy the night with one's mere scorning.
And tear the darkness and so mar light,
Denser than pitch, as night that has no morning,
A night that has no starlight!
Can one destroy a night with one's mere scorning?

Hope that burns in the windows of the Inn
Is extinguished, is dead for ever!
On a moonless night can one find refuge for sin
In spite of all his wild endeavour?
—The Devil has snuffed out all the candles in the Inn.

Adorable Sorceress, lovest thou thy damnation?
Say, knowest thou the Irremissible?
Remorse, as poisonous as thine own irritation,
Poisonous as hearts that hate their Hell?
Adorable Sorceress, lovest thou thy damnation?

The Irreparable gnaws with his accursed tooth
Our Soul, shame's punishment,
And he attacks the defences of our youth,
Our youth in banishment.
The Irreparable gnaws with his accursed tooth.

—I have often seen, in the depth of a Theatre diurnal,
Inflamed by an orchestra fabulous,
A fairy awaken, in a sky infernal,
A dawn of day miraculous;
I have often seen, in the depth of a Theatre diurnal,

Garbed in light simply, in gauze, in gold, a Being
Hurl down the enormous Satan;
My heart that knows not ecstasy is fore-seeing
A Theatre when the Powers of Evil greaten
Always—always in vain—the gauze-winged Being!

The Cracked Bell

IT IS SWEET AND BITTER, on the winter nights, for our Vices
To hear, near the fire that palpitates and smokes,
Our far-off memories and our vast surprises
Rise to the sound of the carillon the wind evokes.

Wonderful is the bell whose throat is vigorous
That, despite its age, being utterly content,
Casts always in the air its cry prodigious,
Like an old soldier who watches under his tent!

My soul is cracked, and when in its weariness,
With its songs it broods over the night world's loneliness,
It happens that its voice—one's misbegotten!—
Is like the death-rattle of a wounded man forgotten
Under a heap of the dead, beside a lake of blood,
And who dies immensely in that huge solitude.

The Flask

THERE ARE STRONG PERFUMES for which all matter amasses
Its odour—as if they penetrated the glasses.
Sometimes in opening an Oriental coffer scentless, dusty,
Whose lock is grating and reluctant and rusty,

Or in a deserted house where Circe's thinning
Scents turned Arachne to a spider for her spinning,
One finds an old yellow flagon that survives,
From which surges a living soul that thrives.

Ghastly chrysalids—the much more ghastly sleeping
Of shivering beings in the tapestries we are steeping
In colours which take flight, such as sea-caves,
And tints of azure—frozen roses—and gold waves.

Here is the memory of an intoxication
In the troubled air; the eyes close; annihilation
Seizes the vanquished soul and then consumes
Itself amongst the odour of its perfumes.

It destroys its own self near a gulf in a blinding sheet
Where—like Lazarus malodorous in his winding-sheet—
It moves in its awakening the spectral corpse that's dead,
An old tired love's, sepulchral, hallucinated.

Then, when I shall be lost in the Insanity
Of all that is most sinister in one's Vanity,
When I am thrown, an old flagon desolated,
Dusty and foul, abject, viscous, cracked and desecrated,

I shall be thine own coffin, amiable Pestilence!
The witness of thy force and of thy virulence,
Dear poison prepared by the angel's adorable wine,
That gnaws me, O life and death of my heart divine!

The Owls

UNDER THE YEW-TREE's heavy weight
The owls stand in their sullen fashions,
Like Pagan gods of Pagan passions
They dart their eyes and meditate.
Unmoving they stare with living flame
Until the end of the melancholy
Hour sees the oblique sun set in folly,
And darkness falls in shades of shame.
Their aspect to the wise man teaches
All that he needs, all he beseeches,
Tumult and change and discontent;
The man drunk of a shadow that passes
Keeps always the imperishable scent
That makes the wind change and the grasses.

The Beautiful Boat

MY DESIRE IS TO RESPIRE thy charms that are divine
And all in thee that is more beautiful than wine,
All this desire of mine
Is to paint the child whose fashions are malign.

When thou dost wander, thy skirt balances to and fro
In the wind's embraces from the seas that flow,
I see in thee a painted show,
Following an ardent rhythm, languid and slow.

On thy large neck, so pure and undefiled,
Thy dear head flaunts itself like dancers wild,
And I, the Exiled,
Follow thy subtle footsteps, majestic child!

My desire is to respire thy charms that are divine
And all in thee that is more beautiful than wine,
All this desire of mine
Is to paint the child whose fashions are malign.

Thine ardent breasts advance to meet the air,
Triumphant as the silk that hides them, and rare
As dancing-girls in vair
That leave thee to the winds that are most fair.

Provoking breasts, with their red points of roses!
Secret to none, as any shy rose that uncloses,
Where perfume with scent dozes
Delirious to the hearts wherein no rest reposes!

When thou dost wander, thy skirt balances to and fro
In the wind's embraces from the seas that flow,
I see in thee a painted show,
Following an ardent rhythm, languid and slow.

Thy noble legs under their draperies bewitching
Torment obscure desires, set my nerves twitching,

Like two Sorcerers pitching
Black drugs to a snake whose ardent coils are itching.

Thy lovely arms that wave luxuriously
Like unto shining coiling boas furiously
Press one's heart obstinately
And leave me, thy Lover, lonely as the Sea.

On thy large neck, so pure and undefiled,
Thy dear head flaunts itself like dancers wild,
And I, the Exiled,
Follow thy subtle footsteps, majestic child!

Heauton Timoroumenos [TO J.G.F.]

I SHALL STRIKE, being more cruel
Than my hatred, your sweet mouth
Scented as the sorcerous South!
And from your red lids, O my jewel,

In my throat's thirst, as I revel,
Shall gush water that quenches fire,
And my implacable desire
On your salt tears shall bring evil,

As a vessel from a distance
Where my heart's intoxication
Shall drink your sobs, alleviation
Of my passionate persistence!

Am I a wrong note that unites me
With the voracious symphony
Of that diviner Irony
Which in sensation smites and bites me?

She is in my voice the shrill shrew, calling!
She is black poison in all my blood; alas,
I am the sinister looking-glass
Where the Medusa sees snakes crawling!

I am the plague, the knife, the treason!
The cheek that feels the wound! I reel,
All my limbs quartered on the wheel,
That reels before me without reason!

I am of my own heart the Vampire, token
Of one compelled to the condemnation
Of laughter's uttermost damnation,
Who must wreak in hell what I have wroken!

Spleen (I)

PLUVIOSE, against the entire City irritated,
Pours from its great urn a cold that's tenebrous
Over the pale dead in the graveyard inundated
By sheer mortality and rains ruinous.

My cat seeking his strange litter ironically
Twists his thin body cruel and curious;
A Poet's shadow wanders in the gutter, wearily
Uttering the cries of a phantom infamous.

The bourdon makes lament and the firewood smokes
To the sound of the swinging pendulum that chokes,
Whilst in a game full of foul-hearted perfumes,
The fatal heritage of an old woman, an old maid's,
The tragical Knave of Hearts and the Ace of Spades
Hiss sinister-wise at dead loves their Death consumes.

Spleen (II)

I HAVE MORE MEMORIES than a thousand years.

A certain desk that holds balances and arrears,
Verses and criminal trials and romances

And certain women's tresses (after our dances!)
Hides much more secrets than my brain can hide.
It is a cavern, a Pyramid on either side,
That holds more dead people than the common noonlight.
—I am an abhorred grave and hated by the moonlight,
Where like remorse trail worms infuriated,
That always try to madden my dearest dead.
I am an ancient boudoir filled with passions
And with pale roses faded in their fashions,
Where Boucher's plaintive pastels fill the room
With an astonishing and intense perfume.

Nothing equals the horror of these long days crawling
When all the storm winds blow and the snows are falling,
And Ennui, dead fruit of incuriosity,
Assumes the proportions of Immortality—
—From this time forward, matter—can one scan it?—
You are no more than a block of fearful granite
Around whose base some sacred serpent curled.
—An ancient Sphinx forgotten by the world,
Forgotten on the map, wild with her error,
Sings only in the sunsets of her terror.

Spleen (III)

I AM LIKE THE KING of a land of rains and ditches,
Young and yet old, impotent among my riches,
Who, scorning the bows of his tutors and of his Priests,
Endures the weariness of his savage Beasts.
Neither his hawks nor his game can ever divert him,
Nor can his people who die before him hurt him.
He says of a woman: "Who can ever test her?"
He is unmoved by the ballads of his jester;
His bed is like a tomb one finds in Cadiz,

Nor can this fine Prince in his wanton Ladies
Excite their passions, nor when his wine smells musty,
Admire to excess their dresses lewd and lusty.
The wise men who make gold for him never could
Extirpate the corrupt element in his blood.
For these baths of blood the Romans used, remember
Who can, his sins from July to December,
Have never warmed this cold corpse stupefied,
Where instead of blood the green waters of Lethe glide.

Spleen (IV)

WHEN THE DULL DIRE SKY weighs like a heavy cover
Over the sobbing spirit in prey to Pagan rites,
And when upon the stern horizon one can discover
A day made blacker than our infamous nights;

When the entire earth is changed into a prison
Where Hope, like a wicked night Bat that has forgotten
The way, goes beating its wild wings from the floor arisen
And knocks its head against the ceilings rotten;

When the immense winds in the sky, like strong storm-riders,
Howl into barred windows and walls with pouring rains,
And when the silent and sinister people of the Spiders
Spread their inextricable webs in our sorry brains,

Suddenly the bells leap with intense fury thundering,
Hurling up to the sky their ferocious howling,
Like unseen spirits that are forever wandering,
That sob their hearts out at the cloud that's scowling.

And ancient state-carriages, without music, like erotic
Shades defile very slowly in my sad spirit, and sinister Hope,
Weeping like one who is vanquished, and anguish, despotic,
Set on my skull their black flags, in the wind's scope.

Mists and Rain

WINDS OF AUTUMN, winters dipped in mud,
I love you, sleepy seasons, with my blood,
And praise you that you hide my heart below
A vaporous shroud that all the tombstones know.

In this great plain where cold as rain I stood
In the long nights when the weather-vanes creaked like wood,
My soul renewed itself with sudden heat, and lo!
My spirit opened its wings like a croaking crow.

Nothing is sweeter to the ravaged heart that clings
To frost that whitens the whole space of things,
Than the sad certainty of being hallucinated,
Except the aspect of a nightless noon,
—If it were not, on a night without a moon,
For two to sleep with sorrow on a hazardous bed.

To a Red-Haired Beggar Girl

MY WHITE GIRL with red-gold tresses,
Let not this one of thy dresses
Leave bare all the poverty
Of thine ardency,

For me, poet, soul's my study,
All that's sad in thy mad body
Has beside its pure completeness
Sin's suave sweetness;

Thou dost wear with more perfection
Than a jesting-girl's dilection
Velvet shoes that have the passion
Of some fashion.

Instead of rags, there's no adorning
Like a superb court gown for morning
Wear, in certain folds one feels are
Where thy heels are;

Let instead of silken stockings
For the rakes and for their mockings
On thy leg a golden garter
Their taste martyr;

Let the loose knots be unveiling
For our sins the unavailing
Brightness of thy breasts that glisten
(Let me listen);

That for thy entire undressing
Thine arms on their own arms pressing
Chase with mutinous grace what lingers
In their fingers;

—Pearls that spell the soul's disaster,
Sonnets of Belleau our master,
In thy lovers one discovers
Rhyming lovers;

Flocks of rhymesters and cut-purses
Dedicate to thee their verses.
How thy slippers, dear, they ogle
Like a bogle!

Many a page where many a sword is,
Many a Ronsard where many a lord is,
Shall for thy sake make a sonnet
And dream upon it.

Thou shalt count in beds what laden heads
Shall have possession of thy maidenheads,
Here a Valois, then a Kingless
Man that's stingless.

—Yet at last thou must go spying
A certain ruined creature lying
On the threshold of some tavern,
Vefour's cavern;

Then with eyes where all that's cruel
Shines, for a mere trifling jewel
That I cannot (I forgive thee!)
Give thee;

Go then, with no more adornment
Than the perfume of the morn meant,
Than the divine impurity
Of thy purity!

The Irremediable

AN IDEA, A FORM, a Being created,
Hurled from the sky and fallen in,
A Styx as miry and as leaden as Sin,
Where no eye of the sky has penetrated;

An Angel, an imprudent traveller benighted,
Tempted by his passion for all deformity,
In the depths of nightmares, dire enormity
Struggling with shadows self-invited,

With infernal anguishes coquetting!
Against a backwater gigantic
That sings as it surges like madmen frantic,
And is in the darkness pirouetting;

A wretch bewitched by a wise wild wizard,
Groping forever and forever falling
Into the void where the reptiles are crawling,
Seeking for a key and finding a vizard;

A damned soul descending without lamplight
Into a gulf where stupefaction
Turns to an abject putrefaction,
Down eternal staircases that give but damplight;

A ship seized in the Pole, arisen
From some deep places where strange men snare men,
Seeking to find like flying airmen
How it has fallen into this prison;

—Sad symbols, shadowing the imperfect
Fortune that to fools is as irremediable
As the certainty that the Devil in Hell
Has made, as God made, all things perfect!

Face to face now and none dissembles
That a heart is its mirror absolutely!
Deep dark Pits of Truth, where veritably
One livid star in the wan sky trembles,

A lighthouse ironical and infernal,
Torches of grace Satanical,
Glory unique, diabolical,
—Conscience in Evil is Eternal!

Dawn

THE AWAKENING sang in the courts of all the barracks,
And the morning wind breathed on the lanterns like their arracks.

This is the hour when the swarms of dreams injurious
Twist on pillows youths who are much too curious;
Where, like an aspect that palpitates with dread,
The lamp on the daylight makes a spot that's red;
Where the soul, under the weight of the body peevish,
Fights with the lamp and the daylight, these being thievish.
Like a face covered with tears that the winds misshape,

The air is full of the shivers of things that escape,
And the man is weary of writing and the woman of loving.

The houses begin to smoke and the ever roving
Wanton women of pleasure, with their eyelids vivid,
Mouths open, sleep stupidly and awaken livid.
The poor women, with lean thin breasts, where poverty lingers,
Breathe on their firebrands and breathe upon their fingers.
It is the hour when the niggard lines of the wild bed
Exaggerate the travail of women in their childbed;
Like a sob broken by a blood that foams and chokes,
The cry of the cock lacerates the air that smokes;
A sea of mists bathes the walls of the edifices,
And those dying in the hospitals, dreaming of precipices,
Utter their last death-rattle in their last surmises.
The debauched went home, worn out by all their vices.
The yellow dawn in robes of red and green shivering,
Advanced slowly over the deserted sad Seine quivering,
And sombre Paris, rubbing its eyes, began to seize
Its heavy tools, warmed by the breath of the breeze.

Evening Twilight

THE NIGHT COMES, friend of the Criminal, suddenly;
It comes with wolfish steps and cruel passions; the sky
Closes upon itself like an immense alcove,
Man, furious, changes himself into a beast wild with love.

O night, adorable night, one's adoration,
Desired by all who lie and say: To-day in our prostration
All of us have worked! It is the night that solaces
Spirits devoured by the woes of loneliness,
The obstinate wise man who has all things read,
And the worn out labourer who returns to bed.
Yet the unclean demons in the atmosphere

Heavily wake before they have seized on fear,
And fly and frighten the penthouses and the shutters.
Across the strange gleams the wind torments, there mutters
In all the streets intoxicated Prostitution,
Like a heap of ants that dig their restitution;
Everywhere Prostitution becomes more difficult
As one who leads spirits into ways occult;
Stirring in the heart of the city the utter filth
Of the enriching gutter's plague-green spilth.
One hears here and there the kitchens noisily shrieking,
The orchestras thunder, the theatres are squeaking,
In the dining-rooms, where one gambles, one surprises
The prostitutes and the sharpers and all their Vices,
And the Thieves, who have no mercy nor no truce,
Must to-day begin their work, thanks to the deuce,
So as to force upon the doors and the cash boxes
And live and dress their mistresses, their Doxies.
Awaken, my soul, at this grave moment and adore
Thy God and hear no more the city's roar.
At this hour the sorrows of the sick are not diminished!
The sombre night seizes them by the throat—they have finished
Their destiny and go toward the gulf, maid, nun;
The hospital is filled with their sad sobbing—more than one
Shall never again find perfumed soup in his room,
By the fireside, at night, nor his mistress's perfume.

Why is it that these, beyond their sin's forgiving,
Have never lived nor known the art of living?

Satan's Litanies

O THOU, WISEST OF ANGELS in Heaven's mazes,
God betrayed by Fate and deprived of praises,

O Satan, have pity of my intense misery!

O Prince of Exiles, to whom God has done wrong,
Who, being vanquished, vanquishes the strong.

O Satan, have pity of my intense misery!

Thou who knowest all, King of the wings of Thunder,
Healer of Evils, that leave God in wonder.

O Satan, have pity of my intense misery!

Who to accursed Animals that have lived on lies
Teachest by love the taste of Paradise.

O Satan, have pity of my intense misery!

O Thou, who of Death, thine ancient and mad mistress,
Engenders madder Hope—deceived by this tress!

O Satan, have pity of my intense misery!

Thou who canst damn upon a scaffolding
A criminal who conspired against a King.

O Satan, have pity of my intense misery!

Thou who knowest in what hidden lands rare Spices
Are hid where thy jealous God hid precious vices.

O Satan, have pity of my intense misery!

Thou who knowest the secrets of the Arsenals that keep
The people of Metals shrouded in deep sleep.

O Satan, have pity of my intense misery!

Thou whose huge hand conceals the precipices
From the Somnambulist stumbling on Hell's abysses.

O Satan, have pity of my intense misery!

Thou who dost rub with oil and balm the old bones
Of benighted drunkards fallen on the stones.

O Satan, have pity of my intense misery!

Thou who to give to man his ultimate passion
Makes him mix madness with a wanton's fashion.

O Satan, have pity of my intense misery!

Thou who didst seal an intolerable sign
On Midas, of all misers the most malign.

O Satan, have pity of my intense misery!

Thou whose cult of rags and plagues and scarlets
Excites the eyes, incites the hearts of Harlots.

O Satan, have pity of my intense misery!

Staff of Exiles, conspirator's lamp, high Priest,
Who confesses hanged men in some bloody Feast.

O Satan, have pity of my intense misery!

Father of those who in his huge derision
God the Father chased from Paradise in perverse vision,

O Satan, have pity of my immense misery!

Glory and praise to Thee, Satan, in the heights,
Of Heaven where thou didst reign, and in the immense nights
Of Hell where, in the deep silence pregnant thou broodest!
Let my soul repose under the Tree of Science, rudest
Of deaths in life, until that ultimate Hour
Sound, for our sakes, on Hell's eternal Tower!

The Woman Servant

THE WOMAN SERVANT of whose heart you had been jealous—
—Does she sleep under the turf who had been zealous?
We ought to give her certain flowers, to-morrow's.
The dead, the poor dead, they have much greater sorrows,

And when, lifter of the old trees, the cold October
With his melancholy wind that makes men sober,
Certainly, they must find us, the living, ungrateful,
Who sleep, as they do, warmly, who yet are hateful,
Whilst, devoured by black dreams and violent visions,
Without bedfellows, without even their derisions,
Old skeletons travelled by the worm, hell's splinter,
They feel fall over them the snows of winter,
And without friends see fly Eternity
Replacing the rags of their mere nudity.

When the firewood hisses and sings, if at the night time
I see her sit in the chair, if that were the right time,
A very blue and very cold night of December's,
And I found her crouched in my room, beside the embers—
Grave, and coming from her bed eternal,
Were to brood over her great child with eyes maternal,
What could I say to this soul, what words could follow
Words, if I saw fall tears heavily from her eyelids hollow?

A Martyred Woman

SKETCH BY AN UNKNOWN MASTER

IN THE MIDST OF FLASKS, of stuffs, spangled, moth-consumed,
And of objects voluptuous,
Of marbles, pictures and of robes perfumed
Which trailed in folds luxurious,

In a warm room where never a warm wind passes,
The air is fatal and dangerous,
Where bouquets, dying in their thin coffins of glasses,
Exhaled their last sighs dolorous,

A headless corpse pours out like a river smoking,
On a pillow that slakes its thirst,

A red and living blood, of which the linen is soaking
With the avidity of the Accursed.

Like a pale vision that engenders shadows and obsesses
The enchantment of eyes too cruel,
The head, with its immense mass of sombre tresses,
With many a precious jewel,

On the night table, like a ranunculus
Reposes, and, void as Orient dyes,
A vague intense regard makes ridiculous
The horribly revulsed eyes.

On the bed, stark naked trunk's exposure,
In the most complete abandonment
Of the fatal beauty and of its dire disclosure
Of what God gave it and its scent;

A rose-red stocking, with gold coins, on the leg that barters,
Remains like one's memory;
And like secret eyes that flame, her famous garters
Dart rays of sombre mystery.

The singular aspect of this sinister solitude
And of a great portrait languorous,
With eyes provocative as her impure attitude,
Reveal a passion tenebrous,

A guilty joy that feasts like beasts and revels
Full of infernal kisses,
Exultant as the swarm of evil devils
That writhe in the curtain's abysses;

And yet, to see how thin in their secret passion
The shoulder emaciated,
The thighs that are too pointed in their fashion
Like a reptile irritated,

She is so young! Her spirit exasperated
And her senses and her incenses,

Were they not made for the hounds of Hell, lacerated
As her flesh that cries and her senses?

The vindictive man that you could not have, when you were
    living,
Satiated as if with fire,
Did he not penetrate your inert flesh with the unforgiving
Immensity of his desire?

Answer, impure corpse! And by thy tresses rigid,
Lifting thee with an arm feverishly,
Tell me, fearful head, has he not on thy teeth frigid
Fashioned his last kisses furiously?

Far from the jesting world, far from the crowd's impurity,
Far from the mobs incurious,
Sleep in peace, sinister Sorceress, in thy purity,
In thy tomb mysterious;

Thine immortal frame, over which sweet dreams hover,
Shall meet after his breath
Is out of him, thy most unfaithful lover,
In the shadow we name death.

Moesta Et Errabunda

TELL ME, DOES THY HEART FLY far from thee, Agathe,
From the darkness to the foul City on the Sea,
Toward another sea as fair as any agate,
Divine as any maid's virginity?
Tell me, does thy heart fly far from thee, Agathe?

The sea, only the vast sea consoles our labours!
What Demon has damned the Sea, some hell-bringer
Of more than sinister Saracenic sabres
To the sheer sublimity of a death-flinger?
The sea, only the vast sea consoles our labours!

Carry me far from the city, O meagre maggot!
Far from Paris where the wind's made of our weeping!
Is it certain that the sad mad heart of Agathe
Says: Far from cruel crimes and criminals' sleeping,
Carry me far from the City, O meagre maggot!

How far you are, Paradise perfumed, painted,
Where love and joy are mixed and sin is sunken,
When all one's love is by some passion tainted,
When the mad heart is tragically drunken!
How far you are, Paradise perfumed, painted!

But the green Paradise has other gardens,
That lure in the void where kisses are divine,
Where the violins dying in the act of Pardons
Mix in the words with our own blood our wine.
But the green Paradise has other gardens,

The innocent Paradise, full of furtive pleasures,
Is it more distant than the Indian sea?
Can one recall with cries of listless leisures
And animate with a voice of active agony
The innocent Paradise full of furtive pleasures?

I Have Not Forgotten

I HAVE NOT FORGOTTEN, adjacent to the City,
Our pure white house, when we were wise and witty,
The great Pomona and its ancient Venus
And the naked busts of the figures that came between us;
—And the sun, that shone before our days were ended,
Behind the window, where we enjoyed the offended
Eyes of the Gods, who pitiless to all sinners,
Saw all our lazy and luxurious dinners,
Where we composed, adoring the sunsets, the fashions
Of Latin Lovers who had assuaged their passions.

Causerie

You are an autumnal sky the spirit knows!
Sadness within me rises like the sea,
And leaves, in its ebbing, on my lip morose,
The bitterness of inexorable misery.

—Thine hand glides in vain over my breast, inhuman;
What it seeks, dear, is a place—can one sweeten it?
Ravaged by the ferocious claws of the woman—
Seek not my heart; the monsters have eaten it.

My heart is a tavern withered by its sin,
Intoxication and self-slaughter entered in:
—A perfume wanders over your naked breast!

O Beauty, plague of souls, our soul's unrest!
With thine eyes of fire, furious as the feasts,
Calcine these rags spared by the raging beasts!

To a Creole Lady

In a perfumed land the Oriental sun caresses,
I have known, under purple tinged trees beside a ford,
Near palm trees which excited the eyes to idlenesses,
A creole woman whose beauty was ignored.

Her complexion is hot; the brown-skinned Enchantress
Has languors as she passes across the sward;
Slender and straight she walks with leisured loveliness,
Do not her eyes say unto her: "I am adored"?

If you should go, Madame, to the land of glory,
On the margins of the Seine you would read the story
Of the wars of France and of her manor-houses,

You would make, in the deep shades that no sun tracks,
Germinate sonnets in a Poet's heart that drowses,
That your eyes would make more cringing than your Blacks.

Damned Women (*I*)

DELPHINE ET HIPPOLYTE

IN THE LIGHT OF LANGUISHING LAMPS in their recesses,
On perfumed cushions by their own scent scented,
Hippolyte dreams of the ravishing caresses
The curtained skies have never yet frequented.

Her eyes are by the wind of a tempest troubled,
That have in them the intensity of a division
Of one who, when the sight of him is doubled,
Hates the obscure vision of his derision.

In her eyes all the fantasies of her fashion
Show her sad stupor, her sensuality,
Her shaken sighs, the accents of her passion,
And of her rare beauty the fragility.

Filled with a furious joy, at her feet extended,
Delphine desires her with her eyes' fierce fires,
As a strong animal on his prey undefended
Fastens his teeth and dies of his desires.

Strange beauty kneeling before beauty stranger,
Superb, she breathes in deep, voluptuously,
The wine of her triumph, nothing now can change her,
As her feverish frenzy rises furiously.

She seeks in the other's eyes where her cruel crime is,
The silent song that chants her secret pleasure,
And in her gratitude, for what sublime is,
Her eyelids beat and her foot dances their measure.

—"Hippolyte, dear heart, thy passion's bud uncloses,
In the mere act of its long quivering,
In the harvesting of the fairest of thy roses
To violent desires itself delivering.

My kisses are as light as a bird's feathers
That fell out of the mists of evening's errors,
Kisses like beggars in the dusty weathers
That have but these as shelter for their terrors.

They shall pass over thee and not discover thee
In our dim alcove hidden from our City.
Hippolyte, O turn thy face, I will bend over thee,
Thou, my soul and my body, my all and my pity,

Turn towards me thine eyes, let futurity
Flame in thy dear regards, embalm them finely:
I would lift thy veils for more of night's obscurity,
To sleep with me in thee and die divinely!"

Hippolyte, lifting her young visage, irritated:
—"I am not ungrateful and have no repentance,
My Delphine, I suffer and am disquieted,
As after a night's repast, over sin's last sentence.

I feel melt in me I know not what obsession,
As if some ghosts in flesh risen up in body
Led me in all their horrible procession
To where the very sunset's stained and bloody.

Have we entered any reincarnations?
Explain, if thou canst, my fear that beats within me:
I shiver with dread at all of our creations,
And yet my mouth is thine and thou art in me.

Do not regard me thus, my predilection,
Thou that I love forever in love's sedition,
Even if thou wert my sister in election,
And the very beginning of my own perdition!"

Delphine, shaking her tragic tresses, erotic,
Writhing like a Sibyl shaken as her spell is,
With fatal eyes, replies in tones despotic:
—"Who before Love dare speak of where our hell is?

There is a curse on those who dream of peril
And would the first in their stupidity
Fathom problems unsolvable and sterile,
And mix with honesty love's cupidity!

He who would unite in a cadence magical
Shadow with heat and night with noontide's flaming,
Shall never warm his body's aspect tragical
In this red sun that loves and knows no shaming!

Go, if thou wilt and find a man that's cruel,
Offer a virgin heart to his senseless kisses:
Thou shalt bring to me, livid, a loveless jewel,
Thy stigmatised breasts, not knowing yet what this is!

Shall our passions here ever be contented?"
But, the child, seeing some sorrow from her escaping,
Cries suddenly:—"I feel in my being demented
An abyss that is my heart, an abyss gaping,

Burning as a volcano, deep as the empty spaces!
Never with this monster shall I be satiated,
Nor my throat refreshed save with the Furies' graces,
That burn me to the blood intoxicated.

Our closed curtains might bring isolation,
And lassitude's repose under the doom-stones:
I shall find in thy breast annihilation.
Then sink forever underneath the tomb-stones!"

Descend, descend, Lesbians lamentable,
Descend the way that leads to hell infernal;
Plunge in a deep gulf where crime's inevitable,
Flagellated by a wind driven from the skies eternal,

Where all your torments, and for all the ages,
Mad shadows, never at the end of your desires,
Shall never satisfy your furious rages,
And your chastisement be born of loveless fires.

Never a ray of light shall illuminate your caverns;
By the holes in walls miasmas insinuating
Shall flame as lanterns that have lighted taverns,
Your bodies with foul perfumes permeating.

The sharp sterility of your lasciviousness
Shall change your skin into discoloration,
And the furious wind of your concupiscence
Make your flesh spin in the wind of dislocation.

Far from the living world, in condemnation,
Wander as wolves after a ghostly vanity;
Make of your destiny, souls disordered, your damnation,
And escape the duplicity of your insanity!

Damned Women (II)

LIKE BROODING BEASTS they lie on the wet sands sloping,
Turning their eyes in the direction of the Seas,
Feet stretching out to feet and their hands groping,
They endure strange spasms and bitter agonies.

Some, their breasts seized with their intoxication,
Hiding themselves in the sombre depths of the woods,
Utter love's words, who, swift for their damnation,
Feel in their bodies the responses of the blood's;

Others, like sisters, see from the rocks emerging,
Apparitions in the forms of fornications,
Where Saint Anthony saw, as small sly serpents surging,
The naked purple breasts of his temptations;

There are, that as they hear the panthers growling
In the mute hollows of their Pagan lairs,
Call thee to save them from love's fevers howling,
O Bacchus, luller asleep of ancient cares!

And others, whose breasts love all the Scapularies,
Hiding a whip for scourge under their vestures,
Mix, in the sullen nights when midnight marries
Midnight, their foaming lusts with stricken gestures.

O martyrs, O demons, O monsters, O virgin
Unvirginal, who hate the venom of the skies,
Seekers after the Infinite, who see surge in
Their spirits an immensity of cries,

You that in your Hell my soul seeks hallucinated,
I love you more than one who loves a City,
For your sad sorrows, for your thirsts unsatiated,
And for your loveless loves that know no Pity!

Love and the Skull

LOVE IS SEATED on Humanity's
Skull that must be nameless,
On this throne and its Profanities
With his laughter shameless,

Breathes upon the whirling bubbles
In the wintry weather,
That rejoin the world's worst troubles
In the swirling ether.

The globe frail as words unspoken
Soaring up and screaming,
Spits his wasted soul that's broken
In the act of dreaming.

I hear the sad skull's sobs atrocious
To the bubble that diminishes:
"This game ridiculous and ferocious—
What then if it ever finishes?

For what in the air they mouth that's cruel,
Assassin, is what matters,
Monster, my morbid love, my jewel,
My blood, my flesh, it shatters!"

Beatrice

As I WAS WANDERING in my wanton fashion
Complaining not of Nature's cruel passion,
And sharpening my thoughts as one that wandered
As on my heart my poignard I had squandered,
I saw in midday over my head descending
A ghastly cloud that with a storm was blending
Its inhuman self with a troop of demons vicious,
Like little cruel dwarfs, curious, pernicious,
That gazed upon me with sudden stupefaction
As on an admired madman who is out of action,
And as they winked and chuckled and made a gesture
They shook off every scrap of their rare vesture.

"Is this really the Caricature of an evil Creature,
This shadow of Hamlet and certainly not his feature,
His hair dishevelled, as he sees his City,
Might one not have for him a sense of pity,
For this mere knave, for this mere malefactor,
Who is known to be an abominably bad actor,
Who wants to interest us only with the thickets,
With eagles and with flowers and with death's wickets,
As to us, writers of old plays dramatic,
He howls his phrases—from an empty attic?"

I might have—had my pride only been sundered,
Received these demons' shocks and never wondered!—
Turned suddenly my head and its vain vanity
On those obscure beings whose sheer insanity
Had caused a crime the sun might tremble at,
Had they not have cursed—can I ever dissemble that?—
My very heart's queen who with impish laughter
Devoted me and them to the hereafter.

Tomb of a Cursed Poet

IF ON A MIDNIGHT near a new Inn
One by an act of charity,
Behind a very ancient ruin
Buried your body famously,
At the hour when the cold clouds hide her,
The Moon, along with small things rotten,
Sees the webs woven by the spider
And viper's vipers are begotten:
You shall hear the ululation
On your head's condemned damnation
Of the wolves that howl in the leaves,
The cries of famished Sorceresses,
The lusts of men in whore's caresses,
And the plots of the dark thieves.

The Cask of Hate

HATE IS THE BARREL of the pale Danaides;
Vengeance with enormous arms utterly frantic
Precipitates into the void darkness of the Seas
Huge buckets full of blood and of snakes that antic.

The Demon in his abysses has made secret hollows
Through which fly sweating more than a thousand years,
After his heedless victims Hate hastily follows,
Makes bleed their bodies, galvanised by his shears.

Hate is a drunkard at the far end of a Tavern,
Who feels always his intense thirst born of his drink
Multiply himself like a hydra in a Cavern.

—But the jolly drunkards know to what depths they sink,
And that Hate endures this pang redoubtable
Of never having slept even in Hell.

A Journey to Cythera

MY HEART SWUNG BIRDLIKE in its intense distraction,
And soared in the cordages, hung heavily by its grip:
Under me swayed and surged the white-sailed ship
Like a radiant angel filled with intoxication.

What is this sad dark Isle? It is Cythera whose birth
Was famed in songs, made famous as the fashions
Of the most ancient and most adulterous passions:
It is a beautiful and a barren earth.

—Island of sweet secrets and of hearts savorous!
The superb ghost of the ancient Venus here finds room
To add her perfume to the sea's salt perfume
That fills one's spirits with cares calamitous!

Green Island where many a dazzling sunflower dozes
Under its scented, demented infatuation,
Where the sad sighs of one's heart in adoration
Burn and turn like incense over a garden of roses—

And shudder eternally in odours orgiastic!
—Cythera is only a ruin mocked by the skies,

A rock-strewn desert troubled by angry cries.
I saw upturned a singular thing—fantastic!

It was not even a shrine as one might take it,
Where the young priestess, amorous of her warm sheets,
Wandered, her body burning with secret heats
As the warm winds left her entirely naked.

But as we suddenly came on the sea's track
That might have been enough to trouble the swift sea-swallows,
We saw on an immense height a hideous gallows,
Stark on the naked sky and cypress black.

Ferocious birds perched on their pasture in desecration,
Destroying with rage a hanged man's flesh, once pure,
Each one planted, as a sharp tool, its beak impure
In the bleeding corners of this putrefaction;

The eyes were two holes, and from the belly violated
The horrible entrails hung between his thighs,
And these fiends, gorged with their hideous merchandise,
Having clawed him left him absolutely castrated.

Under his feet, a horde of infamous beasts
Turned round and round him in their stupefaction:
A much more infamous beast in agitation
Whirled on himself made furious for these feasts.

Cythera's child, for whom none had ever predicted
Such extreme tortures and such extreme insults,
In the expiation of thine infamous cults
And of thy passions that the grave interdicted,

Ridiculous hanged creature, thine are mine own sorrows!
I felt at the aspect of thy thin limbs wavering,
Rise to my teeth like some violent vomiting
The acrid flood of all one's lost to-morrows;

But, before thine atrocity, O poor devil,
I have felt all the beaks and the jaws like the anthers

Of lacerating ravens and of dead black panthers
That assassinated my flesh like veritable spawns of evil.

—The sky was lovely and how fair the Sea;
For me that instant was at once black and bloody,
Alas! and I had turned as a shroud turns ruddy
And my buried heart writhed in its agony.

In thine isle, O Venus, I found only upthrust
A Calvary symbol whereon mine Image hung,
—Give me, Lord God! to look upon that dung,
My body and my heart, without disgust!

Cain and Abel

RACE OF ABEL, drink and be sleeping:
God shall smile on thee from the sky.

Race of Cain, in thy filth be creeping
Where no seeds of the serpents die.

Race of Abel, thy sacrifices
Shall flatter the nose of the Seraphim;

Race of Cain, shall thy devil's devices
Come to an end in any Inn?

Race of Abel, time for thy seed-time
And for thy cattle to be accursed.

Race of Cain, shall there not bleed time
In thine entrails that howl with thirst?

Race of Abel, warm thy belly in Caverns
When the midnight hour is stark.

Race of Cain, tremble in thy taverns
As thou hearest the jackals bark.

Race of Abel, fear not pollution!
God begets the children of nights.

Race of Cain, in thy heart's solution
Extinguish thy cruel appetites.

Race of Abel, drowse and be trembling
As the lice in the haunted wood!

Race of Cain, on the roads dissembling
Trail thy progeny that cries for blood!

Ah, race of Abel, thy carrion's bloody
And shall follow the smoking soil!

Race of Cain, thy head that's muddy
Is not made for the viper's coil.

Race of Abel, let thy shame be shriven:
The sword is vanquished by the rod!

Race of Cain, mount up to thy heaven
And cast from heaven to the earth thy God!

Franciscae Meae Laudes

VERSES COMPOSED FOR A MODEST, LEARNED AND PIOUS WOMAN

Songs from mine exasperation,
Dear girl, lithe-limbed, of my creation,
In heart's solitude's crispation.

This intricately disseminated,
A woman too delicate to be hated,
Who saves our souls our God created!

As in Lethe fulminated,
I shall drain your kisses violated
In your magnetism impregnated.

When the tempest of our Vices
Shall shatter the shrines of sacrifices,
Lo, the Divinity swathed in spices,

As the sailor's star that hovers
Over many sleepless lovers,
I shall hang my heart on shrines she covers.

Well-water that is full of virtue,
Eternal spring of youth desert you
Never while my kisses hurt you!

What was soiled, burn with aspersion;
What was ribald, to wrath's reversion;
What was nerveless, to hell's perversion!

For my hunger, tavern-raven,
Light my midnight, cavern-paven,
With hell's perils straight to haven.

Add to venom venomous,
Scented breath, male, odorous,
Senses strange and savorous!

My lean languid limbs set quivering
No chaste hints of your delivering,
Water dyed from pinions shivering:

Golden jewels coruscated,
Salt bread, Francisca, never tasted,
Divine wine on your beauty wasted!

The Ghost

LIKE THE ANGELS with eyes of mauve
I shall return to thine alcove,
And towards thee in silence glide
Where the shades of the night abide;

I shall give thee, brown girl, soon
Kisses colder than the moon
And the caresses of a snake
Around a ditch, that coils awake.

When there dawns the morning frigid,
Thou shalt find my place there, rigid,
Until there comes the terrible night.

In thy passionate heart no truth is,
Where thy life and where thy youth is,
I, I shall reign over thee by fright.

Metamorphoses of the Vampire

AND YET THE WOMAN, who all things remembers,
Writhing her limbs as serpents on the embers,
Beating her breasts, as if herself she hated,
Utters these words by her musk impregnated:
—"I, my lips are moist, and I know the science
Of losing in a bed's depths my defiance;
I dry all tears of all that have the passion
For these my breasts, my laughter is their fashion.
I replace, for those men who see me naked,
The sun, the moon, the stars, so must you take it!
I have, dear learned man, the power to rifle
Flesh in my velveted arms, the strength to stifle
Certain, when I am naked, such igniting
To furnace-heat, as they my flesh are biting,
Who on this mattress swoon, these to enslave me:
The impotent angels would be damned to save me!"

When out of all my bones she had sucked the marrow
And as I turned to her, in the act to harrow
My senses in one kiss, to end her chatter,
I saw a gourd that was filled full with foul matter!

I closed mine eyes, all my body shivering,
And when I opened them, in the dawn's quivering,
I saw at my side a puppet of derision
Who had made of its blood too much provision,
Then fragments of a skeleton in confusion
That of themselves made a mere mist of illusion,
Or of a sign-board at the end of a batten
The winter wind swung, as it seemed, in Latin.

The Joyous Dead Man

IN A FOUL EARTH covered with snails and with stones
I shall dig for mine own self an immense tomb,
Where I shall full of ease extend my ancient bones
And sleep in oblivion like a shark on the spume.

I hate the Testaments. I hate the graves and the thrones;
Rather than implore pity from the waste world's wide womb,
Living, I would love to invite the crows with the crones
To make bleed my infernal carcass my sins consume.

—O worms! Dark demons without ears and without eyes,
You shall see come to you a dead man before Death dies!
Living philosophers, sons of hell's putrefaction,

You shall go across my ruin with remorseless tread,
You shall tell me if there is more torture in Hell than Damnation,
For that soulless body dead amongst the dead!

Sadness of the Moon

TO-NIGHT THE MOON DREAMS with more idleness;
Like a beautiful woman, who on her cushions rests,
And who with her delicate hand loves to caress,
Before she sleeps, the contour of her breasts.

Dreaming of love she finds in love's decisions
A sense of dying, very ardently she swoons,
And with closed eyes sees pass before her visions
Of suns that are burning and of the swooning moons.

When sometimes she lets fall upon her bosom
Her fragrant scent that odorous seems to blossom,
A certain Poet, sleepless because his art

Excites him, finds that her scent excites his passion,
Fragments of opals flash after their fashion:
He hurls against the sun the cries of his Heart.

The Fountain of Blood

SOMETIMES I HAVE SEEMED TO HEAR my frozen blood
Flow with the rhythm of a fervent flood,
I hear it flowing as the swooned sexual Senses,
Just as I feel my wound: the pain intense is.
Across the city where it seems most vile
I cease my breathing for a certain while;
Blood quenches the thirst of every living creature
And covers in red nature's ill-favoured feature.

I have desired of subtle and of sorcerous wine
To send asleep my subtle fears that keep
My senses drunken and my mind malign.
I have sought only in love an odious sleep,
But love to me is no more than a mattress of needles
Made to give drink to the cruel girls one wheedles!

Music

THE IMMENSITY OF MUSIC seizes me like the Sea!
Toward my star that's pale

Under a misty sky I furiously
Set myself to the sail;

And standing there near to the heaving helm
As the foam fails from me,
I mount and I descend and the waves overwhelm
The ship's sides the night veils from me;

I feel vibrate in me the passionate revulsions
Of a ship that shrieks like a wolf:
The wild wind and the tempest and its convulsions
Over the sombre gulf

Lull and annul me—and become monstrously the mirrors
Of my insensate errors!

The Pipe

I AM THE PIPE of a Great Joker;
One sees, in contemplating my mien
Of an Abyssinian, that his Queen
Knows that my master's a great smoker.

If he sees a woman he can choke her,
And I smoke exactly like the hovel
In which one reads a naughty novel:
He sees her cheeks covered with ochre.

I lull his soul with my own Litany
That from my mouth on fire like fretwork
Rises and twists around the network,

I twine around him wild-wood dittany
That heals the languor of his heart
And heals his spirit by mine art.

Destruction

THE DEMON AGITATES HIMSELF at my side, I follow him;
He swings around me always in the air infernal;
I feel him burn me hideously, I swallow him,
He fills me with a desire culpable and eternal.

He sways, knowing my great love of art, strange incenses,
Takes the seductive form of women over amorous,
And under a knave's most specious of pretences,
Accustoms my lips to love-potions infamous.

He leads me, under the regard of God who is deathless,
In the midst of—broken with fatigue and breathless—
Those deserted plains of Ennui, with cheeks painted—

And casts in my eyes that are filled with the last Illusion
Wounds wide-open, blood-red vestments that are tainted,
And the magnificence of Destruction and of Delusion!

Lesbos

MOTHER OF LATIN GAMES and Grecian graces,
Lesbos, whose kisses are magnificent,
Hot as the nights and fresh as foreign faces,
These have the passions of girls malevolent,
—Mother of Latin games and Grecian graces,

Lesbos, where the kisses are profoundly throbbing,
As seas in storms that furiously are forming
Into huge waves, the hearts of virgins sobbing
Deeper than love and in their bosoms swarming:
Lesbos, where the kisses are profoundly throbbing.

Lesbos, where the Phrynes in their superb acting
Give voice to all the winds that fly between us,
The Paphian stars in envy are contracting
A love for Sappho, jealous of no Venus!
—Lesbos, where the Phrynes in their superb acting,

Lesbos, land of nights hot and languorous,
That make at their mirrors, in their sterility,
Hollow-eyed girls, of their bodies amorous,
Caress the ripe fruits of their nubility—
Lesbos, land of nights hot and languorous,

Let Plato frown who had no sense of virtue;
You draw your pardon from your own excesses
Of amorous kisses, nothing now can hurt you,
Unexhausted in your Lesbian caresses.
Let Plato frown who had no sense of virtue.

Eternity around you seemed to harden
All of respite that keeps you all from pity
In the immensity of an expected pardon
From an unknown and very distant City.
Eternity around you seemed to harden.

Who of the Gods will dare to judge you ever
And give you up to certain hard conditions,
Whose balances are simply one's endeavour
To save oneself from self and self's perditions?
Who of the Gods will dare to judge you ever?

Just or unjust, which do you want for reason,
Virgins sublime? What shall we have hereafter
In matters of love and in matters of treason,
When heaven and hell shall echo back our laughter?
—Just or unjust, which do you want for reason?

For Lesbos has chosen me as the least ruinous
Of Poets to sing of the Virgins, lovely, idle,
For from a child I was admitted to the mysterious,

Frantic laughter that has nor bit nor bridle;
For Lesbos has chosen me as the least ruinous

Of Poets who without the least confusion
Keep watch over the passions of these daughters
Of fruitful Lesbos women, into the illusion
Of all that wanders between the winds and waters.
A Poet who without the least confusion

Knows the sea's passions, how the storm-waves harden,
And that around the rock for all its sobbing
The sea one night shall give Lesbos back for pardon
The adored dead body of Sappho, lifeless, throbbing,
For the sea's passion, where the storm-waves harden!

Of the male Sappho, the Poet and the Lover,
Fairer than Venus in her pallid pleasures!
—Azure is vanquished by the spots that cover
The tenebrous circle traced by the mad measures
Of male Sappho, the Poet and the Lover!

Fairer than Venus on the world arising
And pouring the treasures of her charms unwonted,
And her youth's beauty for the sun's surprising
On the old Ocean of her daughter enchanted:
Fairer than Venus on the world arising!

—Of Sappho who died of too much passionate dreaming,
When, insulting the Rite and the Cult invented,
She had given her body to her loved Phaon, scheming
More than all body's pride: genius demented
Of Sappho who died of too much passionate dreaming.

And since this time Lesbos is self-lamented,
And, despite the cries of the Universe perverted,
Intoxicates herself, herself tormented,
Whose cries are heard along her shores deserted.
And since this time Lesbos is self-lamented!

The Two Good Sisters

DEBAUCH AND Death are two detestable Hags,
Rich and ribald and of kisses prodigal,
Whose virginal limbs are always draped in rags,
Whose fervent ardours are demi-virginal.

To the Sinister Poet, enemy of man's money-bags,
Favourite of Hell, Courtesan and Cardinal,
Tombs and brothels show, under the infernal flags,
A bed remorse frequented never, maniacal.

And the coffin and the alcove pregnant to bestir me
Offer to all of us, like two sisters, listless leisures,
Fearful sweetnesses and intolerable pleasures.

Debauch, with unclean arms, when will you enter me?
O Death, when will you, her rival, her wiles being quaffed,
On her black cypresses your infected myrtles ingraft?

The Soul of Wine

ONE NIGHT, THE SOUL OF WINE sang in all the bottles;
"Man, towards you I thrust, O dear disinherited,
Under my prison of glass, my red wax throttles,
A song of one's light love's hallucinated!

I know that on the flaming hill one surrenders
One's pain and sweat and the heat of the sun furious,
For out of one's veritable spirit life one engenders,
But I shall not be ungrateful or injurious.

I feel an immense joy when I fall in a room
Into a man's throat worn by his work, some knave's,
So much so that his warm breast is a sweet tomb,
Better than when I exist in my frozen caves.

Do you ever hear the riotous, rough refrains of the Sundays,
And the hope that in my breast is like a scent?
Elbows on the table, shirt-sleeves pulled up, on Mondays
You will glorify me and you will be content.

I shall make glow of the eyes of your dear wife ravished;
To your son I shall give force to cling and to nestle
Against the frail athlete of life on whom I have lavished
The oil that strengthened the muscles of those who wrestle.

I shall let fall in you, vegetable that no man curses,
The precious grain sown by the Sower eternal,
So that from our love might emerge my passionate verses
That shall return towards God from the Hells infernal!"

The Wine of the Rag-Pickers

OFTEN, IN THE RED FLARING LIGHT of the night lamps,
When the wind beats the flame before the night decamps,
In the heart of an old suburb, a labyrinth, foul,
Where humanity growls in storms while the skies growl,

One sees a rag-picker nodding his head, we know it,
Stumbling and hitting the walls like any Poet,
Who, while hating his spies, his subjects, not his Muses,
His heart exults in plans his sense confuses.

He swears on oath, he dictates laws sublime,
Knocks down the wicked and forgets the time,
And under the firmament where no fiends can hurt you,
He astonishes himself with his own proper virtue.

Yes, those people who endure their own vexation,
Travailed and tormented by their exasperation,
Jaded and martyred under wild wastes the wind harries,
In a confused vomiting of our enormous Paris,

Return, perfumed by odorous wines and thus,
Followed by their friends curious and furious,
With all the splendour of the ancient hours,—
—Triumphant arches, flags and banners and flowers,

Arise before them by some solemn magic!
And in the luminous orgy strange and tragic
Of clarions, of the sun, of cries, of drums, there is enough
To intoxicate the people drunk with love!

It is thus that across frivolous Vanity and Humanity
The wine ran gold, the Pactolus of Insanity;
And in men's throats it sings its fierce achievement,
And reigns by its gifts like Kings in some upheavement.

So as to drown rancour and to lull the indolence
Of those accursed creatures who die in wickedness,
God, seized with remorse, made sleep for everyone:
Man added Wine, the sacred son of the Sun!

The Lovers' Wine

TO-DAY SPACE IS SPLENDID and idle!
Without bit, without spurs, without bridle,
Let us ride on wine's back, for wine is
As divine as the sky divine is!
As two angels of cruel evil
That follow the tracks of the Devil,
The wings of the creature we follow
On the wings of the winged Apollo.
Now in the air we are swaying,
On the whirlwind's wings that are fraying
The way where delirium takes us;
And the Devil knows we are praying
Without respite for the soul that forsakes us,
To find dreams when the dawn awakes us!

The Lonely Man's Wine

THE SINGULAR REGARD of a wanton woman dissembling
Her nerves which glide toward you like one's duty
Neglected when the wandering moon is trembling
Before she bathes the nakedness of her beauty;

The last gold coins in a gambler's fingers; confessing
What else, the lewd kiss of the meagre Adeline?
The sounds of a music encircling and caressing,
Like the cry of human sorrow toward the Unseen,

Nothing of this is worthy, O profound bottle,
Of your pregnant belly's penetrating balms that throttle
Some Poet's throat, who loses and wins the odds;

You offer him hope, youth, but not life's slavery,
—And pride, this treasure of all knavery,
That makes us triumphant and equal with the Gods!

The Assassin's Wine

MY WIFE IS DEAD and I am living!
Now I can drink till I am drunk.
When I returned my purse had shrunk,
My very fibres, unforgiving!

No King is more luxurious;
The air is pure, splendid the weather.
—That summer that we spent together
When I was furiously amorous!

—This terrible thirst tears me in tatters,
And yet I need the intoxication
Of wine that holds her grave's damnation
And nothing more; nay, nothing matters.

I hurled her into the depths of a pit,
And I pushed over her what her grave meant:
The whole heap of the hideous pavement
—Forget her? As soon as I cease to spit!

And in the name some souls have shrunken
From which nothing can unknot us—
Not even the demons that begot us—
When we had reason to be drunken,

I sent her word—the obscure night we had—
To meet me, as in our old folly.
She came! What madness to be jolly!
We are all of us more or less mad!

She was intolerably jolly,
Yet tired: and I who loved her, I,
Loved her too much;—and that is why
I said to her: Out of life's folly!

Alas, as one can comprehend me,
These drunkards, in their dreams invidious
To make of wine a shroud? Perfidious
These nights of mine that bite and rend me.

This invulnerable concupiscence
As the machines that the roads splinter,
Has never known, in summer or winter,
Love veritable in magnificence,

With all its sombre incantations,
And all its retinues infernal
Of Phials of poison, its diurnal
Clanking of chains, bones, dislocations!

—I am alone and free from slaughter!
And I shall be dead drunk to-night;
Then, perhaps, before my soul takes flight,
The earth shall be my bed, earth's daughter,

Never to waken me from slumber!
The chariot with its heavy wheels—
Mad thought that in my spirit reels!—
May in its rages without number

Destroy my guilty head and level
All of my limbs. Let the loud hills nod!
I shall mock myself as I mock my God,
The Holy Table and the unholy Devil!

Death of the Lovers

WE SHALL HAVE BEDS filled with strange scents odorous
And deep divans like graves where the suns shine,
And stranger flowers that are more savorous
Than these under the skies that shine like wine.

Vying with each other in their last heats languorous,
Our hearts shall be two vast torches, mad, malign,
Which shall reflect their lights luxurious
In our twin spirits, mirrors of the Divine.

On a night made of rose and blue after our fashion,
We shall exchange an unique flash wherein our passion
Shall sob like Circe's snared by her strange Spells:

Then shall an angel shadowing our shames
Revive, after their descent into their hells,
The mirror tarnished and the deathlike flames.

Death of the Poor

IT IS DEATH WHO GIVES US LIFE in excitation,
It is the end of life, the one hope, the one delight,

That, divine elixir, is our Intoxication
And which gives us the heart to follow the endless night.

Across the skies and the snow and our exultation,
This exhales in us and gives us an appetite
In the famous Inn inscribed on the Book of Damnation,
When we can always eat, sleep and write;

Where there is an Angel who holds in his hands magnetic
Slumber and the great gift of dreams ecstatic,
And who remakes the bed of the poor who are naked;

It is the God's glory, it is the mystical attic,
The poor man's purse, our sense of the dramatic,
The thirst of the Unknown skies and the Thirst to slake it!

Death of the Artists

How MANY TIMES must I shake my stupid shins
Before I kiss your hideous visage, Caricature?
To hit the mark, O mystical quadrature,
How many, O quiver, lose of my javelins?

We lose our soul in subtle plots to save our sins,
We must demolish many a sinister Signature,
Before we seize the great Creature's nomenclature,
Whose infernal desire throbs in our sensitive skins!

There are those who have never known their Idol,
And these damned Sculptors and their Capuchins
Who at the Confessional absolve our sins,
Have but one hope, O Paris, for some bridal!

And as the whirling world before us spins,
Let Death rush to the abyss fast in Hell's gins!

Prose Poems

The Stranger

"WHOM DO YOU LOVE BEST, enigmatical man, tell me? Your father, your mother, your sister, or your brother?"

"I have neither father, nor mother, nor sister, nor brother."

"Your friends?"

"You use a word whose meaning is thus far unknown to me."

"Your country?"

"I do not know in what latitude it is situated."

"Beauty?"

"Willingly had I loved Beauty, Goddess and Immortal."

"Gold?"

"I hate it as you hate God."

"What, then, do you love, extraordinary stranger?"

"I love the clouds, the clouds that pass, eternally, the marvellous clouds."

Plans

HE SAID TO HIMSELF, as he wandered about in a great and lonely park: "How beautiful she would be in an elaborate and stately court dress, descending the marble steps of a palace, opposite great lawns and fountains, and seen through the atmosphere of a lovely night. For she has the natural air of a princess."

Later, while passing along a street, he stopped before a picture shop, and finding in a folio a print of a tropical landscape, he said to himself: "No! It's not in a palace that I wish to possess her. We wouldn't feel at home there. Besides, the walls covered with gold would leave no room to hang her picture; in those solemn galleries there would not be a single cosy corner. Surely, it is *here* that I should live to cultivate my life-dream."

And, while studying the details of the print, he continued mentally: "At the seashore, a lovely wood cabin, surrounded by all those fantastic and shining trees whose names I have forgotten; in the air, an intoxicating, indefinable odour; in the cabin, a powerful perfume of rose and of musk; in the distance, behind our little domain, the tops of the masts rising and falling on the swell; around us, beyond the room full of rosy light filtering through the blinds, a room strewn with fresh mats and heavily scented flowers, with rare couches of a Portuguese rococo, made of a heavy, dark wood (where she would lie, so serene, so carefully fanned, smoking a faintly opiumed tobacco!), and beyond the timbered floor, the noisy twittering of birds intoxicated with the light, and the idle chatter of little Negresses; and at night, as an accompaniment to my dreams, the plaintive songs of the melodious trees, the sighs of the melancholy cassowary! Yes, here surely is the setting I seek. What have I to do with palaces?"

And farther on, as he was walking along a wide avenue, he saw a neat little inn, where two laughing girls were leaning from a window brightly hung with checkered calico curtains. And at once he said to himself: "My thought must be a great vagabond since it went so far to seek what is so near. Pleasure and happiness can be found in the first inn one comes to, in the inn discovered by chance, and so full of delights. A roaring fire, colourful earthenware, a fair supper, a strong wine, and a very wide bed with sheets a bit rough, but fresh. What could be better?"

Returning home alone, at the hour when wisdom's advice can be heard above the buzz of activity, he said to himself: "I have had, today, in my dreams, three dwelling places in which I found equal pleasure. Why compel my body to move about, since my soul travels so easily? And what is the use of carrying out any plan, since the plan in itself is sufficient joy?"

The Despair of the Old Woman

THE LITTLE SHRIVELLED UP old woman rejoiced when she saw the pretty child whom everyone adored and strove in every way to charm,—this pretty being as frail as was the little old woman herself, as toothless, as devoid of hair. And she came closer, that the child might see the joy in her face, and laugh with her. But the terrified child struggled under the caresses of the little decrepit old woman, and filled the house with his yelpings. Then the old woman retired into her eternal solitude, and she wept in a corner, saying to herself: "Ah! for us, miserable old females, the time has passed when we could please, when we could please even the innocent; and now we terrify the little children we want to love."

The Double Room

A ROOM which is like a reverie, a room truly *spiritual,* where the stagnant atmosphere is lightly tinged with pink and with blue. There the soul bathes in idleness, perfumed by regret and desire. There is something in it of the twilight, a glow of rose and of blue, a dream of felicity during an eclipse. The pieces of furniture have prostrated, lengthened, languid forms; they seem to dream, to be gifted with a somnambulistic life, like plants and minerals. The fabrics have a silent speech, like flowers, like skies, like setting suns. On the walls no artistic abominations. Relatively to the pure dream, to the unanalysed impression, definite art, positive art, is blasphemy. Here, all has the sufficient clearness and the delicious obscurity of harmony. An infinitesimal scent of the most exquisite choice, with which is mingled a slight humidity, swims in this atmosphere, where the slumbering spirit is lulled by the sensations of a hothouse. Muslin rains abundantly before the windows and the bed;

it scatters itself in snowy cascades. On this bed the Idol sleeps, the sovereign of dreams. Whence came she hither? Who brought her hither? What magic power has installed her on this throne of reverie and of pleasure? What matters it? I see her, I know her. Those are her eyes whose flame traverses the twilight; those subtle and terrible mirrors that I recognize by their fearful malice! They attract, they subjugate, they devour the glance of the hapless ones who gaze upon them. Often have I studied them, those black stars which excite curiosity and admiration.

To what benevolent demon do I owe the delight of being thus surrounded with mystery, with silence, with peace and with perfumes? O beatitude! That which we usually call life, even in its greatest moments, has nothing in common with this supreme life which is now mine and which I savour minute by minute, second by second! Lo! There are no more minutes, there are no more seconds. Time has disappeared; it is Eternity which reigns, an Eternity of bliss!

But, loud and terrible, a knock resounds on the door, and, as in an infernal dream, it seems to me that a pickaxe has struck me in the stomach. And now a Spectre enters. It is a tipstaff who comes to torture me in the name of the law; an infamous concubine, who comes to cry misery and to add the trivialities of her life to the sorrows of mine; or else the errand-boy of a newspaper who asks for the rest of the manuscript.

The paradisiacal room, the Idol, the sovereign of dreams, the *Sylphide,* as the great Chateaubriand used to say,—all this magic disappears at the spectre's brutal knock. Horror! I remember, I remember! Yes; this hovel, this abode of eternal Ennui, certainly is mine. Here are the stupid, dusty, ugly pieces of furniture; the chimney without flame and without embers, soiled with spittings; the sad windows on which the rain has traced furrows in the dust; the revised or unfinished manuscripts; the diary where the pencil has marked sinister dates! And this perfume of another world, with which my cunningly perfected senses were intoxicated is replaced, alas! by a foul odour of tobacco mixed with I know not what loathsome damp. One breathes here only the rancidity of desolation. In this narrow world, so full of disgust, only one known object smiles at me; the phial of laudanum, an old and terrible friend; but, like all one's women friends, alas! pregnant with caresses and treacheries.

Yes! Time has reappeared, now reigns as sovereign, and with this hideous old man returns his demoniacal retinue of Memories, Regrets, Spasms, Fears, Anguishes, Nightmares, Wraths and Nerves. I assure you that the seconds are strongly and solemnly accentuated, and that each one, issuing from the clock, says: "I am Life, unbearable, implacable Life!"

There is only one Second in life whose mission is to announce good news, that particular *good news* which causes inexplicable fear. Yes! Time reigns; he has reassumed his brutal despotism. And he drives me, with his double goad as if I were a bull,—"And gee up, then, moke! sweat, then, slave! Live, then, damnèd soul!"

The Confiteor of the Artist

How POIGNANT IS THE FALL of an Autumn day! Poignant as bodily pain, for there are certain exquisite sensations whose vagueness does not preclude intensity; and there is no point more stabbing than that of the Infinite. How blissful it is to drown one's gaze in the immensity of sky and sea! Solitude, silence, the incomparable chastity of the azure; a little sail shivering on the horizon, which by its minuteness and its isolation parodies my irremediable existence; the monotonous melody of the swell,—all these things think in me, or else I think in them (for in the grandeur of reverie the ego is soon lost!). They think, I say, musically and picturesquely, without quibblings, without syllogisms, without deductions.

Yet, whether these thoughts arise out of me or soar from the things themselves, they become too intense. Sensual energy creates restlessness and positive suffering. My nerves in their extreme tension give out only shrill and painful vibrations. Now the depth of the sky dismays me; its limpidity exasperates me. The insensibility of the sea, the immutability of the spectacle, revolt me. . . . Ah, must we suffer eternally, or eternally fly from the beautiful? Nature, pitiless enchantress, ever victorious rival, leave me! Cease to tempt my desires and my pride! The study of the beautiful is a duel in which the artist cries out with fear before he is vanquished.

To Everyone His Chimera

UNDER A WIDE GREY SKY, on a wide dusty plain, without roads, without grass, without one thistle, without one nettle, I met several men who stooped as they walked. Each of them carried on his back an enormous Chimera, as heavy as a sack of corn or of coal, as heavy as the accoutrement of a Roman foot-soldier. But the monstrous Beast was not an inert weight; on the contrary, it enveloped and oppressed the men with its elastic and powerful muscles; with its two vast claws it hooked itself to the breast of its mount; its fabulous head surmounted the man's forehead, like one of those terrible helmets by which the ancient warriors hoped to add to the terror of their enemies.

I questioned one of these men, and I asked him where they were going. He told me he did not know, nor did the others, but that evidently they were going somewhere, because they were driven onward by an invincible need of walking.

I noticed one curious thing: none of these travellers seemed to be exasperated by the ferocious beast that clasped his neck and squatted on his back; they seemed to consider the Beast a part of themselves. All these weary and serious faces showed no signs of despair; under the splenetic cupola of the sky, their feet plunged in the dust of a land as desolate as that sky, they wandered on and on with the resigned aspect of those who are condemned to hope forever. The procession passed beside me and sank into the atmosphere of the horizon, at the point where the rounded surface of the planet escapes from the curiosity of the human eye. For several moments I persisted in my endeavour to fathom this mystery; but before long an irresistible indifference came over me, and I was more horribly overwhelmed by it than were they themselves by their crushing chimeras.

The Clock

THE CHINESE TELL TIME by looking at the eyes of cats. One day a missionary, wandering in the environs of Nankin, noticed that he had forgotten his watch, and asked a small boy what time it was. The child of the Celestial Empire hesitated; after a moment he replied: "I shall tell you." Almost immediately afterwards he returned, holding in his arms a very fat cat, and, to use a colloquial expression, gazing into the whites of its eyes, he affirmed without hesitation: "It is not quite noon." Which was true.

As for me, if I lean towards my fair Féline, so felicitously named, who is at once the honour of her sex, the pride of my heart and the perfume of my spirit, whether at night or by day, in sunshine or in opaque darkness, I always distinctly see the hour in the depths of her adorable eyes, always the same hour, vast, solemn, great as space, without division of minutes or of seconds—a motionless hour not marked on any clock, and yet which is as light as a sigh, as swift as a glance.

And if some intruder were to disturb me while my gaze rested on this charming dial, if some rude and intolerant genie, some Demon of ill omen came to me and said: "What do you gaze at so searchingly? What do you seek in the eyes of this being? Do you see the hour there, prodigal and idle mortal?" I should reply without hesitation: "Yes, I see the hour: it is Eternity!"

Is not this, Madame, a truly praiseworthy madrigal and as full of affectation as your precious self? In truth, it has given me so much pleasure to embroider this pretentious compliment, that I shall ask nothing from you in exchange.

A Jester

IT WAS THE EXPLOSION of the New Year; a chaos of mud and snow, traversed by a thousand coaches, shining with toys and with sweets, swarming with cupidity and with despair; the official delirium of a great City, enough to trouble the imagination of the serenest of hermits. In the midst of this hubbub and of this tumult, an ass was trotting rapidly, harassed by a lout who flourished a whip.

As the ass was about to turn the angle of a pavement, a handsome passer-by, gloved, cruelly cravatted, with patent leather boots, imprisoned in newly bought clothes, bowed ceremoniously before the humble beast, and said to it, as he raised his hat: "I wish you a happy New Year!" Then he returned to I know not what comrades of his with a fatuous air, as if he wanted them to add their approbation to his own contentment. The ass never saw this fine jester, but went on trotting zealously to where its duty called it.

As for me, I was seized suddenly by an incommensurable rage against this magnificent fool, who seemed to me to concentrate in himself the entire wit of France.

The Madman and the Venus

WHAT A WONDERFUL DAY! The vast park swoons under the burning eyes of the sun, as youth swoons under Love's domination. The universal ecstasy of things is inarticulate; the very waters seem to sleep. So different from our human feasts is this silent orgy! One would say that an ever-increasing light made inanimate things glitter; that the excited flowers burned with the desire to excel the blue of the sky by the energy of their colours, and that the heat, making visible the perfumes, caused them to rise like smoke towards a star.

Nevertheless, amidst this universal rapture, I see an afflicted being. At the feet of a colossal Venus, one of these artificial fools, one of these willing clowns, whose chief business it is to make Kings laugh when Remorse and Ennui obsess them, made more hideous by a ridiculous and bizarre costume and wearing a fool's cap and bells, is huddled against the pedestal and lifts his weeping eyes towards the immortal Goddess.

And his eyes say: "I am the lowest and the most lonely of men, deprived of love and of friendship, and thus inferior to the lowest of the animals. Nevertheless, I, too, was born able to fathom Immortality and feel Beauty! Ah! Goddess! pity my sadness and my delirium!"

But the implacable Venus gazes out of marble eyes at I know not what, in the distance.

The Courteous Marksman

As the carriage drove through the wood, he told the driver to stop near a shooting gallery, remarking that he would like to take a shot or two, to *kill* Time. To kill that monster: isn't that everyone's most usual and legitimate occupation? Gallantly he offered his arm to his dear, charming and execrable wife, to that mysterious woman to whom he owed so many pleasures, so many sorrows, and perhaps the greater part of his genius.

Several shots missed their mark; one even lodged in the ceiling; and as the charming creature laughed immoderately, making fun of her husband's skill, he suddenly turned, and said to her: "See that doll, there, on the right, with its nose in the air and the haughty expression. Well, dear angel, I am pretending *that it is you!*" And closing his eyes, he let go the trigger. The doll was neatly decapitated.

Then bowing to his dear, charming, execrable wife, his inevitable and pitiless Muse, he respectfully kissed her hand, and added: "Ah! my dear angel, how I do thank you for my skill!"

The Dog and the Flask

"MY BEAUTIFUL DOG, my dear dog, my good bow-wow, come and sniff an excellent perfume I have just bought from the best perfumer in the City."

The dog, waggling his tail, which is, I believe, the sign in these poor beings which corresponds to one's smile and one's laughter, approaches and with his wet nose curiously sniffs the uncorked flask; then, suddenly recoiling with fright, he barks at me reproachfully.

"Ah! miserable dog, if I had offered you a package of excrement, you would have sniffed it with delight and perhaps would have devoured it. Thus, you yourself, unworthy companion of my sad life, are like the public, to whom one must never offer those delicate perfumes that would exasperate it, but only carefully chosen sweepings."

The Evil Glazier

THERE ARE NATURES which are purely contemplative and wholly unfit for action, which, nevertheless, under a mysterious and unknown impulse, act sometimes with a rapidity of which they would never have considered themselves capable. He who, for instance, fearing to find in his porter's lodge some vexatious missive, wanders in a cowardly fashion for a whole hour in front of his door without daring to enter; he who keeps a letter for two weeks without opening it; or he who after six months is still undecided on a step which should have been taken a year earlier. Such men sometimes feel themselves brusquely propelled into action by an irresistible force, like an arrow shot from a bow. The moralist and the doctor, who pretend to universal knowledge, cannot explain from whence so mad an energy suddenly springs in these idle and voluptuous souls, nor how, incapable of accomplishing the simplest and most necessary things, they find at a given moment a glorious courage for the execution of the most absurd and often the most dangerous actions.

One of my friends, the most inoffensive dreamer who ever existed, once set a forest on fire so as to see, he said, whether the flames would spread as rapidly as people generally asserted. Ten times over the experiment failed; but, at the eleventh, it succeeded far too well. Another lighted a cigar while standing next to a powder barrel, *in order to see, in order to know, in order to tempt destiny,* to prove his own energy, to gamble, to know the pleasure of anxiety, for no reason whatever, out of caprice, out of idleness. This is a kind of energy which is caused by weariness or by day deams; and those in whom it manifests itself so obstinately are, in general, as I have said, the most indolent and the greatest dreamers. Another, timid to the point of lowering his eyes before those who glance at him, and who has to muster what remains to him of will in order to enter a café or stop at the box office of a theatre where those who hand him the tickets seem to be invested with the majesty of Minos, of Æacus and Rhadamanthus, will suddenly fall on the neck of an old man passing near him and embrace him enthusiastically before an astonished crowd. Why? Because—because his physiognomy was irresistibly sympathetic to him? Perhaps; but it is more legitimate to suppose that he himself would not be able to say why he had done it.

I have more than once been the victim of these crises and of these impulses that appear to be the action of malicious Demons that possess us and, unknown to ourselves, make us accomplish their most absurd desires.

One morning I got up feeling bad-tempered, sad, worn out with extreme weariness, driven, as it seemed to me, to do something wonderful, to commit some astonishing crime; and I opened the window, alas!

(Take heed, I beg, of this fact, that the spirit of mystification which, in certain people, is not the result of overwork, or of a combination, but of a fortuitous inspiration, seems by the intensity of the desire, to be part of that state of mind which doctors call hysteria and people more thoughtful than doctors, demonism, and impels us, unresisting, to commit many dangerous and unconventional actions.)

The first person I saw in the street was a glazier whose piercing and discordant cry came to me from the pavement below, through the foul and heavy atmosphere of Paris. It would be impossible for me to say why at the aspect of this poor man I was seized with a hatred at once sudden and despotic.

"Halloa! Halloa!" I shouted, calling to him to mount the stairs. At the same time I reflected, not without some gaiety, that the room being on the sixth floor, and the staircase very narrow, the man was bound to experience some difficulty in climbing up all those stairs and would knock the corners of his fragile freight against various obstacles.

At last, he appeared; I examined curiously all his panes of glass, and I said to him: "What! You have no coloured glass? Rose, blue, magical glass, glass worthy of Paradise? What impudence! How dare you wander about in poor neighbourhoods without glass through which one may see some beauty in life!" And I pushed him violently in the direction of the staircase, where he stumbled, grumbling.

I went over to the balcony and took up a little flowerpot, and when I saw the man just outside the door, I let fall my war engine on the outer edge of his hooks, and the shock making him fall backward, he somehow managed to break under his poor back what remained to him of his itinerant fortune, and it sounded like the bursting of a crystal palace shattered by lightning. Intoxicated with my folly, I shouted at him furiously: "Life is beautiful! Life is beautiful!"

These nervous jests are not without peril, and one often pays dear for them. But what matters an eternity of damnation to one who has found in a second an infinite joy?

At One O'Clock in the Morning

AT LAST I AM ALONE. I hear no longer
the noise of the belated and weary vehicles. For some hours we
shall possess silence, if not repose. At last! The tyranny of the
human face has disappeared; I suffer only from my own loneli-
ness. At last! I can relax in a bath of shadows! First, a double
turn of the key in the lock. It seems to me that this turn of the
key will intensify my solitude and will strengthen the barriers
that now separate me from the world.

Horrible life! Horrible city! Let us recapitulate our day: hav-
ing seen several men of letters, one of whom asked me if one
could go to Russia by land (he probably thought that Russia
was an island); having disputed handsomely with the Editor of a
magazine who answered every objection by saying: "This is the
opinion of decent people," which implied that all other magazines
are edited by rascals; having greeted twenty people of whom
fifteen were unknown to me; having shaken hands in the same
proportion, and that without having taken the precaution to buy
gloves; having gone during a shower, to the rooms of a dancing-
girl who wanted me to design for her a costume of *Vénustre;* hav-
ing tried to court the favour of the Manager of a Theatre, who
said as he ushered me out: "Perhaps you ought to call on Z: he's
the heaviest, the stupidest and the most celebrated of all my play-
wrights; with him you might perhaps come to some understand-
ing. Go to see him, and then we shall see"; having boasted (why?)
of several villainous actions I had never committed, and having
in a cowardly fashion denied certain other misdeeds that I accom-
plished with joy, an offence of boasting, a crime against human
respect; having refused a simple favour to a friend, and having
given a recommendation to a perfect knave: oh! what a relief to
have finished with all that!

Discontented with myself and discontented with everyone, I
should like to redeem myself and feel a little pride, in the silence
and solitude of the night. Souls of those I have loved, souls of

those I have sung, fortify me, sustain me, remove from me the lies and the corrupting vapours of the world, and you, Lord, my God! grant me the grace to fashion a few beautiful verses which will prove to me that I am not the lowest of men, that I am not inferior to those I despise.

Crowds

IT IS NOT GIVEN to every man to take a bath in the multitude: to enjoy crowds is an art; and only he to whom in his cradle a fairy has bequeathed the love of masks and disguises, the hate of home and the passion of travel, can plunge, at the expense of humankind, into a debauch of vitality.

Multitude, solitude: equal and interchangeable terms to the active and fertile poet. He who does not know how to people his solitude, does not know either how to be alone in a busy crowd.

The poet enjoys this incomparable privilege, to be at once himself and others. Like those wandering souls that go about seeking bodies, he enters at will the personality of every man. For him alone, every place is vacant; and if certain places seem to be closed to him, it is because in his eyes they are not worth the trouble of visiting.

The solitary and thoughtful stroller derives a singular intoxication from this universal communion. He who mates easily with the crowd knows feverish joys that must be for ever unknown to the egoist, shut up like a strong-box, and to the sluggard, imprisoned like a shell-fish. He adopts for his own all the occupations, all the joys and all the sorrows that circumstance sets before him.

What men call love is small indeed, narrow and weak, compared with this ineffable orgy, this sacred prostitution of the soul which gives itself up wholly (poetry and charity!) to the unexpected as it occurs, to the stranger as he passes.

It is good sometimes that the happy people of this world should learn, were it only to humble their foolish pride for an instant, that there are higher, wider, and rarer joys than theirs. The founders of colonies, the shepherds of nations, the missionary priests, exiled to the ends of the earth, doubtless know something of these mysterious intoxications; and, in the midst of the vast family that their genius has raised about them, they must sometimes laugh at the thought of those who pity them for their chaste lives and troubled fortunes.

The Old Mountebank

EVERYWHERE THE HOLIDAY CROWD lolled about, made merry, and scattered in all directions. It was one of those days of ceremony to which mountebanks, acrobats, lion-tamers and wandering tradesmen, wearily look forward in the hope that they will make up for the bad seasons of the year. On such days as these it seems to me that the people forget everything, sorrow and work; they become like children. For the young it is a day of freedom, with the horror of school dismissed for twenty-four hours. For the old it is an armistice concluded with the malevolent powers of life, a respite from the universal struggle and strife. Even the man of the world and the man concerned with spiritual labours escape with difficulty the influence of this public festivity. They unwillingly absorb their share of this carefree atmosphere. As for me, like a true Parisian, I never fail to make a tour of the booths that are so joyously decorated on these days of official celebration.

The competition between the booths was, in fact, formidable; they howled, bellowed, bawled. There was a medley of cries, of brass detonations and of the explosion of fireworks. The grotesques and the Jocrisses convulsed the features of their tanned faces, hardened by the wind, the rain and the sun. With the self-possession of actors sure of the effect, they bandied witty phrases and jests, as solid and as ponderous as Molière's comedy. The Hercules, proud of the enormity of their limbs, with hardly any foreheads or skulls, rather like apes, strutted about majestically in tights that had been washed for the occasion only the night before. The dancing-girls, lovely as fairies or as princesses, jumped and skipped under the fire of the lanterns which covered their skirts with sparks.

All was light, dust, cries, joy, tumult; some spent, others earned; both equally joyous. Children clung to their mother's petticoats in order to obtain a sugar-stick, or climbed on their father's shoulders to have a better view of some juggler as dazzling as a god. And pervading all, dominating the perfumes, was the odour of the frying-pan which seemed to be the incense of this feast.

At the end, at the extreme end, of the row of booths, as if, shameful, he had exiled himself from all these splendours, I saw a poor mountebank, bent, broken down, decrepit, a ruin of a man, with his back against one of the posts of his shed; a shed more miserable than that of the most brutalized savage, and the distress of which two smoking and guttering candles made even more evident.

Everywhere, joy, profit, debauch; everywhere the certainty of bread for the morrow; everywhere the frenzied explosion of vitality. Here, absolute misery, misery made more horrible for being wrapped in rags whose contrasting patches, the result rather of necessity than of art, produced a comical effect. The miserable man did not laugh! He neither wept nor danced, nor gesticulated, nor cried; he did not sing a gay or a sorrowful song; nor did he beg. He was mute and motionless. He had given up; he had abdicated. His destiny was done.

But how profound, how unforgettable the glance he cast over the crowd and on the lights, whose moving flood stopped a few steps from his repulsive misery! I felt my throat seized by the terrible hand of hysteria, and it seemed to me that my eyes were blinded by those rebellious tears they would not surrender.

What could I do? Of what use would it be to ask the unfortunate man what curiosity, what marvel he had to show in that stinking darkness, behind his ragged curtain?

Indeed, I dared not: and though the reason for my timidity

may make you laugh, I confess that I feared to humiliate him. I had just resolved to put some money on the counter as I passed, hoping that he would divine my intention, when a sudden wave of movement in the crowd, caused by I know not what disturbance, carried me away from him.

And, on my way back, obsessed by this vision, I tried to analyse my sudden sorrow, and I said to myself: "I have just seen the picture of an old man of letters who has outlived the generation which he amused with his brilliance; of an old poet without friends, without family, without children, degraded by his misery and by the ingratitude of the public, and into whose booth the forgetful world will no longer enter!"

Windows

HE WHO LOOKS IN through an open window never sees as much as he who looks at a window that is shut. There is nothing more profound, more mysterious, more fertile, more sinister, or more dazzling, than a window, lighted by a candle. What we can see in the sunlight is always less interesting than what transpires behind the panes of a window. In that dark or luminous hole, life lives, life dreams, life suffers.

Across the waves of roofs, I see a woman of mature years, wrinkled, and poor, who is always bending over something, and who never goes out. From her face, from her dress, from her gestures, out of almost nothing, I have made up the woman's story, or rather her legend, and sometimes I say it over to myself, and weep.

If it had been a poor old man, I could have made up his just as easily.

And I go to bed, proud of having lived and suffered in others.

Perhaps you will say to me: "Are you sure that it is the true story?" What does it matter, what does any reality outside of myself matter, if it has helped me to live, to feel that I am, and what I am?

The Widows

VAUVENARGUES SAID that in the public gardens there were paths haunted principally by disappointed ambition, by miserable inventors, by abortive glories, by broken hearts, by all those tumultuous and cheated souls in whom the last sighs of a storm have not subsided, and who recoil from the insolent stare of the joyous and the idle. These shadowy retreats are the trysting places of the cripples of life.

It is especially towards these places that the Poet and the Philosopher love to direct their avid conjectures. This is their richest grazing-ground. For if there is a spot they disdain to visit, as I have already intimated, it is where the joy of wealth is most evident. This turbulence in the void holds nothing to attract them; on the contrary, they feel themselves irresistibly drawn towards whatever is weak, ruined, saddened, orphaned. An experienced eye is never deceived. In these rigid or broken-down traits, in these hollow or dull eyes, where gleam the last flashes of the struggle, in these deep and many wrinkles, in these slow and halting steps, one deciphers immediately the innumerable tales of deceived love, of misunderstood devotion, of unrewarded efforts, of hunger and cold, humbly, silently endured.

Have you ever observed the poor widows seated alone on the benches of the parks? Whether they wear mourning or not they are easily recognized. Besides, there is always something lacking in the mourning worn by the poor, an absence of harmony which makes it even more distressing. They are forced to chaffer even with grief. Those who are rich wear their mourning elegantly.

Who is the saddest and most saddening of the widows? Is it the one who is dragging by the hand a child to whom she cannot tell her thoughts? or is it the one who is always alone? I don't know. I spent long hours, once, following one of these afflicted women; rigid, upright, wearing a worn-out shawl, she had in her being all the pride of a Stoic.

She was evidently condemned, by absolute solitude, to the habits of an old celibate, and the masculine character of her mor-

als added a mysterious piquancy to their austerity. I don't know
in what miserable café or by what means she procured her food.
I followed her to a lending library, and I saw her, with bright eyes
that once were burnt by tears, looking over the newspapers in an
attempt to find some news which seemed to have a powerful and
personal interest.

Then, in the afternoon, under an autumn sky, one of those skies
from which descend crowds of regrets and memories, I saw her
seated in a lonely place in the gardens, far from the crowd, where
she seemed to be listening to one of those concerts of regimental
music which gratifies the Parisian taste. This was no doubt the
little debauch of this innocent old woman (or of the purified old
woman), the well-earned consolation for one of those heavy days
without friends or gossip, or pleasure, which God had been send-
ing her for many years, and three hundred and sixty-five times a
year.

And yet another: I am never able to prevent myself from cast-
ing a glance, if not universally sympathetic, at least curious, on
the crowd of outcasts who stand close together outside the enclo-
sure of a public concert. The orchestra flings festal songs across
the night, songs of triumph and of pleasure. Gowns trail and
gleam; glances are exchanged; idlers, weary of their idleness, loll
about, pretending indolently to savour the music. Here are only
wealth and happiness; nothing is here that does not breathe and
inspire carelessness and the pleasure of floating idly on the stream
of life,—unless we except the rabble leaning against the outer rail-
ing where, as it watches this shining inner furnace, it hears from
time to time a fragment of music; sent forth gratis at the wind's
will.

There is nothing more interesting than this reflection of the
pleasures of the rich in the depths of poor people's eyes. But on
this day, in the midst of a crowd dressed in blouses and in calico,
I saw a being whose dignity offered a curious contrast to the sur-
rounding triviality. She was a tall, majestic woman, with so noble
an air that I have never seen her equal in any collection of aristo-
cratic beauties of the past. A perfume of lofty virtue emanated

from all her person. Her face, so sad arïd thin, was in perfect accord with her mourning. She also, like the lower classes with whom she was standing and yet never saw, gazed on this luminous world with profound eyes, as she listened to the music, now and then nodding her head. A strange sight! "Certainly," I said to myself, "this poverty, if this indeed be poverty, has nothing to do with sordid avarice: so noble a face convinces me of that. Why then does she remain of her own will in the midst of that crowd when she seems so strangely out of place?" But as I curiously passed by her, I thought I found the reason. The stately widow held by the hand a child who like her was dressed in black; reasonable as was the price of admission, this money was perhaps to be used to provide a necessity for her little boy, or better yet, a superfluity, a toy.

And she went home, doubtless on foot, meditating and dreaming, alone, always alone; for children are turbulent, selfish, without sweetness and without patience; and they cannot even, like the thoroughbred animal, like dogs or cats, serve as the confidant of our lonely grief.

The Wild Woman and the Little Mistress

"REALLY, MY DEAR, you weary me beyond measure and beyond all pity; to hear you sigh, one would say that you suffered more than those old women who glean the harvest-fields and the old beggar women who pick up crusts of bread outside the tavern doors. If at least your sighs expressed remorse, they would do you some honour; but they only indicate satiety and the weariness of repose. And, besides, you are always repeating useless words: 'Love me well; I have such need of you. Console me here and caress me there.' Come now, let me try to cure you; we shall perhaps find a way of doing it, for a few coins, at some fair, and without going very far.

"Look carefully at this solid iron cage in which this hairy

monster, whose form, vaguely enough, resembles yours, is throwing himself about, howling like a soul in hell, shaking the bars like an orang-outang exasperated by exile, imitating to perfection, now the circular leaps of the tiger, now the stupid slouch of the polar bear.

"This monster is one of those animals one generally calls 'my angel'! that is to say a woman. The other monster, he who is shouting at the top of his voice, a stick in one hand, is a husband. He has chained his legitimate wife as if she were a wild beast, and he exhibits her at the fairs around town, with the permission of the authorities, of course.

"Pay attention! See with what voracity (perhaps not simulated!) she pulls to pieces the living rabbits and the squealing fowls her keeper throws to her. 'Enough,' says he, 'you shouldn't spend all you have in one day'; and after this wise remark, he cruelly tears the prey from her, the divided intestines dangling for an instant between the teeth of the ferocious beast, of the woman, I mean.

"Now another stroke of the stick to quiet her! For she turns her terrible eyes glaring with greediness on the food of which she has been deprived. Good God! The stick isn't the kind that clowns use! Do you hear it smack despite the hairy covering? Now her eyes begin to protrude, now she howls *more naturally*. In her rage she flares all over, like the iron one beats on an anvil.

"Such are the conjugal manners of these two descendants of Adam and of Eve, these works of your hands, O my God! This woman is undoubtedly miserable, although after all, perhaps, the titillating enjoyments of glory are not unknown to her. There are miseries more incurable, miseries without compensation. But in the world into which she was cast, she has never been able to believe that any woman deserved any other destiny.

"Now it is our turn, most precious of women! After seeing the Hells with which the world is populated, what do you suppose I think of your pretty hell, you who lie only on fabrics as soft as your skin, who eat only cooked meat, and for whom a careful servant carves the daintiest morsels? What meaning do you suppose there can be for me in these sad sighs that rise from your perfumed breast, my well-nourished coquette? And all these affectations found in books, and this constant melancholy, calculated to inspire in the onlooker quite another sentiment than pity? In truth, I am seized at times with a desire to teach you what is the worst of all woes.

"To see you thus, dear delicate creature, with your feet in the filth and your eyes turned vaporously towards the sky as if to demand from it a King, one would say you were like a little frog invoking an ideal. If you scorn the small joist (which I am supposed to be, don't you know?) beware of the crane *who will eat you, gobble you and slay you for its pleasure!*

"Poet that I am, I am not the dupe you would like to believe, and if you weary me too often with your *precious whimperings,* I shall treat you like the *wild woman* that you are, or I shall throw you out of the window, like an empty bottle."

The Cake

I WAS TRAVELLING. The landscape in the midst of which I was seated was of an irresistible grandeur and sublimity. No doubt, at that moment, something passed from it into my soul. My thoughts fluttered with a lightness like that of the atmosphere: vulgar passions, such as hate and profane love, seemed to me now as far away as the clouds that floated in the chasms beneath my feet; my soul seemed to me as vast and as pure as the dome of the sky that enveloped me; the remembrance of earthly things came as faintly to my heart as the thin tinkle of the bells of unseen herds, browsing far, far away on the slope of another mountain. Across the little motionless lake, black with the darkness of its immense depth, there passed from time to time the shadow of a cloud, like the shadow of an airy giant's cloak, blown across the sky. And I remember that this rare and solemn sensation, caused by a vast and perfectly silent movement, filled me with mingled joy and fear. In a word, thanks to the enrapturing beauty about me, I felt that I was at perfect peace with myself and with the universe; I believe that in that state of beatitude and in my complete forgetfulness of all earthly evil, I had even come to think that after all those newspapers were not so ridiculous which maintained that man was born good; when, incorrigible matter renewing its exigencies, I sought to refresh my weariness and satisfy an appetite caused by so lengthy a climb. I took from my pocket a large piece of bread, a leathern cup, and a small bottle of a certain elixir which the chemists at that time sold to tourists, to be mixed, on occasion, with liquid snow.

I was quietly cutting my bread when a slight noise made me look up. Before me stood a little ragged urchin, dirty and dishevelled, whose hollow eyes, wild and supplicating, devoured the piece of bread. And I heard him gasp, in a low, hoarse voice, the word: "Cake!" I could not help laughing at the appellation with which he thought fit to honour my bread, so nearly white, and I cut off a big slice and offered it to him. Slowly he came up to me, never taking his eyes from the coveted object; then, snatching it out of my hand, he stepped back quickly, as if he feared that my offer was not sincere, or that I had already repented of it.

But at the same instant he was knocked over by another little savage who had sprung from I know not where, and who was so exactly like the first that one might have taken them for twin brothers. They rolled over on the ground together, struggling for the possession of the precious prize, neither apparently willing to share it with his brother. The first, exasperated, clutched the second by the hair; the latter seized his brother's ear between his teeth, and spat out a little bloody piece with a superb oath in dialect. The legitimate proprietor of the cake tried to hook his little claws into the usurper's eyes; the latter, in turn, did his best to throttle his adversary with one hand, while with the other he endeavoured to slip the prize of war into his pocket. But, heartened by despair, the loser pulled himself together, and sent the victor sprawling with a blow of the head in his stomach. Why describe a hideous fight which indeed lasted longer than their childish strength seemed to promise? The cake travelled from hand to hand, and changed from pocket to pocket, at every moment; but, alas! it changed also in size; and when at length, exhausted, panting and bleeding, they stopped from the sheer impossibility of continuing, there was no longer any cause for the feud; the slice of bread had disappeared, and lay scattered in crumbs like the grains of sand with which it was mingled.

This sight had darkened the landscape for me, and dispelled the joyous calm in which my soul had been basking; I remained saddened for quite a long time, saying over and over to myself: "There is, then, a wonderful country in which bread is called cake, and is so rare a delicacy that it is enough to cause a literally fratricidal war!"

The Gifts of the Fairies

THERE WAS A GREAT ASSEMBLY of the Fairies, convoked for the purpose of distributing gifts among all the babes newborn within the previous twenty-four hours.

These ancient and capricious Sisters of Destiny, these strange Mothers of Joy and of Sorrow, were very diverse: some had a sombre, sulky aspect, others looked mischievous and frolicsome; some were young, and had always been young; others were old, and had always been old.

All fathers who had faith in Fairies had come, each carrying his new-born babe in his arms.

The Gifts, the Talents, Good Luck, Invincible Circumstances, all were heaped beside the tribunal, like prizes on the platform at commencement time. The difference here was that the Gifts were not the recompense for some effort, but on the contrary, were a favour granted to a person who had not yet lived, a favour that might determine his destiny and become quite as much the source of his misery as of his happiness.

The poor Fairies were very excited, for there was a great crowd of petitioners; and the intermediate world, placed between Man and God, is just as subject as we are to the terrible law of Time and its vast progeny, the Days, the Hours, the Minutes, the Seconds.

As a matter of fact, they were just as bewildered as Ministers on court day, or as clerks in the government pawnshops when a national holiday authorises the gratuitous return of articles in pawn. I even believe that they looked from time to time at the hands of the clock with as much impatience as those human judges who, seated on the Bench since early morning, cannot keep from dreaming of their dinner, their family and their beloved slippers. If, in supernatural justice, there is a little precipitation and chance, we must not be astonished to find that the same may be true of human justice. We, ourselves, should be unjust judges in such a case.

So on this day certain strange blunders were committed, which we might consider strange if prudence, rather than caprice, were a distinctive, eternal characteristic of Fairies. Thus the power of magnetically attracting fortune was bestowed upon the sole heir of a very wealthy family, who, not having been gifted with any sense of charity, nor with any great desire for the most obvious of the material things of life, was, later, to find himself prodigiously embarrassed by his millions.

Thus the love of Beauty and poetic Power were given to the son of a melancholy wretch, a quarryman by trade, who could not, in any fashion, aid the talent, nor relieve the needs of his deplorable progeny.

I have forgotten to tell you that the distribution, on these solemn occasions, is without redress, and that no gift can ever be refused.

All the Fairies had arisen, believing their toilsome task was done; there remained not a single gift, not a single largesse to throw to all this small fry, when an honest fellow, a poor little tradesman he was, I believe, rose up and seizing the Fairy nearest to him by her robe of multi-coloured vapours, cried: "Oh, Madam! You have forgotten us! There's still my little boy! I don't want to have come here for nothing."

The Fairy might have been embarrassed, for nothing more was

left. However, she remembered in time a well known law, which is rarely applied in the supernatural world inhabited by the Fairies, the Gnomes, the Salamanders, the Sylphides, the Sylphs, the Nixes, the Water-sprites, those impalpable Deities, friends of man, who are often constrained to adapt themselves to his passions—I mean that law which concedes to Fairies in similar cases, that is to say when the supply of gifts is exhausted, the faculty of still giving one additional and exceptional gift, always providing that she have sufficient imagination to create it immediately.

So the good Fairy replied, with a self-possession worthy of her rank: "I give your son—I give him—the *Gift of pleasing!*"

"But please how? Please? Please why?" obstinately demanded the little shopkeeper, who was doubtless one of those reasoners, so commonly heard, who are incapable of grasping the logic of the Absurd.

"Because! because!" replied the enraged Fairy, turning her back on him; and rejoining the retinue of her companions, she said to them: "What do you think of this vain little Frenchmen who wants to understand everything, and who, having obtained for his son the best of the Gifts, dares to question and to discuss the Indisputable?"

The Counterfeit Coin

As we walked away from a tobacco shop, my friend sorted his money very carefully; he slipped the small gold coins into the left pocket of his waistcoat; into the right, the silver coins; into the left pocket of his trousers, a lot of coppers; and finally, into the right, a silver two-franc-piece he had particularly examined. "A strange, minute distribution!" I said to myself. On our way, we met a poor man who held out his cap to us with a trembling hand. I know nothing more disturbing than the mute eloquence of those supplicating eyes, in which the sensitive man who knows how to read can find so much humility and so much reproach. He will see in the tearful eyes of a whipped dog this same deep and complex emotion. My friend's donation was much larger than mine, and I said to him: "You are right; once we ourselves have had the pleasure of being astonished there is no greater pleasure than that of causing surprise to others." "I gave him the counterfeit coin," he quietly replied, as if to justify his prodigality.

My poor mind, always looking for difficulties where there are none (what a tiresome faculty nature has given me!), suddenly conceived the idea that my friend's action was prompted by a desire to make this an eventful moment in the life of this poor devil, and perhaps also to learn the various consequences, either fatal or otherwise, which might result from a counterfeit coin being found in a beggar's possession. Might it not be multiplied into real coins? Might it not also be the cause of his imprisonment? A baker, a tavern-keeper, for instance, might have him arrested as a counterfeiter or for circulating counterfeit money. And it was possible, too, that the coin might become, for some poor little speculator, the nucleus of a fortune that would quickly vanish. And so played my fantasy, lending wings to my friend's thought, and drawing all possible conclusions from all possible hypothesis.

Suddenly he interrupted my reverie by repeating my own words: "Yes, you are right; there's no greater pleasure than that of surprising a man by giving him more than he expects."

I looked straight into his eyes, and I was terrified to see that they shone with unmistakable candour. I saw then clearly that he had wanted to be charitable and, at the same time, make a good deal; to win forty *sous* and the Kingdom of Heaven; to get into paradise thriftily; to acquire without expense the reputation of being a charitable man. I might almost have pardoned in him the desire for that criminal experience I had attributed to him but a short while ago; I might have found it curious, singular, that he should amuse himself by implicating the poor; but I shall never forgive the absurdity of his motive. There is no excuse for being wicked, but there is some merit in knowing that one is wicked; and the most irreparable vice is to do evil through sheer stupidity.

Invitation to the Journey

THERE IS A WONDERFUL LAND, a land of Cockaigne, they say, which I dream of visiting with an old friend. It is a strange land, lost in the mists of our North; it might be called the East of the West, the China of Europe, so freely does a warm and capricious fancy flourish there, so patiently and persistently has that fancy illustrated it with rare and delicate vegetation.

A real land of Cockaigne, where everything is beautiful, rich, quiet, genuine; where order holds up the mirror to luxury; where life is rich, and sweet to breathe; where disorder, tumult, and the unexpected are shut out; where happiness is wedded to silence; where even cooking is poetic, rich and highly flavoured all at once; where everything, dear love, is made in your image.

You know that feverish sickness which comes over us in our stark miseries, that nostalgia for unknown lands, that anguish of curiosity? There is a country made in your image, where all is beautiful, rich, quiet, and genuine; where fancy has built and decorated a western China, where life is sweet to breathe, where happiness is wedded to silence. It is there that we should live, it is there that we should die!

Yes, it is there that we should breathe, dream, and draw out the hours with an infinity of sensations. A musician has written an "Invitation à la Valse": who will be the one to compose the "Invitation au Voyage" that we can offer to the beloved, to the chosen sister?

Yes, it would be good to live in this atmosphere, where slower hours contain more thoughts, where clocks strike happiness with a deeper and more significant solemnity.

On shining panels, or on gilded leather of a sombre richness, discreetly repose the impassive pictures, calm and deep as the souls of the painters who created them. The sunsets which so richly colour the walls of dining-room and drawing-room, are sifted through beautiful hangings or through tall wrought windows, leaded into many panes. The furniture is large, strange, and fantastic, provided with locks and secrets like subtle souls. Mirrors, metals, fabrics, pottery and the art of the goldsmith, play for the eyes a mute and mysterious symphony; and from all things, from every corner, from the cracks of drawers and from the folds of draperies, there emanates a singular odour, a "forget-me-not" of Sumatra, which is, as it were, the soul of that dwelling.

A real land of Cockaigne, I tell you, where all is beautiful, clean, and shining, like a clear conscience, like a bright array of kitchen copper, like splendid jewelry, like variegated gems. All the treasures of the world have found their way there, as into the house of a hard-working man to whom the whole world is indebted. Strange country, excelling others as Art excels Nature, where Nature is refashioned by dreams, where she is corrected, embellished, remoulded.

Let the alchemists of horticulture seek and seek again, let them set ever further and further back the boundaries to their happiness! Let them offer prizes of sixty and of a hundred thousand florins to him who will solve their ambitious problems! For me, I have found my "black tulip" and my "blue dahlia!"

Incomparable flower, recovered tulip, allegoric dahlia, it is there, is it not, in that beautiful country, so calm and so full of dreams, that you should live and flower? There, would you not be framed within your own analogy, and would you not see yourself reflected, as the mystics say, in your own "correspondence"?

Dreams, always dreams! and the more delicate and ambitious the soul, the further do dreams estrange it from possible things. Each man carries within himself his natural dose of opium, ceaselessly secreted and renewed, and, from birth to death, how many hours can we reckon of positive pleasure, of successful and decided action? Shall we ever live in, shall we ever pass into, that picture which my mind has painted, that picture made in your image?

These treasures, this furniture, this luxury, this order, these perfumes, these miraculous flowers, are you. They are you, too, these great rivers and these quiet canals. These vast ships that drift down them, laden with riches, and from whose decks rise the monotonous songs of labouring sailors, they are my thoughts which slumber or rise and fall on your breast. You lead them gently towards the sea, which is the infinite, while mirroring the depths of the sky in the crystal clearness of your soul; and when, weary of the surge and sated with the products of the East, they return to their port of birth, it is still my thoughts, now enriched, that return to you from the infinite.

The Poor Boy's Toy

I WANT TO SUGGEST an innocent diversion. There are so few amusements which are not sinful! When you go out in the morning with the evident intention of sauntering along the highways, fill your pockets with little penny toys—such as the flat Polichinelle who is moved by a single wire, the Blacksmith who strikes the anvil, the horseman and his horse whose tail is a whistle—and beside the taverns, under the trees, bestow your gifts upon the poor unknown children whom you will meet. You will see their eyes open wide. At first they will not dare to take it; they will doubt their happiness. Then their hands will suddenly snatch the gift, and they will take to their heels like cats that go a long way off to eat the morsel you have given them, having learned to be mistrustful of men.

On a road, behind the railings of a vast garden, at the end of which appeared the white walls of a pretty, sunlit château, a handsome, rosy-cheeked boy stood, dressed in those country clothes that are so full of daintiness. The luxury, the freedom from care, the habitual sight of riches, make these children so pretty that one might believe they were made of a different composition than the children of mediocrity or of poverty.

There lay on the ground beside him a splendid toy, as fresh as its owner, polished, gilded, dressed in a purple robe, covered with feathers and glass beads. But the child was not interested in his favourite toy, and this is what he gazed at : on the other side of the railing, in the road, between the thistles and the nettles, there stood another boy, thin, dirty, sooty, one of those outcast brats in whom an impartial eye could discover beauty, if, like the eyes of the connoisseur that suspect an ideal picture under the coating of carriage varnish, one were to remove the disgusting patina of misery.

Through these symbolical bars separating two worlds, the high road and the château, the poor boy showed the rich boy his own toy, which the latter examined greedily as if it were a rare and unknown object. Now, this toy, that the little sloven teased, disturbed and shook inside a wired box, was a living rat! His parents, through economy, no doubt, had taken the toy from life itself. And the two children, laughing at one another fraternally, displayed teeth of an equal whiteness.

The Temptations, or Eros and Pluto and Glory

LAST NIGHT, two superb Satans and a She-Devil, no less extraordinary, ascended the mysterious staircase by which Hell assaults Man's weakness while he sleeps, and secretly communicates with him. And they came and stood gloriously before me, upright, as if on a platform. A sulphurous splendour emanated from these three personages, and they stood out against the opaque background of night. They looked so proud and so dominating, that at first sight I took the three of them for real Gods.

The face of the first Satan was of an ambiguous sex; the lines of his body had the softness of the ancient Bacchus. His large languishing eyes, of a dark and uncertain colour, were like violets still wet with the heavy tears of the storm, and his half-opened lips were warm incense burners exhaling rich perfumes; and whenever he sighed, the warmth of his breath enkindled the aromatic insects fluttering about.

Around his purple tunic was corded, like a girdle, a glistening serpent which, with lifted head, languorously turned towards him eyes like embers. From this living girdle were hung shining knives and surgical instruments, alternating with phials filled with sinister liquors. In his right hand he held another phial which contained something luminously red, and which had for label these strange words: "Drink, this is my blood, a perfect cordial"; in his left, a violin which he doubtless played to express his sorrows and his pleasures, and to spread abroad the contagion of his folly at the midnight *Sabbats*. From his delicate ankles trailed several links of a broken chain of gold, and when the consequent annoyance made him lower his gaze, with intense vanity he contemplated his toe nails, brilliant and gleaming like well-polished stones. He gazed on me with eyes full of inconsolable hurt, eyes from which flowed an insidious intoxication, and he said to me in a singing voice: "If you wish, if you wish, I shall make you the lord of souls, and you shall be master of living matter, even more than the sculptor can be master of clay: and you shall know the pleasure, forever reborn, of escaping from yourself to find oblivion in others, and of attracting other souls until they are lost in yours."

And I answered him: "Ever so many thanks! I don't want this precious lot of beings who, no doubt, are no better than my poor little self. Although I can remember some shameful things, I don't want to forget anything; and even if I would not recognize you, you old monster, your mysterious cutlery, your doubtful phials, the chains with which your feet are entangled, are symbols which explain clearly enough the inconveniences of your friendship. Keep your presents."

The second Satan had none of this tragic and smiling aspect, none of these beautiful insinuating manners, none of this delicate and perfumed beauty. He was a large man, with a fat face and no eyes; his heavy paunch hung down over his thighs, and every inch of his skin was gilded and covered, like a tattooing, with a crowd of little moving figures representing the numerous forms of universal misery. There were little emaciated men who were deliberately hanging themselves from a nail: there were thin, deformed little gnomes whose supplicating eyes implored alms even more eloquently than their trembling hands; and old mothers, who carried abortions that clung to their withered breasts. And there were many others.

The fat Satan tapped his immense belly with his fist, and it gave forth a long, resounding clash of metal, that died away to a vague moaning uttered by countless human voices. He laughed, impudently showing his bad teeth, an enormous, idiotic laugh like that of certain men the world over after they have dined too well.

And this one said to me: "I can give you that which obtains all, that which is worth all, that which replaces all." And tapping his monstrous belly, the sonorous echoes provided a commentary on his coarse speech.

I turned away from him in disgust, and I replied: "To be happy, I don't require the misfortune of others; and I don't want riches burdened with all the miseries pictured on your skin like wallpaper."

As for the She-Devil, I should lie if I did not confess that at first sight I found in her a bizarre charm. To describe this charm, I can compare it to nothing better than the faded beauty of women who never seem to age further, and whose loveliness has all the poignant magic of ruins. She seemed haughty yet awkward, and her eyes, though tired, had a fascinating power. What struck me most was the mystery of her voice, in which I recognized the most beautiful *contralti* tones and also a little of that hoarseness caused by incessant drinking of brandy.

"Do you want to know my power?" said the false goddess in her charming and paradoxical voice. "Listen." She put to her mouth a gigantic trumpet, beribboned like a reed-pipe with the names of all the newspapers of the universe, and into this trumpet she shouted my name, which rolled across space with the sound of a thousand thunders, and returned to me in a reverberating echo from the most distant planet.

"The Devil!" I cried, almost won over. "Here is something valuable!" But upon looking more closely at the seductive virago,

I seemed vaguely to remember her as one whom I had seen clinking glasses with some scoundrels of my acquaintance; and the raucous sound of the brass brought to my ears I know not what memory of a prostituted trumpet.

So I answered with utter disdain: "Go! I'm not one who will take to wife the mistress of certain men whose names I prefer not to mention."

Certainly I had every reason to be proud of so courageous an abnegation. But unfortunately I awakened, and all my strength left me. "In truth," said I to myself, "I must have been slumbering heavily to have shown such scruples. Ah! if they would return when I am awake, I wouldn't be so fastidious." And I invoked them in a loud voice, begging them to pardon me, offering to dishonour myself as often as need be in order to deserve their favours; but I must have deeply offended them, for they have never returned.

Evening Twilight

THE DAY IS OVER. A great restfulness pervades those poor minds wearied by the day's work, and their thoughts now take on the dim and tender colours of twilight.

Nevertheless from the mountain top there comes to my balcony, through the transparent clouds of evening, a great clamour, made up of a multitude of discordant cries, that distance changes to a mournful harmony, like that of the rising tide or of a brewing storm.

Who are the hapless ones to whom evening brings no calm; to whom, as to the owls, the coming of night is the signal for a witches' sabbat? This sinister ululation comes to me from the dark house of refuge on the mountain; and, in the evening, as I smoke, and behold the quiet of the immense valley, filled with houses, each of whose windows seem to say, "Here is peace, here is domestic happiness!" I can, when the wind blows from the heights, lull my astonished thought with this imitation of the harmonies of hell.

Twilight excites madmen. I remember I had two friends who were made quite ill by the twilight. One of them ignored all the social and friendly amenities, and flew at the first-comer like a savage. I have seen him throw at a waiter's head an excellent chicken, in which he imagined he had discovered some insulting hieroglyph. Evening, harbinger of profound delights, spoilt for him the most succulent things.

The other, a prey to thwarted ambition, became more bitter, more gloomy, more troublesome as the daylight dwindled. Kindly and sociable by day, he was pitiless in the evening; and it was not only on others, but also on himself, that he vented the rage of his twilight mania.

The first died insane, unable to recognize his wife and child; the second is still the restless victim of a perpetual disquietude; and, if all the honours that republics and princes can confer were heaped upon him, I believe that the twilight would still quicken in him a burning desire for imaginary distinctions. Night, which filled their minds with its own darkness, brings a light to mine; and, though it is by no means rare for the same cause to bring about two opposite results, I am always, as it were, perplexed and alarmed by it.

O night! O refreshing darkness! You summon me to an inner feast, you deliver me from my anguish! In the solitude of the plains, in the stony labyrinths of some capital, twinkling of stars or sputtering out of street-lamps, you are the fireworks of the goddess Liberty!

Twilight, how gentle you are and how tender! The rosy glow that still lingers on the horizon, like the last agony of day under the conquering oppression of night; the flaring candle-flames that stain with dull red the last glories of the sunset; the heavy draperies that an invisible hand draws out of the depths of the East, all these resemble those complex feelings that war on one another in the heart of man at the solemn moments of life.

Would you not say it was like one of those strange costumes

worn by dancers, in which the veiled beauties show through the dark and transparent gauze of a gorgeous skirt, as the happy past pierces through the darkness of the present? And the wavering stars of gold and silver with which it is spangled, are they not those fires of fancy which only blaze well against the deep mourning of night?

Solitude

A PHILANTHROPIC JOURNALIST tells me that solitude is bad for a man; and in support of his contention, he quotes, as unbelievers always do, the words of the Church Fathers. I am aware that the Demon likes to frequent barren country, and that the Spirit of murder and of lubricity becomes extraordinarily inflamed in solitary places. Yet it is possible that solitude might be dangerous only for those idle and wandering souls who people it with their Chimeras and their passions. It is certain that a talkative man, whose supreme pleasure consists in speaking from a pulpit or from a platform, would seriously run the risk of becoming stark mad on Robinson Crusoe's island. I do not insist that my journalist possess all of Crusoe's courageous virtues, but I do say that he must not issue a writ of accusation against the lovers of solitude and of mystery.

There are individuals in our chattering races who would accept the supreme punishment with less repugnance if they were allowed to make a long oration from the scaffold without fear of an untimely interruption by the drums of Santerre. I do not pity them, because I suspect that their oratorical effusions give them as much pleasure as is found by others in silence and in meditation; only I despise them.

I desire above all that my accursed journalist let me amuse myself in my own way. "Don't you ever feel the need of sharing your pleasures?" he asked me in that very nasal and apostolic tone. You see how subtly envious he is! He knows that I disdain his, and he thrusts himself into mine, the miserable spoil-sport!

"The tragedy of not being able to be alone!" says La Bruyère somewhere, as if to shame those who rush into a crowd to forget themselves, in the fear, no doubt, that their own loneliness will prove unbearable.

"Almost all our misery comes from not having been able to keep to our own room," said another wise man, Pascal, I believe, who thus summons to meditation in their cells all those distracted people who seek happiness in activity and in a form of prostitution I might call Fraternity, if I wanted to speak the beautiful language of my time.

A Thoroughbred

SHE IS QUITE UGLY, and yet how delightful she is! Time and Love have marked her with their claws, and have cruelly taught her how much of youth and of freshness are spent every minute and for every kiss. She is really ugly; she is an ant, a spider, if you prefer, a skeleton even; but she is also drink, balm, sorcery! In one word, she is exquisite. Time could not disturb the sparkling harmony of her carriage, nor the indestructible elegance of her figure. Love has not changed the sweetness of her childish breath; Time has not touched one hair of her abundant tresses, from which like wild perfumes arises all the devilish vitality of southern France: of Nîmes, Aix, Arles, Avignon, Narbonne, Toulouse, cities blessed by the sun, cities charming and amorous. Time and Love tried to tear her to pieces; they never hurt the vague but eternal charm of her boyish figure. Worn, perhaps, but not weary, and still heroic, she reminds one of those thoroughbred horses whom the true lover of horses will always recognize, even when they are harnessed to a hired carriage or to a heavy waggon.

Moreover, she is so sweet and so fervent. She loves as one loves in the autumn; the approach of winter seems to light a new flame in her heart, and her servile affection is never irksome.

The Fair Dorothy

THE SUN OVERWHELMS the town with its direct and terrible light; the sand is dazzling, and the sea glitters. The torpid world sinks feebly into its siesta, a siesta which is a kind of savorous death and during which the drowsy sleeper enjoys the exquisite sensation of annihilation.

Yet Dorothy, strong and proud as the sun, moves through the deserted street, a gleaming, black blot on the light, the only living creature at this hour, under the wide sky. As she advances, her slender waist indolently sways above her full hips. Her clinging dress of bright and rose coloured silk, contrasts vividly with her dark complexion, and moulds her tall form, the curve of her back and her pointed breasts. Her red parasol, sifts the light and, casts over her dark face the blood red rouge of its reflection. The weight of her abundant blue-black tresses bends her delicate head backward and gives her an idle and triumphant air. Heavy earrings tinkle faintly in her tiny ears. From time to time the sea breeze lifts a corner of her loose skirt and uncovers her superb shining limbs; and her feet, like the feet of a marble goddess hidden in some European museum, leave their faithful imprint on the fine sand. For Dorothy is so great a coquette that the pleasure of being admired means more to her than pride in her freedom and, although she is free, she walks without slippers.

She moves forward gracefully, full of the joy of life, and smiling as if she perceived far off in space a mirror reflecting her bearing and her beauty. At this hour when even the dogs whimper with pain under the biting sun, what strong impulse thus bestirs our indolent Dorothy, fair and cold as bronze? Why has she left her little cabin, so daintily furnished: where flowers and mats make a perfect boudoir at so little cost; where she takes such pleasure in combing her hair, in smoking, in being fanned or in looking at herself in the mirror of her great feathered fans, while the sea, which breaks on the shore a short distance away, provides a powerful, monotonous accompaniment to her vague reveries, and while the iron pot in which a ragoût of crabs with rice and saffron, is being cooked at the far end of the court-yard, wafts to her its exciting perfume?

Perhaps she has an assignation with some young officer, who, in other lands, has heard his comrades speak of the famous Dorothy. Unquestionably the simple creature will implore him to describe the ball at the opera, and she will ask him whether she could go there with bare feet, just as she goes to the Sunday dances, where even the old Kaffir women become intoxicated and mad with joy; and also if the beautiful women of Paris are all more beautiful than she.

Dorothy is admired and petted by everyone, and she would be perfectly happy if she were not obliged to hoard piastre after piastre in order to ransom her little sister, who is at least eleven and already ripe, and so lovely! Kind Dorothy will no doubt succeed; the child's master is so miserly, far too miserly to conceive of any other beauty than that of gold pieces!

Be Drunken

BE DRUNKEN, ALWAYS. That is the point; nothing else matters. If you would not feel the horrible burden of Time weigh you down and crush you to the earth, be drunken continually.

Drunken with what? With wine, with poetry or with virtue, as you please. But be drunken.

And if sometimes, on the steps of a palace, or on the green grass in a ditch, or in the dreary solitude of your own room, you should awaken and find the drunkenness half or entirely gone, ask of the wind, of the wave, of the star, of the bird, of the clock, of all that flies, of all that sighs, of all that moves, of all that sings, of all that speaks, ask what hour it is; and wind, wave, star, bird, or clock will answer you: "It is the hour to be drunken! Be drunken, if you would not be the martyred slaves of Time; be drunken continually! With wine, with poetry or with virtue, as you please."

The Eyes of the Poor

AH! YOU WANT TO KNOW why I hate you to-day. It will probably be less easy for you to understand than for me to explain it to you; for you are, I think, the most perfect example of feminine impenetrability that could possibly be found.

We had spent a long day together, and it had seemed short to me. We had promised one another that we would think the same thoughts and that our two souls would become one soul; a dream which is not original, after all, except that, dreamed by all men, it has come true for none.

In the evening you were a little tired, and you sat down outside a new café, at the corner of a new boulevard, still littered with plaster yet already proudly displaying its unfinished splendours. The café glittered. The very gas-jet burned with the ardour of a beginner, and sturdily illuminated the blinding whiteness of the walls, the dazzling glass in the mirrors, the gilt of the cornices and mouldings, the chubby-cheeked pages leading hounds straining at the leash, the ladies laughing at the falcons on their wrists, the nymphs and goddesses carrying fruits and pies and game on their heads, the Hebes and Ganymedes holding out at arm's-length little jars of bavaroise or parti-coloured obelisks of mixed ices: all history and all mythology was here placed at the service of the gourmand. Right before us, in the roadway, stood a man of about forty years of age, with a weary face and a greyish beard, holding a little boy by one hand and carrying on the other arm a child too weak to walk. He was acting as nurse-maid, and had brought his children out for their evening walk. All three were in rags. Their faces were extraordinarily serious, and the six eyes stared fixedly at the new café with the same admiration, yet manifested differently in each according to his age.

The father's eyes said: "How beautiful! how beautiful! One would think that all the gold in this poor world had found its way to those walls." The boy's eyes said: "How beautiful! how beautiful! But it's a house which people like us cannot enter." As for the little one's eyes, they were too fascinated to express anything but stupid and utter joy.

Song-writers say that pleasure ennobles the soul and softens the heart. The song was right that evening, so far as I was concerned. Not only was I deeply moved by this family of eyes, but I felt rather ashamed of our glasses and decanters, which were so much larger than our thirst. I turned to look at you, dear love, that I might read my own thoughts in you; I was gazing deep into your eyes, so beautiful and so strangely sweet, your green eyes that are the home of Caprice and under the sovereignty of the Moon, when you said to me: "I can't stand those people staring with eyes like saucers! Couldn't you tell the head waiter to send them away?"

So hard it is to understand one another, dearest, and so incommunicable is thought, even between people who are in love!

The Generous Gambler

YESTERDAY, WHILE SAUNTERING with the crowd on the boulevard, I felt a mysterious Being brush past me whom I had always wanted to know, and whom I recognized immediately, in spite of the fact that I had never seen him. He had, doubtless, a similar desire about me, for he gave me, in passing, a significant wink which I hastened to obey. I carefully followed him, and was soon descending behind him into a subterranean dwelling, furnished with dazzling luxury without parallel among any of the superior Parisian homes. It seemed strange to me that I could have passed that delightful retreat so often without discovering the entrance. An exquisite, an almost intoxicating atmosphere prevailed, which made one forget almost instantly all the dull horrors of life; here one breathed a sombre beatitude, like that which the lotus eaters must have known, when, set ashore on an enchanted isle, basking in an eternal afternoon, the desire was born within them, to the soothing sounds of melodious cascades, never again to return to their homes, their women, their children, and never again to be tossed about by the waves of the open sea.

In this house there were strange faces of men and of women, faces distinguished by a fatal beauty that I seemed to have seen before, in ages and in countries that I could not precisely recall, and which inspired in me a brotherly sympathy rather than that fear which is usually aroused at the appearance of a stranger. If I should try to describe in some way or other the singular expression of their glances, I would say that never had I seen eyes gleam more brightly with the horror of boredom and the immortal desire to be alive.

As for my host and myself, when we sat down we were already old and perfect friends. We ate, and we drank deeply of all sorts of extraordinary wines, and—what is no less extraordinary—it seemed to me, after several hours, that I was no more intoxicated than he.

However, gambling, that superhuman pleasure, interrupted our copious libations at various intervals, and I ought to say that while playing a rubber, I staked and lost my soul with heroic light-heartedness and indifference. The soul is so intangible a thing, often so useless and sometimes so troublesome, that I was hardly more disturbed at this loss than if I had dropped my visiting-card in the street.

We spent long hours smoking cigars, and their incomparable savour and perfume filled my soul with longing for unknown delights and places yet unseen, and, intoxicated by all this bliss, in an access of familiarity which did not seem to displease him, I dared to exclaim, as I lifted a glass filled to the brim: "To your immortal health, Old Goat!"

We talked of the universe, of its creation and of its future destruction, of the great idea of the century—namely, of Progress and Perfectibility—and, in general, of all kinds of human infatuations. On this subject his Highness had an inexhaustible number of irrefutable jests, and he expressed himself with a suavity of diction and a quietly comic humour such as I have never found in any of the most famous conversationalists in the world. He explained to me the absurdity of the different philosophies that have thus far possessed men's minds, and deigned even to talk to me in confidence of certain fundamental principles, which I am not at liberty to share with anyone.

He complained in no way of the evil reputation which he enjoyed the world over; he assured me that he himself was the one most interested in the destruction of *superstition;* and he confessed to me that, as concerns his own power, he had only once known fear, and that was on the day he had heard a preacher, more subtle than his colleagues, cry from the pulpit: "My dear brethren, when you hear the progress of knowledge praised, do not ever forget that the Devil's cleverest trick is to persuade you that he does not exist!"

The memory of this famous orator brought us naturally to the subject of Academies; and my strange host declared to me that at times, he was not averse to inspiring the pens, the words and the consciences of pedagogues and that, although invisible he was almost always present in person at academic meetings.

Encouraged by so much kindness, I asked him if he had any news of God, and if he had seen him recently. There was a note of sadness in his voice as he replied, with great unconcern: "We bow to each other when we meet, but like two old noblemen whose innate good breeding cannot quite efface the memory of an old grudge."

It is doubtful whether his Highness had ever given so long an audience to a simple mortal, and I feared to be presumptuous.

Finally, as the trembling dawn whitened the windows, this famous personage, sung by so many poets, and served by so many philosophers who unwittingly work for his glory, said to me: "I want you to remember me agreeably, and I want to prove to you that I—of whom so much ill is spoken—am sometimes a *good devil,* to use one of your vulgar expressions. In order to make up for the irretrievable loss of your soul, I shall give you the stake you would have won if fate had been with you—namely, the ability to solace and conquer, during your life-time, that strange propensity for Boredom, which is the source of all your maladies and of all your miseries. Never shall you express a desire that I will not help you to realize; flattery and even adoration will be yours; you will lord it over your vulgar equals; money and gold and diamonds and fairy palaces will seek you out and will beg you to accept them, without your having to make the least effort to obtain them; you will change your home and fatherland as often as your fancy may dictate; you will be drunk with pleasure, without ever growing weary, in charming, sunny lands, where the women are as fragrant as the flowers. . . ." Thereupon he stood up and bid me goodbye with a charming smile.

Had it not been for the fear of humiliating myself before so great an assembly, I would have fallen willingly at the feet of this generous gambler, to thank him for his extraordinary munificence. But after I had left him, an incurable mistrust gradually took possession of me; I dared no longer believe in such prodigious happiness; and as I went to bed, mumbling the prayer which idiotic habit still brought to my lips, I drowsily repeated: "My God, oh Lord, my God! Make the Devil keep his word with me!"

A Hemisphere in Tresses

LET ME INHALE SLOWLY, slowly, the odour of your hair, let me plunge my face into it like a man who thirsts and drinks the waters of a spring, let me wave your tresses with my hand like a perfumed handkerchief, shaking out my memories in the air. If you could but know all that I see, all that I feel, all that I hear in your hair! My soul wanders over its perfume as the souls of other men wander over music.

Your hair contains a dream, filled with masts and sails; it contains the wide seas whose monsoons carry me towards happy climes, where the sky is more blue and more profound, where the atmosphere is perfumed by fruits, and leaves and the skin of human beings.

In the ocean of your tresses, I see a harbour swarming with melancholy chants, with vigorous men of all nations, and with ships of all types, defining their delicate and complicated architecture on an immense sky vibrating with eternal heat.

In the caresses of your tresses, I live again the languor of long hours spent on a divan, in the lounge of a beautiful ship, lulled by the imperceptible motion of the harbour, between pots of flowers and refreshing water-jars.

In the passionate warmth of your tresses, I inhale the odour of tobacco mixed with the odour of opium and of sugar; in the night of your tresses, I see shine the infinity of the tropical azure; on the downy shores of your tresses, I am intoxicated by the mingled odours of tar, musk and cocoa-oil.

Let me slowly bite your heavy black hair. When I nibble at your flexible and rebellious tresses, it seems to me that I am feeding upon memories.

The Cord

To EDOUARD MANET

"ILLUSIONS," MY FRIEND SAID TO ME, "are perhaps as innumerable as the relations of men between themselves, or of men with things. When the illusion disappears, that is to say when we see the being or the fact just as it is outside ourselves, we experience a curious sentiment, composed partly of regret at the disappearance of that phantom, and partly of agreeable surprise at the novel sight of the real fact. If there exists a phenomenon that is unchanging, trite, obvious, and of such a nature as to make deception about it impossible, it is maternal love. It is as difficult to imagine a mother without maternal love as a light without heat; therefore is it not perfectly proper to attribute to maternal love all a mother's actions and words relative to her child? And yet, listen to this little story of how I was singularly mystified by this most natural of illusions.

"My profession as a painter leads me to observe very attentively the faces, the physiognomies, that I see wherever I go. You know what pleasure we derive from that particular faculty which makes life keener in our eyes and more significant than to other men. In the remote quarter where I live, and where vast grass-grown spaces still separate the houses, I frequently observed a child whose exceptionally bright, clever face fascinated me. He often sat for me, and I would change him into a little gypsy, or into an angel, or sometimes into a mythological Cupid. I painted him holding the violin of the vagabond, the Crown of Thorns and the nails of the Passion, and the Torch of Eros. I was so taken with the boy's humours that one day I asked his parents, who were poor people, to let me have him, promising to dress him well, to supply him with a little money and to give him no other work than that of cleaning my brushes and running my errands. This child, kept properly clean, was charming, and the life that he led with me seemed to him a paradise, compared with what he had endured in his own poverty-stricken home. But I ought to say that the little fellow often astonished me by his strange and precocious fits of sadness, and that he very soon manifested an immoderate fondness for sugar and liqueurs; so much so that one day, when I ascertained that in spite of my repeated admonitions, he had committed another theft of this nature, I threatened to send him back to his parents. Then I went out, and my business kept me away from home quite a while.

"Imagine my horror and my astonishment when, upon my return, the first thing I saw as I entered the house was the boy, my playful little companion, hanging from the top of that cupboard! His feet almost touched the floor; a chair, which he must have kicked away with his feet, was overturned beside him; his head was twisted convulsively over one shoulder; his swollen face, and his eyes, staring with a fearful fixity, made me think for a moment that he was still alive. To cut him down was not as easy as you might imagine. He was already quite stiff, and I was singularly loath to let him drop to the floor. I had to hold him up with one arm, and cut the cord with my free hand. That done, I was still not through. The little monster had used a very thin cord which had cut deeply into the flesh, and with a small pair of scissors I now had to pry into the swollen wound and find the cord, so as to free his neck.

"I forgot to tell you that I had called loudly for help, and that all my neighbours had refused to come to my assistance; they were restrained by that deep-rooted prejudice, held by civilized people, for some reason or other never to have anything to do with a hanged man. Finally a doctor came, who declared that the child had been dead for several hours. When, later on, we had to undress him for the burial, the corpse was so stiff that we had to give up trying to bend his limbs, and tore and cut his clothes in order to get them off.

"The police superintendent, to whom naturally I had to report the accident, looked at me suspiciously, and said: 'This is a shady affair!' prompted, I suppose, by an inveterate professional desire to terrify, whatever the facts, the innocent as well as the guilty.

"There remained a supreme duty to perform, the mere thought of which caused me terrible anguish: the parents had to be informed. My feet literally refused to take me to them. Finally, courage came to me. But, to my great astonishment, the mother was unmoved; not a tear trickled from the corner of her eye. I attributed this strange behaviour to the horror she must be feeling, and I remembered the well-known aphorism: 'The most terrible sorrows are those that are silent.' As for the father, he simply said, with a stupid, sleepy air: 'After all, it is probably just as well; he was sure to come to a bad end!'

"The corpse was laid out on my divan, and, assisted by a servant girl, I was busy with the final preparations when the mother entered my studio. She wanted, she said, to see her son's corpse. I could not, of course, prevent her from dwelling upon her misfortune; I could not refuse her this supreme and sombre consolation. At last she asked me to show her the place where her son had hanged himself. 'Oh, no, Madame,' I answered her, 'that will distress you.' And as my eyes involuntarily sought the ghastly cupboard, I perceived with disgust and horror and anger that the nail was still fixed in the partition, with a long piece of cord still hanging from it. I rushed over to tear off those last vestiges of the tragedy, and I was on the point of throwing them out of the open window, when the poor woman seized my arm and said in a tone of voice I could not resist: 'Oh, sir! Let me have them! Please let me have them!' I felt certain that despair had so upset her mind that she was seized now with tenderness for that which had been the cause of her son's death, and wanted to keep it as a horrible and precious relic—so she took possession of the nail and string.

"Everything was over at last. I had only to get back to work, perhaps a little more feverishly, than usual, in order to shut out the haunting memory of that little corpse whose ghost, with its big, staring eyes, harried me. But the next day I received a packet of letters; some from my fellow-lodgers, others from my neighbours; one from the first floor; another from the second; still another from the third, and so on; some in a jesting style, as though trying to hide the sincerity of their demand; under an apparent lightness of tone others, clumsily shameless and ill-spelt; but all with the same object in view, namely, to obtain from me a piece of the fatal and beatific cord. Of those who signed them, the greater part, I must admit, were women and not men; but all, you may believe me, were not of the common or lowest class. I have kept these letters.

"And then, suddenly, it came to me in a flash, and I understood why the mother was so eager to have that piece of string, and how she planned to console herself.

Vocations

IN A LOVELY GARDEN, where the rays of an autumnal sun seemed to be pleasantly lingering, under a green sky in which aureate clouds floated like travelling continents, four handsome children, four boys, no doubt tired of their games, began to talk.

One said: "Yesterday I was taken to the theatre. In great, gloomy palaces, beyond which could be seen the sky and the sea, men and women, looking grave and sad, but far more beautiful and far better dressed than those we see elsewhere, spoke in melodious voices. They threatened each other, they pleaded, they grieved, and often they gripped the dagger that was thrust through their girdles. Ah! that was splendid! The women were more beautiful and much taller than those who come to our house, and though their big, sunken eyes and their fiery cheeks gave them a terrifying appearance, you could not help loving them. They frightened you, they made you want to weep, and yet you were glad. And then, what is still more strange, they made you want to dress just as they were dressed, say and do the same things, and speak in the same voice."

One of these four children, who for some seconds had ceased listening to his friend, and was staring strangely at some point in the sky, said suddenly: "Look, look over there. Do you see *him?* He's sitting on that lonely little cloud, that little fire-coloured cloud, that is drifting slowly. *He,* too, seems to be looking at us."

"But who?" asked the others.

"God!" he replied in a tone of perfect conviction. "Ah! He's already far off; in a moment you will not be able to see him at all. He must be travelling, to visit all the countries. There, he's going to pass behind that row of trees that is almost on the horizon . . . and now he is going down behind the belfry. Ah! He's gone!" The child remained a long while looking in that direction, and while he gazed at the line that separates the earth from the sky, his eyes reflected his inarticulate ecstasy and regret.

"Isn't he stupid, talking about that God of his, whom he alone can see?" said the third, a tiny fellow, yet full of surprising vivacity and vitality. "I'll tell you something that happened to me and which never happened to you, something more interesting than your theatre or your clouds. A few days ago, my parents took me with them on a journey, and, as there were not enough beds for all of us in the inn where we stayed, it was decided that I was to sleep in my nurse's bed." He made his friends come closer, and continued in a lower voice. "It's a funny feeling, let me tell you, not to be sleeping alone and to be in a bed with your nurse, in the dark. I couldn't sleep, so while she slept I amused myself by running my hand over her arms, and her neck and her shoulders. Her neck and arms are bigger than those of other women, and her skin is so soft, so soft—just like notepaper or tissue paper. I found this such fun that I would have kept it up if I had not been afraid, first of waking her, and then of I don't know what. So I buried my head in her hair which hung down her back, heavy as a horse's mane, and, let me tell you, it smelled just as wonderfully as the flowers in the garden at this minute. Try it, sometime, if you get the chance, and you'll see."

The young author of this wonderful revelation, while telling his story, had his eyes wide open, as if still astonished at what he had experienced, and the rays of the setting sun, as they touched the red curls of his dishevelled hair, changed them, as it were, into a sulphurous halo of passion. It was easy to predict that this lad would not waste his life seeking Divinity in the clouds; rather would he often find it elsewhere.

Finally the fourth said: "You know I never have a good time at home; they never take me to the theatre; my tutor is too stingy; God never concerns himself about me and my boredom; and I haven't even a fine-looking nurse to pamper me. It has often seemed to me that my greatest delight would be always to keep going straight ahead, without knowing where, without anyone bothering about it, and of always seeing new countries. I am never happy anywhere, and I always think I should be happier else-where than there where I happen to be. Well, at a recent fair held in a neighbouring village, I saw three men who live exactly as I should like to live. You fellows didn't notice them. They were tall, almost black, and very proud, though they were in rags, and they looked as if they needed help from no one. Their great dark eyes became absolutely brilliant when they played their music; such astonishing music that it made me want to dance, weep, or do both at once, and it would have driven me mad if I had heard much more of it. One, as he drew his bow across his violin, seemed to tell his sorrows, and the other, making his tiny hammer skip over the notes of a little piano that hung from his neck by a leather strap, seemed to be making fun of his comrade's lamentation, while the third clashed his cymbals from time to time with extraordinary violence. They were so pleased with themselves that they kept on playing their wild music, even after the crowd had dispersed. Finally, they picked up the coins that had been tossed to them, loaded their baggage on their backs, and went their way. I wanted to find out where they lived, so I followed them at a distance, until they reached the edge of the forest, and then it suddenly came to me that they lived nowhere.

"Then one of them said: 'Shall we put up our tent?'

" 'Lord, no,' said the other, 'it's such a wonderful night!'

"The third said, as he counted the collection: 'These people here have no sense of music, and their women dance like bears. Fortunately, in less than one month, we shall be in Austria, where we shall find pleasanter people.'

" 'Perhaps it would be better to start for Spain; the season is getting on. We ought to get away before the rains, and wet nothing but our throats,' said one of the two others.

"As you see, I have remembered everything. Then each one drank a mug of brandy and fell asleep, his face turned towards the stars. At first I wanted to ask them to take me with them and to teach me how to play their instruments; but I did not dare, probably because it's always very difficult to make any kind of a decision, and also because I was afraid of being overtaken before I was outside of France."

The uninterested attitude of the three other boys gave me food for reflection. They already considered the little fellow *queer*. I looked at him closely. There was something in his eyes and in his forehead which betokened that fatal precocity which generally alienates sympathy, and which, I don't know why, excited mine to such a pitch that for a moment I had the strange idea that I might find a brother who was unknown to me.

The sun had set. The solemn night came into its own. The children parted, each one going, unconsciously, according to chance or circumstance, to consummate his destiny, to scandalise his kindred and to gravitate either towards glory or towards dishonour.

An Heroic Death

FANCIOULLE was an admirable buffoon,
and almost a friend of the Prince. But for persons professionally
devoted to the comic, serious matters have a fatal attraction, and,
although it may seem strange that ideas of patriotism and liberty
should despotically seize upon the brain of a player, one day
Fancioulle joined a conspiracy formed by some discontented
nobles.

There are respectable men everywhere who will go to the au-
thorities and denounce those individuals of atrabilious disposi-
tion who seek to depose princes, and reconstitute society without
consulting it. The lords in question were arrested, together with
Fancioulle, and doomed to certain death.

I could readily believe that the Prince was almost sorry to find
his favourite actor among the rebels. The Prince was neither
better nor worse than any other prince; but an excessive sensibil-
ity caused him to be, in many cases, more cruel and more despotic
than his equals. Passionately enamoured of the fine arts, more-
over an excellent connoisseur, he had an insatiable desire for
pleasure. Indifferent enough in regard to men and morals, himself
a true artist, he feared no enemy but Ennui. Had the writing of
anything which did not tend exclusively to pleasure, or to wonder,
which is one of the most delicate forms of pleasure, been per-
mitted in his domain, the extravagant efforts that he made to flee
or to vanquish this tyrant of the world would certainly have
earned for him, from some stern historian, the epithet of "mon-
ster." This Prince's great misfortune was that he had no theatre
vast enough for his genius. There are young Neros who stifle
within too narrow confines, and whose names and good intentions
will never be known to future ages. Providence lacked foresight
when she gave this one faculties greater than his dominions.

Suddenly the rumour spread that the sovereign had decided to
pardon all the conspirators; and the origin of this rumour was the
announcement of a special performance in which Fancioulle

would play one of his best *rôles*, and at which even the condemned nobles, it was said, were to be present,—an evident sign, added shallow minds, of the generous tendencies of the offended Prince.

From a man so naturally and wilfully eccentric, anything was possible, even virtue, or mercy, especially if he could hope to find in it some unexpected pleasure. But to those who, like myself, had succeeded in penetrating further into the depths of this sick and curious soul, it was infinitely more probable that the Prince wished to estimate the theatrical ability of a man condemned to death. He wanted to take advantage of the occasion and make a physiological experiment of *capital* interest, to discover to what extent the usual faculties of an artist could be changed or modified by the extraordinary situation in which he found himself. Whether, beyond this, he had made up his mind to show mercy is a point which has never been determined.

At last, the great day arrived, and the little court displayed all its pomp; and it would be difficult to conceive, without having seen it, what splendour the privileged classes of a little state with limited resources can display on a really solemn occasion. And this occasion was doubly solemn, both for the wondrous exhibition of luxury, and for the mysterious and moral interest involved.

The Sieur Fancioulle was especially fine in parts either silent or little burdened with words, such as are often the principal ones in those fairy plays which aim to represent symbolically the mystery of life. He came upon the stage lightly and with perfect ease, which in itself lent some support, in the minds of the nobles in the audience, to the idea of kindness and forgiveness.

When we say of an actor, "There is a good actor," we are using a formula which implies that under the character-part we can still distinguish the actor, that is to say, art, effort, will. Now, if an actor should succeed in being, in relation to the character which it is his business to portray, what the finest statues of antiquity, miraculously animated, living, walking, seeing, would be in relation to the general, confused idea of beauty, this would be, undoubtedly, a singular and unheard-of case. Fancioulle that evening, was, a perfect idealisation, which it was difficult not to suppose living, possible, real. As the buffoon came and went, as he laughed, wept, and was convulsed, there was an indestructible aureole about his head, an aureole invisible to all, but visible to me, in which were strangely blended the rays of art and a martyr's glory. Fancioulle, by I know not what special grace, introduced something divine and supernatural into even the most extravagant buffooneries. My pen trembles, and an emotion I still feel brings tears to my eyes, as I try to describe to you this never-to-be-forgotten evening. Fancioulle proved to me, in a peremptory, irrefutable manner, that the intoxication of art is better qualified than aught else to veil the terrors of the gulf; that genius can act on the brink of the grave with a joy that makes it lose all sight of the grave, living, as it does, in a paradise where any thought of destruction and of the grave can never enter.

The entire audience, *blasé* and frivolous as it was, soon fell under the all-powerful sway of the artist. Not a thought remained of death, of mourning, or of torture. They all blissfully surrendered to the manifold delights that are felt when in the presence of a masterpiece of living art. Manifestations of joy and of admiration repeatedly shook the walls of the building with the fury of continuous thunder. The Prince himself ecstatically joined in the applause of the court.

Nevertheless, to a discerning eye, his emotion was not unmixed. Did he feel defeated in his power as a despot? humiliated in his art of striking terror into hearts, and chill into souls? frustrated in his hopes and deceived in his conjectures? Such suppositions, not exactly justified, yet not absolutely unjustifiable, passed through my mind as I watched the face of the Prince. A new pallor slowly overspread his habitually pale features, as snow overspreads snow. His lips became more tightly compressed, and his eyes lighted up with an inner fire like that of jealousy or of spite, while he ostensibly applauded the talents of his old friend, the strange buffoon, who jested so well with death. At a certain moment, I saw his Highness turn towards a little page, stationed behind him, and whisper in his ear. The roguish face of the pretty child lit up with a smile, and he quickly left the Prince's box, as if to execute some urgent command.

A few minutes later a shrill, prolonged hiss interrupted Fancioulle in one of his greatest moments, and rent alike every ear and heart. And from the corner of the theatre, from whence this unexpected note of disapproval had sounded, a child darted into a corridor, stifling his laughter.

Fancioulle, shaken, roused out of his dream, closed his eyes, re-opened them almost immediately, extraordinarily wide, then opened his mouth as if to breath convulsively, staggered forward a few steps, backward a few steps, then fell to the boards, stark dead.

Had the hiss, swift as a sword, really cheated the hangman? Had the Prince himself suspected the perfectly murderous efficacy of his ruse? We may doubt it. Did he regret his dear and inimitable Fancioulle? It is sweet and but right to believe so.

The guilty nobles attended a play for the last time. That same night they were effaced from life.

Since then, many mimes, rightly appreciated in different countries, have played before the court of ——; but none of them has ever been able to recall to mind the marvellous talents of Fancioulle, or to attain the same *favour*.

The Desire to Paint

UNHAPPY PERHAPS THE MAN, but happy the artist who is torn by desire!

I burn to paint her who came to me so rarely and who fled so rapidly, like some beautiful thing reluctantly left behind by a traveller when he vanishes into the night. How long it is since she disappeared. She is beautiful, and more than beautiful; she is astounding. In her, all is dusk, and all that she inspires is nocturnal and profound. Her eyes are two caverns where mystery vaguely gleams, and her glance illuminates like lightning; it is a flash in the darkness. I would compare her to a black sun, if one could conceive of a black star radiating light and happiness. But she makes me think rather of the moon, which must have marked her with its baleful influence; not the white moon of idylls, which is like a cold bride, but the sinister and intoxicating moon, suspended in the depths of a stormy night tormented by racing clouds; not the peaceable and discreet moon visiting the slumber of innocent men, but the moon torn from the sky, vanquished and rebellious, that the Thessalian Sorceresses cruelly compelled to dance on the terrified grass!

Behind her little forehead lie a tenacious will and a predatory instinct. Yet, in the lower half of that disturbing face, where quivering nostrils inhale the unknown and the impossible, laughter bursts with an inexpressible grace from a wide mouth, red and white and beautiful, that brings to mind the miracle of a superb flower blossoming in volcanic soil. There are women who arouse the hunger to master and possess them; but this one inspires in me the desire to die slowly beneath her gaze.

The Favours of the Moon

THE MOON, who is caprice itself, looked in through the window while you lay asleep in your cradle, and said to herself: "This child pleases me."

And she came softly down her staircase of clouds, and passed noiselessly through the window-pane. Then she leaned over you with a mother's supple tenderness, and she painted her colours upon your face. That is why your eyes are green and your cheeks extraordinarily pale. It was from looking at this visitor, that your eyes became so strangely wide; and she clasped her arms so tenderly about your bosom that ever since you have been close to tears.

Then, in the flood of her joy, the Moon filled the room with a phosphorescent atmosphere, like a luminous poison; and all this living light thought and said: "My kiss shall be upon you for ever. You shall be beautiful as I am beautiful. You shall love that which I love and which loves me: water and clouds, night and silence; the vast, green sea; the formless and multiform water; the place where you shall never be; the lover whom you shall never know; unnatural flowers; perfumes which madden; cats that swoon on top of pianos and whimper like women, in hoarse, sweet voices!

"And you shall be loved by my lovers, courted by my courtiers. You shall be the queen of green-eyed men whose breasts I have also clasped in my nocturnal caresses; of those who love the sea, the vast tumultuous green sea, the formless and multiform water, the place where they are not, the woman whom they do not know, the sinister flowers that look like the censers of some unknown religion, the perfumes that disturb the will, and the wild and voluptuous beasts that are the emblems of their folly."

And that is why, dear accursed spoilt child, I lie now at your feet, seeking to find in you the image of the fearful goddess, the prophetic godmother, the corruptive nurse of all the moonstruck of the world.

Already!

A HUNDRED TIMES ALREADY the sun had sprung up, radiant or sad, out of the immense vat of the sea whose rim was only vaguely discernible; a hundred times it had plunged anew, now glittering or sullen, into its immense bath of night. For days and days we contemplated the other side of the firmament, and deciphered the celestial alphabet of the antipodes. All the passengers groaned and complained. You would have said that the approach to land intensified their suffering. They said, "When shall we have done with a sleep disturbed by the waves and troubled by a wind that snores louder than we? When shall we be able to digest in an arm-chair that stays in place?"

Some of them thought of their homes, and were lonesome for their sulky, unfaithful wives, and their shrill progeny. All were so taken with the picture of the invisible land that they might, I believe, have eaten grass with more appetite than the beasts.

Finally, a coast was sighted; and as we came nearer, we saw that it was a magnificent, a lovely land. It seemed as if the music of life came from it in a vague murmur, and that from its shores, rich in verdure, a delicious fragrance of flowers and fruits was wafted for miles. Immediately, everyone was happy; bad tempers were forgotten. All quarrels were abandoned, all mutual wrongs forgiven; duels which had been arranged were erased from the memory, and rancour blew away like smoke.

I alone was sad, inconceivably sad. Like a priest bereft of his Deity, I could not, without deep distress, tear myself away from this monstrously seductive sea, this sea so infinitely varied in its fearful simplicity, and which seemed to contain within itself, and to portray by its high spirits, its appearance, its anger and its smiles, the moods, sufferings and ecstasies of all the souls who had lived, who are living and who shall live!

In saying farewell to this incomparable beauty, I was profoundly dejected; and that is why, when each one of my companions said: "At last!" I could only cry: "*Already!*"

And yet this was the earth, the earth with all its sounds, its passions, its comforts, its feasts; it was a rich and magnificent earth, full of promise, which sent out to us a mysterious perfume of rose and of musk, and from whose shores the music of life came to us in an amorous murmur.

Which Is True?

I KNEW A CERTAIN BENEDICTA who filled earth and air with ideals; and from whose eyes men learnt the desire for greatness, beauty, glory, and for everything that strengthened their belief in immortality.

But this miraculous child was too beautiful to live long. She

died only a few days after I had come to know her, and I buried
her with my own hands, one day when Spring wafted the contents
of its censer even as far as the graveyard. I buried her with my
own hands, well sealed in a coffin of wood, perfumed and incor-
ruptible as an Indian casket.

And as I stood gazing at the place where I had hidden my treas-
ure, all at once I saw a little person singularly like the deceased.
She was trampling on the fresh soil with strange, hysterical vio-
lence, and was laughing and shouting: "I am the real Benedicta!
and a vile slut I am, too! And to punish you for your blindness
and folly, you shall love me as I really am!"

But I was furious, and I answered: "No! no! no!" And to add
emphasis to my refusal, I stamped my foot so violently that my
leg sank up to the knee in the earth over the new grave, and like a
wolf caught in a trap, I remain fastened, perhaps for ever, to the
grave of the ideal.

The Thyrsus

To FRANZ LISZT

WHAT IS A THYRSUS? According to the
moral or poetical meaning, it is a sacerdotal emblem in the hand
of priests or of priestesses, celebrating the divinity whose inter-
preters and servants they are. But physically, it is only a stick, a
mere stick, a hop pole, a vine prop, dry, hard and straight. Around
this stick, in capricious twists and twirls, stalks and flowers frolic
and play, some sinuous and free, others drooping like bells or like
overturned cups. An astonishing glory radiates from this confu-
sion of lines and of soft, brilliant colours. Is it not as though the
curve and the spiral were paying court to the straight line, and
dancing about it in silent adoration? And all these delicate co-
rollas, all these calyxes, these perfumes and colours, are they not
executing a mystic fandango around the hieratical stick? And yet,
where is the imprudent mortal who would dare to decide whether
the flowers and the vine branches were made for the stick, or

whether the stick was not a mere pretext for displaying the beauty of the vine branches and the flowers? The Thyrsus is an illustration of your astonishing duality, mighty and venerated master, dear Bacchant of mysterious and passionate Beauty. Never did wood nymph, exasperated by the invincible Bacchus, shake her Thyrsus over the heads of her distracted companions with more energy and more caprice, than you wave your genius over the hearts of your brothers. The stick represents your will, straight, constant and unshakable; the flowers, the wandering of your fantasy around your will; it is the feminine element executing alluring pirouettes around the male. Straight line and arabesque, intention and expression, inflexibility of the will, flexibility of the word, unity of the end, variety of the means, all-powerful and indivisible amalgam of genius, what analyst would have the odious courage to divide and to separate you?

Dear Liszt, through the mists, beyond the rivers, above the cities where the pianos sing your glory, where the printing-press translates your wisdom, wherever you may be, in the splendours of the Eternal City or in the mists of those dreamy lands consoled by Cambrinus, improvising songs of delight or of ineffable sorrow, or confiding to paper your abstruse meditations, singer of eternal Pleasure and of eternal Anguish, philosopher, poet and artist, I salute you in immortality!

Portraits of Mistresses

IN A MAN'S BOUDOIR, that is to say in the smoking-room of a fashionable house of ill-fame, four men sat smoking and drinking. They were neither young nor old, ugly nor handsome; but, old or young, they bore the unmistakable mark of veterans of joy, an indescribable something, a cold, jesting sadness which clearly said: "We have lived intensely, and we are seeking that which we could love and esteem."

One of them turned the conversation to the subject of women.

It would have been more philosophical not to have mentioned it at all; but there are intelligent men who, after a certain amount of drinking, are not averse to banal conversations. Then, one listens to whoever is speaking, just as one might listen to dance music.

"All men," said this one, "were once the age of Cherubin: that period of life when, for want of wood-nymphs, we embrace oak trees, and without disgust. That's the first stage of love; in the second stage, we begin to choose. To be able to deliberate is already a sign of decadence. It is then, really, that we seek beauty. As for me, gentlemen, I am proud to say that quite some time ago I reached the climacteric period of the third stage, when beauty itself will no longer suffice unless it is spiced with perfumes, silks, etc. I must confess that I sometimes aspire, as to some unknown happiness, to a fourth stage wherein I should attain absolute tranquillity. But all my life, except at the Cherubin age, I have been unusually sensitive to the annoying stupidity, the irritating mediocrity of women. What I love most in animals is their candour. Imagine, then, how my last mistress must have made me suffer!

"She was the illegitimate daughter of a Prince. Beautiful, of course; otherwise I should not have chosen her. But she spoilt everything by an ambition that was both ugly and unseemly. She was the kind of woman who always wants to play a man's part. 'You are not a man! Ah! If only I were a man! I am more of a man than you are!' This was the unbearable refrain uttered by those lips that should have released nothing but songs. Whenever I spoke admiringly of a book, a poem, or an opera, she would say immediately: 'Perhaps you think that is very fine; but how do you know what is good?' And then she would argue.

"One fine day she began to study chemistry; and thereafter, between her mouth and mine, there was always a glass mask. And besides all this, she was a prude. If I happened to make love to her too ardently, she would writhe like an irritated sensitive plant."

"How did it all end?" asked one of the three others. "I didn't know you were so patient."

"God saw to it," said he, "that the remedy lay in the evil itself. One day I found this Minerva, so eager for ideal power, closeted with my man servant. The circumstances were such that I had to retire discreetly, to avoid causing them embarrassment. That very night I dismissed them both, after paying all arrears."

"For my part," resumed the man who had interrupted him, "I have only myself to complain of. Happiness came to live with me and I did not recognize it. Destiny allotted to me, not long ago, the enjoyment of a woman who was certainly the sweetest, the most submissive and the most devoted of creatures;—always at my service, and always without enthusiasm. 'Of course I will, since you wish it' was her inevitable reply. If you were to strike this wall or this sofa, you would draw more sighs than the most passionate ardour drew from the breast of my mistress. After we had lived together for a year she confessed to me that she had never known pleasure. I became disgusted with this unequal duel, and the incomparable girl married somebody or other. Later, it occurred to me to go and see her. As she showed me her six handsome children she said: 'Well, my dear friend, the wife is still the virgin she was as your mistress.' Nothing about her was changed. Sometimes I miss her: I should have married her."

The others began to laugh, and a third one said:

"Gentlemen, I have known certain pleasures that you may have neglected. I refer to the comedy in love, the comedy which does not preclude admiration. I admired my last mistress more than you could have, I believe, hated or loved yours. And everybody admired her as much as I did. When we went into a restaurant, everyone would soon stop eating in order to stare at her. Even the waiters and the woman behind the counter would respond to that contagious rapture, to the point of forgetting their duties. In short, I lived for a time with a *living phenomenon*. She ate, chewed, crunched, devoured, swallowed, in the lightest, the most casual manner. For a long time she kept me thus entranced. She had a sweet, dreamy, romantically English way of saying: 'I'm hungry!' She would show her beautiful teeth and repeat those words night and day, in a way that would have both moved and amused you. I might have made a fortune showing her at country fairs as a *polyphagous monster*. I fed her well; yet she left me."

"For a provision merchant, no doubt?"

"Something similar, some sort of official in the commissariat department who, by a form of graft known only to himself, probably manages to supply the poor child with the rations of several soldiers. At least that is what I suppose."

"I," said the fourth, "have suffered terribly, and for just the contrary of that for which feminine selfishness is generally blamed. You, too fortunate mortals, are wrong to complain of the imperfections of your mistresses!"

This was said in a very serious manner, by a man of kindly and sober mien. He had a clerical face, unfortunately brightened by clear grey eyes, by eyes whose glance said: "I will!" or "you must!" or "I never forgive!"

"If you, G——, nervous as I know you to be, and you, K—— and J——, cowardly and frivolous as you are, had been living with a certain woman I knew, you would either have fled or have died. I, as you see, survived. Imagine a woman incapable of committing an error of sentiment or of calculation; imagine an unbearable serenity of character; a devotion without sham and without stress; a kindness without weakness; an energy without violence. The story of my love-affair is like an interminable voyage, vertiginously monotonous, across a surface as pure and polished as a mirror, which might have reflected all my sentiments and my gestures with the ironical accuracy of my own conscience, and in such a fashion that I could not allow myself to make a gesture or to utter an unreasonable sentiment without instantly perceiving the silent reproach of my inseparable spectre. Love appeared to me like a guardian. What follies she kept me from, that I regret never having committed! How many debts paid in spite of myself! She deprived me of all the benefits I might have derived from my personal folly. With a cold, insurmountable rule, she thwarted all my caprices. To make it more unbearable, she never demanded gratitude, once the danger was past. How many times I curbed my desire to seize her by the throat and cry: 'Be imperfect, you wretched woman, so that I can love you without discomfort and without anger!' For several years I admired her, my heart full of hatred. . . . Well, it was not I who finally died!"

"Ah!" said the others, "then she's dead?"

"Yes! It couldn't possibly go on any longer. Love had become for me an insufferable nightmare. Victory or death, as they say in Politics; these were the alternatives forced upon me by destiny! One night, in a wood, near a pond, after a melancholy stroll during which her eyes reflected the peacefulness of the sky, and my heart was shrivelled like Hell. . . ."

"What?"

"How?"

"What do you mean?"

"It was inevitable. I have too strong a sense of justice to beat, outrage or dismiss an irreproachable servant. But I had to reconcile this sentiment with the horror this person inspired in me; I had to get rid of this being without wanting in my respect for her. What else could I have done with her, *since she was perfect?*"

The three others gazed at him with a vague and rather blank look, as though pretending not to understand, and as though tacitly confessing that they did not feel themselves capable of such extreme measures, even though they happened to be sufficiently justified.

Then they sent for more wine, to kill time, whose life is so hardy, and to accelerate life, which flows so slowly.

Loss of Halo

"WHAT! YOU HERE, my dear fellow? You, in a house of ill-fame! You, the drinker of quintessences! You, the eater of ambrosia! This is certainly a surprise!"

"My dear fellow, you know my fear of horses and of carriages. Well, just now, as I was hurrying across the boulevard, hopping about in the mud in order to get through that moving chaos out of which death comes galloping at you from all sides at once, I made a sudden movement, and my halo slipped from my head into the slime of the road. I hadn't the courage to pick it up; I decided that it was pleasanter to lose my insignia than to have my bones broken. And then I said to myself, it's an ill wind that blows no good. For now I can wander about incognito, commit base actions, give myself up to debauchery, like any simple mortal. So here I am, just like yourself, you see!"

"At least you ought to advertise for the halo, or notify the police about it."

"Certainly not! I'm very happy here. You alone have recognized me. Besides, dignity bores me. And I like to think that some miserable poet will pick it up, and shamelessly wear it. How nice to be able to make someone happy—someone I can laugh at! Think of X or of Z! How funny that would be!"

Mademoiselle Lancet

I HAD REACHED THE OUTSKIRTS of the suburb, when, in the light of the gas-lamps, I felt an arm gently seize mine, and heard a voice say in my ear: "Are you a doctor, sir?"

I looked at her; she was a tall, robust girl, with wide-open eyes, a face lightly rouged, and hair waving in the wind with the strings of her bonnet.

"No! I am not a doctor. Let me go."

"O yes! You are a doctor. I can see that. Come home with me. You'll be pleased with me, I can promise you!"

"Certainly I'll come to see you, but not right away. *After the doctor,* you know."

"Ah," said she, still clinging to my arm and bursting into laughter, "you must have your little joke, doctor! I have known many like you. Come!"

I am passionately fond of mystery, because I always hope to be able to unravel it. So I allowed myself to be persuaded by my companion, or rather by this unexpected enigma.

I omit the description of that hovel; one may find it in the pages of many famous old French poets. Only I was struck by one detail Régnier never observed: on the walls there were two or three portraits of celebrated doctors.

How she pampered me! A blazing fire, warm wine, cigars; and as she offered me these good things and lighted a cigar herself, the facetious creature said to me: "Make yourself at home, my dear. This should remind you of your youth and of the good old days at the hospital. But how is it that your hair has turned white? You didn't look like that when you were an interne at L—, a short while ago. I remember that it was you who used to help him with the major operations. There was a man who loved to cut and incise and amputate! It was you who used to hand him the instruments, the threads and the sponges. And when the operation was over, how he would take out his watch and say proudly: 'Five minutes, gentlemen!' Yes, I go everywhere. I know these Gentlemen well."

A few moments later she returned to the old refrain. "You are a doctor, aren't you, dearie?" she repeated, using the familiar form of address.

This absurd insistence made me leap to my feet. "No!" I cried furiously.

"A surgeon, then."

"No! No! Unless it were to cut off your head!" And I cursed her roundly.

"Wait," said she, "you'll see."

She took a packet of papers from the cupboard. They were simply a collection of portraits of the famous doctors of that period, lithographed by Maurin, that for years I had seen offered for sale on the Quai Voltaire.

"Look! Do you recognize this one?"

"Yes! That's X—; besides, his name's at the bottom. I know him personally."

"I knew you did! Look! Here's Z—, who used to say to his class, when speaking of X—: 'That monster whose face betrays the blackness of his soul!' Just because the other wasn't of his opinion about a certain case! How they used to roar with laughter about that, at the medical school, in those days! Don't you remember? Look! Here's K—, who denounced the insurgents he was treating in his hospital. That was the year of the insurrections. Is it conceivable that such a handsome man should have so little heart? And now here's W—, a famous English doctor. I caught him when he came to Paris. Hasn't he an effeminate appearance?"

As I touched a sealed packet lying on the little table, she said: "Wait a bit; those are the internes, and these, in this packet, are the externes."

And she spread out, fan-wise, a stack of photographs of much younger men.

"When we meet again, you'll give me your picture, won't you, dear?"

"But," said I, giving way in turn to my own obsession, "what makes you think I'm a doctor?"

"Because you are so nice and so good to women."

"Queer logic!" I said to myself.

"Oh, I never make a mistake; I have known a great many. I love doctors so much that, without being ill, I go to see them sometimes, only just to look at them. There are some who say to me coldly: 'You are not ill in the least!' But there are others who understand me, because I smile at them."

"And when they don't understand you?"

"Oh then, as I have needlessly disturbed them, I leave ten francs on the mantelpiece.—Those men are so good and so kind!—I discovered in La Pitié a young interne as pretty as an angel, and so polite! And who works, poor fellow! His friends tell me he hasn't a penny, because his parents are too poor to send him any money. That gave me courage. After all, I'm still good-looking, although not very young; so I said to him: 'Come and see me, come and see me often. And don't be bashful; I don't need any money.' I made him understand what I meant; I didn't say it right out; I was so afraid of humiliating him, poor child. And do you know, I have a strange desire that I don't dare mention to him? I want him to come and see me with his case of surgical instruments and his apron, even with a little blood on it!"

She said this very simply, as a man might say to an actress he loved: "I want to see you dressed in the costume you wore when you created that famous part."

Still obstinate, I went on: "Can you remember the exact time and the exact occasion when this singular passion first possessed you?"

I found it hard to make myself understood; finally I succeeded. There was an expression of sadness in her face and, as well as I can remember, she turned her eyes away as she replied: "I don't know—I don't remember."

What strange sights one sees in an immense city, when one knows how to wander and observe! Life swarms with innocent monsters. Oh Lord, my God! You, the Creator; you, the Master; you who have made Law and Liberty; you, the Sovereign who merely looks on, you the Judge who pardons; you who are full of motives and of causes, and who have perhaps instilled in my spirit a taste for horror so that my heart might be converted, as one is healed by the thrust of a blade; Lord, have pity, have pity on all madmen and on all madwomen! O Creator! Can monsters exist in the eyes of Him who alone knows why they exist, how they came to exist, and how they might have averted such a fate?

The Shooting Gallery and the Cemetery

AT THE SIGN OF THE CEMETERY. Tavern. "Curious signboard," our wanderer said to himself, "but certainly one to inspire thirst! I'm sure the proprietor of this tavern knows his Horace and those Poets who were pupils of Epicurus. He may even know about the profound sensibilities of the ancient Egyptians, to whom no feast was complete without a skeleton, or without some emblem of the brevity of life."

He entered, drank a glass of beer while facing the graves, and slowly smoked a cigar. Then it occurred to him to explore the cemetery, where the grass was so high and so inviting, and where so ardent a sun held sway.

For indeed, both light and heat raged there: one would have said that the intoxicated sun was sprawled full length on a magnificent carpet of flowers battened on destruction. The air was filled with an immense buzzing of life—the life of the infinitely minute—interrupted at regular intervals by the crackling of shots from a shooting gallery near by, that burst like champagne corks amid the hum of some mute symphony.

Then, basking in the sun that heated his brain and breathing the atmosphere pregnant with the warm perfumes of Death, he heard a voice whispering from the tomb on which he was seated, and this voice said: "Accursed be your targets and your rifles, turbulent mortals, who care so little for the dead and their divine repose! Accursed be your ambitions, and accursed your designs, impatient mortals, who come to study the art of killing near the sanctuary of Death! If you only knew how easy it is to win the prize, how easy it is to hit the mark, and how little anything matters, excepting Death, you would not tire yourselves so, industrious mortals, and you would prove far less troublesome to the slumber of those who long ago attained the Goal, the only real goal of odious life!"

Knock Down the Poor!

I HAD PROVIDED MYSELF with the popular books of the day (this was sixteen or seventeen years ago), and for two weeks I had never left my room. I am speaking now of those books that treat of the art of making nations happy, wise and rich in twenty-four hours. I had therefore digested—swallowed, I should say—all the lucubrations of all the authorities on the happiness of society—those who advise the poor to become slaves, and those who persuade them that they are all dethroned kings. So it is not astonishing if I was in a state of mind bordering on stupidity or madness. Only it seemed to me that deep in my mind, I was conscious of an obscure germ of an idea, superior to all the old wives' formulas whose dictionary I had just been perusing. But it was only the idea of an idea, something infinitely vague. And I went out with a great thirst, for a passionate taste for bad books engenders a proportionate desire for the open air and for refreshments.

As I was about to enter a tavern, a beggar held out his hat to me, and gave me one of those unforgettable glances which might overturn thrones if spirit could move matter, and if the eyes of a mesmerist could ripen grapes. At the same time I heard a voice whispering in my ear, a voice I recognized: it was that of a good Angel, or of a good Demon, who is always following me about. Since Socrates had his good Demon, why should I not have my good Angel, and why should I not have the honour, like Socrates, of obtaining my certificate of folly, signed by the subtle Lélut and by the sage Baillarger? There is this difference between Socrates' Demon and mine: his did not appear except to defend, warn or hinder him, whereas mine deigns to counsel, suggest, or persuade. Poor Socrates had only a prohibitive Demon; mine is a great master of affirmations, mine is a Demon of action, a Demon of combat. And his voice was now whispering to me: "He alone is the equal of another who proves it, and he alone is worthy of liberty who knows how to obtain it."

Immediately, I sprang at the beggar. With a single blow of my fist, I closed one of his eyes, which became, in a second, as big as a ball. In breaking two of his teeth I split a nail; but being of a delicate constitution from birth, and not used to boxing, I didn't feel strong enough to knock the old man senseless; so I seized the collar of his coat with one hand, grasped his throat with the other, and began vigorously to beat his head against a wall. I must confess that I had first glanced around carefully, and had made certain that in this lonely suburb I should find myself, for a short while, at least, out of immediate danger from the police.

Next, having knocked down this feeble man of sixty with a kick in the back sufficiently vicious to have broken his shoulder blades, I picked up a big branch of a tree which lay on the ground, and beat him with the persistent energy of a cook pounding a tough steak.

All of a sudden—O miracle! O happiness of the philosopher proving the excellence of his theory!—I saw this ancient carcass turn, stand up with an energy I should never have suspected in a machine so badly out of order, and with a glance of hatred which seemed to me of good omen, the decrepit ruffian hurled himself upon me, blackened both my eyes, broke four of my teeth, and with the same tree-branch, beat me to a pulp. Thus by an energetic treatment, I had restored to him his pride and his life.

Then I motioned to him to make him understand that I considered the discussion ended, and getting up, I said to him, with all the satisfaction of a Sophist of the Porch: "Sir, you are my equal! Will you do me the honour of sharing my purse, and will you remember, if you are really philanthropic, that you must apply to all the members of your profession, when they seek alms from you, the theory it has been my misfortune to practice on your back?"

He swore to me that he had understood my theory, and that he would carry out my advice.

Anywhere Out of the World

LIFE IS A HOSPITAL, in which every patient is possessed by the desire to change his bed. This one would prefer to suffer in front of the stove, and that one believes he would get well if he were placed by the window.

It seems to me that I should always be happier elsewhere than where I happen to be, and this question of moving is one that I am continually talking over with my soul.

"Tell me, my soul, poor chilled soul, what do you say to living in Lisbon? It must be very warm there, and you would bask merrily, like a lizard. It is by the sea; they say that it is built of marble, and that the people have such a horror of vegetation that they uproot all the trees. There is a landscape that would suit you, —made out of light and minerals, with water to reflect them."

My soul does not answer.

"Since you love tranquillity, and the sight of moving things, will you come and live in Holland, that heavenly land? Perhaps you could be happy in that country, for you have often admired pictures of Dutch life. What do you say to Rotterdam, you who love forests of masts, and ships anchored at the doors of houses?"

My soul remains silent.

"Perhaps Batavia seems more attractive to you? There we would find the intellect of Europe married to the beauty of the tropics."

Not a word. Can my soul be dead?

"Have you sunk into so deep a stupor that only your own torment gives you pleasure? If that be so, let us flee to those lands constituted in the likeness of Death. I know just the place for us, poor soul! We will leave for Torneo. Or let us go even farther, to the last limits of the Baltic; and if possible, still farther from life. Let us go to the Pole. There the sun obliquely grazes the earth, and the slow alternations of light and obscurity make variety impossible, and increase that monotony which is almost death. There we shall be able to take baths of darkness, and for our diversion, from time to time the Aurora Borealis shall scatter its rosy sheaves before us, like reflections of the fireworks of Hell!"

At last my soul bursts into speech, and wisely cries to me: "Anywhere, anywhere, as long as it be out of this world!"

The Port

ANY PORT is a charming abode for a soul weary of the struggles of life. The spacious sky, the ever-varying architecture of the clouds, the sea's changing colours, the scintillation of the lighthouses, form a prism marvellously adapted to amuse the eyes without ever tiring them. The slender form of the ships, with their complicated rigging that sways with the movement of the waters, helps the soul to preserve a taste for rhythm and for beauty. And for those who have neither ambition nor curiosity, there is a kind of mysterious and aristocratic pleasure in contemplating, while resting on the terrace of a house or leaning against a wharf, the activities of those who set sail and of those who return, of those who still have strength of purpose, and desire to travel or grow rich.

The Good Dogs

To JOSEPH STEVENS

I HAVE NEVER BLUSHED, even before the young writers of my time, for my admiration for Buffon; but today it is not the soul of this painter of pompous nature that I shall call to my aid. No.

I would much prefer to address myself to Sterne, and say to him: "Descend from the sky, or rise from the Elysian fields, oh sentimental jester, oh incomparable jester, and inspire me with a song worthy of you, in honour of good dogs, of poor dogs! Return astride the famous ass that is your inseparable companion in the memory of posterity, and let the ass not forget to carry, delicately held between his lips, his immortal macaroon!"

Avaunt, Academic Muse! I'll have nothing to do with that old prude. I invoke the familiar, the urban, the living Muse, that she may help me to sing the good dogs, the poor dogs, the dirty dogs, those that everyone turns out of doors, as if they were plague-stricken and lousy, everyone except the poor who are their allies, and the Poet who looks at them with fraternal eyes.

Fie on the pretty dog, on the conceited quadruped, Danish, King Charles, pug or lapdog, so delighted with himself that he leaps indiscreetly between the legs or on the knees of the visitor, as if he were sure to please; turbulent as a child, silly as a street-girl, sometimes as insolent and surly as a servant! Fie on those fourfooted serpents, shivering and idle, that are called greyhounds, and that have not even enough flair in their pointed muzzles to follow the trail of a friend, nor enough intelligence in their flat heads to play at dominoes!

To the kennel with all these tiresome parasites!

Let them return to their silken, padded kennels! I sing the dirty dog, the poor dog, the homeless dog, the wandering dog, the mountebank dog, the dog whose instinct, like that of the poor, of the gypsy and of the actor, is marvellously sharpened by necessity, that good mother, that true patroness of intelligence! I sing the unfortunate dogs, be they those that wander alone in the sinuous ravines of immense cities, or those that say with blinking, intelligent eyes, to some forsaken man: "Take me with you, and out of our two miseries we shall perhaps make some sort of happiness!"

"Whither go the dogs?" Nestor Roqueplan once asked in an immortal essay which he has certainly forgotten, and which only I, and perhaps Sainte-Beuve, still remember. Whither go the dogs, do you ask, you inattentive people? They go about their own affairs; love-affairs, business affairs. Through the mist, through the snow, through the mud, in the burning heat, in the streaming rain, they go, they come, they run, they dart under carriages, excited by fleas, by passions, by their needs and their duties. Like us, they have risen early in the morning, and seek a livelihood or pursue their pleasures.

There are some that sleep in a ruined house in the suburbs and come every day at the same hour to seek alms at a kitchen door in the Palais-Royal! There are others that travel in packs for more than five leagues, to partake of food prepared for them out of charity by certain sexagenarian old maids, whose empty hearts go out to the beasts, because foolish man does not want them. There are still others that, like runaway Negroes, frantic with desire, leave their villages from time to time to come to the city and gambol for an hour around some fine bitch, a trifle careless of her toilet, but proud and grateful.

And they are all very punctual, without note-books, without notes and without purses.

Do you know Belgium, the indolent, and have you admired, as I have, those powerful dogs harnessed to the little cart of the butcher, of the baker or of the milk woman, whose triumphant bark betrays their pride at competing with horses?

Here are two that belong to an even more civilized group. Allow me to lead you into the room of an absent mountebank. A bed of painted wood, without curtains, trailing bedclothes spotted with bugs, two straw chairs, an iron stove, one or two broken musical instruments. What miserable furnishings! But please observe those two intelligent beings dressed in clothes at once sumptuous and frayed, wearing caps like troubadours or soldiers, who watch, with the attention of two sorcerers, the nameless thing that simmers over the lighted stove, and out of the centre of which protrudes a long spoon, planted there like one of those aerial masts which announce that the masonry is finished.

Is it not just that such zealous strolling players should take to the road only after having first fortified their stomachs with a strong substantial soup? And can you not forgive the trace of sensuality in the nature of these poor devils who all day long have to endure the indifference of the public and the injustice of a manager who takes all the profits and who, alone, eats more soup than any four actors?

How often have I not smiled and been touched as I contemplated these four-footed philosophers, these obliging, obedient, devoted slaves, that the republican dictionary might well describe as unofficial, if the Republic, far too concerned with the happiness of men, could find a little time to treat with respect the honour of dogs!

And many times I have thought that somewhere (who knows after all?) there may be a special paradise for the good dogs, the poor dogs, the dirty and lonely dogs, to reward so much courage, so much patience and labour. Swedenborg declares that there is one for the Turks and one for the Dutch.

The shepherds mentioned in Virgil and Theocritus expected, as a prize for their songs, a piece of cheese, a well-fashioned flute or a she-goat. The Poet who sang the praises of poor dogs received as his recompense a beautiful waistcoat, whose colour, at once rich and faded, reminds one of autumn suns, of Saint Martin's summers, and of the beauty of mature women. None of those who were at the tavern in the rue Villa Hermosa will ever forget with what petulance the painter stripped off his waistcoat in favour of the Poet, so convinced was he that it was right and proper to sing the praises of poor dogs.

So might a gorgeous Italian tyrant in the great age have offered to the divine Aretino a dagger studded with jewels, or a Court mantle, in exchange for a precious sonnet or a curious satirical poem. And whenever the Poet dons the Painter's waistcoat, he is compelled to think of the good dogs, of the philosophic dogs, of Saint Martin's summers and of the beauty of mature women.

The Mirror

A HIDEOUS MAN enters and stares at his reflection in the looking-glass.

"Why do you look at yourself in the mirror, when your reflection never gives you any pleasure?"

The hideous man replies: "Sir, according to the immortal principles of 1789, all men have equal rights; therefore I have the right to look at myself; and whether with pleasure or with displeasure, concerns only my feelings."

In the name of common sense, I was certainly right; but from the legal point of view, he was certainly not wrong.

The Soup and the Clouds

MY DEAR LITTLE MADCAP FRIEND had invited me to dine with her. Through the open window of the dining-room I watched that ever-changing architecture God fashions out of vapour, those marvellous structures built of the impalpable;

and I said to myself, as I watched: "All those dissolving shapes are almost as lovely as the eyes of my beloved, my fantastic little madcap with the green eyes."

And suddenly I received a violent blow from behind, and I heard a hoarse, charming voice, a voice hysterical and as though made raucous by too much brandy, the voice of my dear little beloved that said: "Are you ever going to take your soup, you damned silly old cloud-merchant?"

Epilogue

WITH HEART AT REST I climbed the citadel's steep height, and saw the city as from a tower, Hospital, brothel, prison, and such hells,

Where evil comes up softly like a flower.
Thou knowest, O Satan, patron of my pain,
Not for vain tears I went up at that hour;

But, like an old sad faithful lecher, fain
To drink delight of that enormous trull
Whose hellish beauty makes me young again.

Whether thou sleep, with heavy vapours full,
Sodden with day, or, new apparelled, stand
In gold-laced veils of evening beautiful,

I love thee, infamous city! Harlots and
Hunted have pleasures of their own to give,
The vulgar herd can never understand.

Arthur Rimbaud

A Season in Hell

A Season in Hell

ONCE, IF I REMEMBER WELL, my life was a feast where all hearts opened and all wines flowed.

One evening I seated Beauty on my knees. And I found her bitter. And I cursed her.

I armed myself against justice.

I fled. O Witches, Misery, Hate, to you has my treasure been entrusted!

I contrived to purge my mind of all human hope. On all joy, to strangle it, I pounced with the stealth of a wild beast.

I called to the executioners while dying to let me gnaw the butt-ends of their guns. I called to the plagues to smother me in blood, in sand. Misfortune was my God. I laid myself down in the mud. I dried myself in the air of crime. I played sly tricks on madness.

And spring brought me the idiot's frightful laughter.

Now, only recently, being on the point of giving my last croak, I thought of looking for the key to the ancient feast where I might find my appetite again.

Charity is that key.—This inspiration proves that I have dreamed!

"You will always be a hyena . . ." etc., shrieks the devil who crowned me with such pleasant poppies. "Attain death with all your appetites, your selfishness and all the capital sins!"

Ah! I'm fed up:—But, dear Satan, a less fiery eye I beg you! And while awaiting a few small infamies in arrears, you who love the absence of the instructive or descriptive faculty in a writer, for you let me tear out these few, hideous pages from my notebook of one of the damned.

Bad Blood

I HAVE THE BLUE-WHITE EYE of my Gallic ancestors, their narrow skull and their clumsiness in fighting. I find my clothes as barbarous as theirs. Only I don't butter my hair.

The Gauls were the most inept flayers of beasts and scorchers of grass of their time.

From them too: idolatry and love of sacrilege; oh! all the vices, anger, lust—lust, magnificent—above all, lying and sloth.

I have a horror of all trades. Masters and workers—base peasants all. The hand that guides the pen is worth the hand that guides the plough.—What an age of hands! I shall never have my hand. Afterward domesticity leads too far. The decency of beggars sickens me. Criminals disgust like castrates: as for me, I am intact, and I don't care.

But who gave me so perfidious a tongue that it has guided and guarded my indolence till now? Without ever making use of my body for anything, and lazier than the toad, I have lived everywhere. Not a family of Europe that I do not know.—I mean families like my own that owe everything to the Declaration of the Rights of Man.—I have known all the sons of respectable families.

HAD I BUT ANTECEDENTS at some point in the history of France! But no, nothing.

It is quite clear to me that I have always been of an inferior race. I cannot understand revolt. My race never rose except to pillage: like wolves with the beast they have not killed.

I remember the history of France, eldest daughter of the Church. A villein, I must have made the journey to the Holy Land; my head is full of roads through the Swabian plains, views of Byzantium, ramparts of Jerusalem: The cult of Mary, compassion for the crucified Christ awake in me among a thousand profane phantasmagoria.—A leper, I am seated among pot-sherds and nettles, at the foot of a sun-eaten wall.—Later, a reiter, I must have bivouacked under German stars.

Ah! again: I dance the witches' sabbath in a red clearing with old women and children.

I can remember no farther back than this very land and Christianity. I shall never have done seeing myself in that past. But always alone; without family; and even the language that I spoke —what was it? I cannot see myself at the councils of Christ; nor at the councils of Lords—representatives of Christ.

What was I in the last century? I find no trace again until to-day. No more vagabonds, no more vague wars. The inferior race has over-run everything: the people—as we say the nation, reason, science.

Oh! Science! Everything has been revised. For the body and for the soul,—the viaticum,—there is medicine and philosophy, —old wives' remedies and popular songs rearranged. And the pastimes of princes and games they proscribed! Geography, cosmography, mechanics, chemistry! . . .

Science, the new nobility! Progress. The world marches on! Why shouldn't it turn?

It is the vision of numbers. We are going toward the *Spirit*. There's no doubt about it, an oracle, I tell you. I understand, and not knowing how to express myself without pagan words, I'd rather remain silent.

Pagan blood returns! The Spirit is near; why doesn't Christ help me by granting my soul nobility and liberty? Alas! The gospel has gone by! The gospel! The gospel.

Greedily I await God. I am of an inferior race for all eternity.

Here I am on the Breton shore. Let the towns light up in the evening. My day is done; I'm quitting Europe. Sea air will burn my lungs; strange climates will tan my skin. To swim, to trample the grass, to hunt, and above all to smoke; to drink liquors strong as boiling metal,—like my dear ancestors around their fires.

I'll return with limbs of iron, dark skin and furious eye; people will think to look at me that I am of a strong race. I will have gold: I will be idle and brutal. Women nurse those fierce invalids, home from hot countries. I'll be mixed up in politics. Saved.

Now I am an outcast. I loathe the fatherland. A very drunken sleep on the beach, that's best.

WE'RE NOT GOING.—Back over the old roads again, laden with my vice, the vice whose roots of suffering have flourished at my side since reason dawned,—that lifts to the skies, belabours me, knocks me down, drags me along.

The last innocence and the last timidity. It is said. Not to display my betrayals and disgusts to the world.

Forward! The march, the burden and the desert, weariness and anger.

To whom shall I hire myself out? What beast should I adore? What holy image is attacked? What hearts shall I break? What lies should I uphold? In what blood tread?

Rather steer clear of the law.—The hard life, simple brutishness,—to lift with withered fist the coffin's lid, to sit, to smother myself. And thus no old age, no dangers: terror is not French.

—Ah! I am so utterly forsaken that to any divine image whatsoever, I offer my impulses toward perfection.

O my abnegation, O my marvelous charity! here below, however!

De profundis, Domine, what a fool I am!

STILL BUT A CHILD, I admired the intractable convict on whom the prison doors are always closing; I sought out the inns and rooming houses he might have consecrated by his passing; *with his idea* I saw the blue sky, and labour flowering the country; in cities I sensed his doom. He had more strength than a saint, more common sense than a traveler—and he, he alone! the witness of his glory and his reason.

On highroads on winter nights, without roof, without clothes, without bread, a voice gripped my frozen heart: "Weakness or strength: why, for you it is strength. You do not know where you are going, nor why you are going; enter anywhere, reply to anything. They will no more kill you than if you were a corpse." In the morning I had a look so lost, a face so dead, that perhaps those whom I met *did not see me.*

In cities, suddenly, the mud seemed red or black like a mirror when the lamp moves about in the adjoining room, like a treasure in the forest! Good luck, I cried, and I saw a sea of flames and smoke in the sky; to the right, to the left all the riches of the world flaming like a billion thunder-bolts.

But to me debauch and the comradeship of women were denied. Not even a companion. I saw myself before an infuriated mob, facing the firing-squad, weeping out of pity for their being unable to understand, and forgiving!—Like Jeanne d'Arc!—"Priests, professors, masters, you are making a mistake in turning me over to the law. I have never belonged to this people; I have never been a Christian; I am of the race that sang under torture; laws I have never understood; I have no moral sense, I am a brute: you are making a mistake."

Yes, my eyes are closed to your light. I am a beast, a Negro. But I can be saved. You are sham Negroes, you, maniacs, wildmen, misers. Merchant, you are a Negro; Judge, you are a Negro; General, you are a Negro; Emperor, old itch, you are a Negro: you have drunk of the untaxed liquor of Satan's still.—Fever and cancer inspire this people. Cripples and old men are so respectable they are fit to be boiled.—The smartest thing would be to leave this continent where madness stalks to provide hostages for these wretches. I enter the true kingdom of Ham.

Do I know nature yet? Do I know myself?—*No more words.* I bury the dead in my belly. Shouts, drums, dance, dance, dance, dance! I cannot even see the time when, white men landing, I shall fall into nothingness.

Hunger, thirst, shouts, dance, dance, dance, dance!

THE WHITE MEN ARE LANDING! The cannon! We must submit to baptism, we must put on clothes, we must work.

My heart has known the stroke of grace. Ah! I did not foresee it.

I have never done evil. Light will my days be and I shall be spared repentance. I shall not have known the torments of the soul half dead to good, whence like funeral candles a grave flame ascends. The fate of the sons of respectable families, the premature coffin covered with limpid tears. Certainly debauch is stupid, vice is stupid; all that is rotten must be cast aside. But the clock will not have succeeded in striking only the hour of pure pain! Am I to be carried off like a child, to play in Paradise forgetful of all sorrow?

Quick! Are there other lives?—Sleep in wealth is impossible. Wealth has always been public property. The keys of knowledge are the gifts of divine love alone. I see that nature is but the display of goodness. Farewell chimeras, ideals, errors!

The reasonable song of angels rises from the saviour ship: it is divine love. Two loves! I can die of earthly love, die of human devotion. I have abandoned souls whose pain will be increased by my going! Among the ship-wrecked you choose me; those who remain, they're my friends, aren't they?

Save them!

Reason is born to me. The world is good. I will bless life. I will love my brothers. These are no longer childish promises. Nor the hope of escaping old age and death. God is my strength and I praise God.

BOREDOM IS NO LONGER MY LOVE. Rages, debauchery, madness,—I have known all their soarings and their disasters,—My whole burden is laid down. Let us contemplate undazed the extent of my innocence. I would no longer be capable of begging the solace of a bastinado. I don't fancy myself embarked on a wedding with Jesus Christ as father-in-law.

I am not a prisoner of my reason. I said: God. I want freedom in salvation: how am I to seek it? Frivolous tastes have left me. No more need of human devotion nor of divine love. No more regrets for the age of tender hearts. Each of us has his reason, scorn and charity; I reserve my place at the top of that angelic ladder of common sense.

As for established happiness, domestic or not . . . no, I cannot. I am too dissipated, too weak. Life flourishing through toil, old platitude! As for me, my life is not heavy enough, it flies and floats far above action, that dear mainstay of the world.

What an old maid I am getting to be, lacking the courage to be in love with death!

If only God granted me celestial, aerial calm, prayer,—like the ancient Saints.—Saints, they're the strong ones! Anchorites, artists such as are not wanted any more!

Farce without end? My innocence would make me weep. Life is the farce we all have to lead.

ENOUGH! HERE IS THE PUNISHMENT.—*Forward, march!*

Ah! My lungs are on fire, my temples roar! In this sunlight night rolls through my eyes: Heart . . . Limbs . . .

Where are we going? To battle? I am weak! The others advance. Tools, weapons . . . time! . . .

Fire! Fire on me! Here! Or I surrender.—Cowards!—I'll kill myself! I'll throw myself under the horses' hoofs!

Ah! . . .

—I shall get used to it.

It would be the French way of life, the path of honour!

Night of Hell

I HAVE SWALLOWED a monstrous dose of poison.—Thrice blessed be the counsel that came to me!—My entrails are on fire. The violence of the venom twists my limbs, deforms and prostrates me. I die of thirst, I suffocate, and cannot scream. It is hell, eternal punishment! See how the fire flares up again! How nicely I burn. Go to it, demon!

I had caught a glimpse of conversion to good and to happiness, salvation. Can I describe the vision? Hell's fire will tolerate no hymns! There were a million charming creatures, a melodious sacred concert, strength and peace, noble ambitions—I don't know what all!

Noble ambitions!

And still this is life!—Suppose damnation were eternal! Then a man who wants to mutilate himself is well damned, isn't he? I think I am in hell, therefore I am in hell. It is the execution of the catechism. I am the slave of my baptism. Parents, you have been my undoing and your own. Poor innocent!—Hell has no power over pagans.

—This is life still! Later the delights of damnation will be more profound. A crime, quick, a crime, that I may fall into nothingness in accordance with human law.

Be quiet, do be quiet! . . . There's shame and reprobation here: Satan who says that the fire is contemptible, that my anger is horribly silly. Enough! . . . Fallacies they whisper to me, sorceries, false perfumes, childish music.—And to think that I possess truth, that I perceive justice: my judgment is sound and sure, I am ripe for perfection. . . Pride.—My scalp is drying up. Pity! Lord, I am afraid. I am thirsty, so thirsty! Ah, childhood, the grass, the rain, the lake on the pebbles, *the moonlight when the bell was chiming twelve* . . . the devil is in the belfry at this hour. Mary! Holy Virgin! . . .—Loathing of my stupidity.

Out there, are they not honest souls that wish me well? . . . Come. . . I have a pillow over my mouth, they do not hear me, they are phantoms. Besides, no one ever thinks of others. Let no one come near me. I must smell scorched I'm sure.

Hallucinations are without number. Truly that is what I have always known: no more faith in history, principles forgotten. I'll keep quiet about that: poets and visionaries would be jealous. I am a thousand times the richest, let us be as avaricious as the sea.

What! The clock of life stopped a while ago. I am no longer in the world.—Theology is serious, hell is certainly *down below*,— and heaven on high.—Ecstasy, nightmare, and sleep in a nest of flames.

What tricks in observation in the country. . . Satan, Old Nick, runs with the wild grain. . . Jesus walks on the purple briars and they do not bend. . . Jesus walked on the troubled waters. The lantern showed him to us, erect, white, with long brown hair. . . on the flank of an emerald wave. . .

I am going to unveil all the mysteries: religious mysteries, or natural mysteries, death, birth, the future, the past, cosmogony, nothingness. I am a master of phantasmagoria.

Listen! . . .

I have all the talents!—There is no one here and there is someone: I would not squander my treasures.—Do you want Negro songs, the dances of houris? Do you want me to vanish, to dive after the *ring?* Is that what is wanted? I will make gold, remedies.

Trust in me then, faith assuages, guides, restores. Come, all of you, even the little children,—that I may comfort you, that my heart may be poured out for you,—the marvelous heart!—Poor men, toilers! I do not ask for prayers; with your faith alone I shall be happy.

—Think of me! It hardly makes me regret the world very much. I am lucky not to suffer more. My life was nothing but sweet follies, it's a pity.

Bah! Let us make all manner of grimaces.

Decidedly we are out of the world. No longer any sound. My sense of touch has left me. Ah! my castle, my Saxony, my willow wood. Evenings, mornings, nights, days. . . How weary I am!

I should have my hell for anger, my hell for pride,—and the hell of sloth; a symphony of hells.

I die of lassitude. It is the tomb, I go to the worms, horror of horrors! Satan, you fraud, you would dissolve me with your charms. I demand my due. I demand it! a thrust of the pitchfork, a drop of fire.

Ah! to rise again into life! to cast our eyes on our deformities. And that poison, that kiss, a thousand times accursed! My weakness, the cruelty of the world! My God, pity, hide me, I behave too badly!—I am hidden and I am not.

It is the fire that flares up again with its damned.

Delirium   (I)

THE FOOLISH VIRGIN, THE INFERNAL BRIDEGROOM

LET'S HEAR NOW a hell-mate's confession: "O heavenly Bridegroom, my Lord, do not reject the confession of the saddest of your handmaidens. I am lost. I am drunk. I am unclean. What a life!

"Forgive me, heavenly Lord, forgive me! Ah! forgive me! How many tears! And how many more tears later, I hope!

"Later I shall know the heavenly Bridegroom! I was born His slave.—The other can beat me now!

"At present I am at the bottom of the world! O my friends. . . no, not my friends. . . Never delirium and tortures like these. . . How stupid!

"Ah! I suffer, I scream. I really suffer. Yet everything is permitted me, burdened with the contempt of the most contemptible hearts.

"At any rate let me tell my secret, free to repeat it twenty times again,—just as dreary, just as insignificant!

"I am a slave of the infernal Bridegroom, the one who was the undoing of the foolish virgins. He is really that very demon. He is not a ghost, he is not a phantom. But I who have lost all reason, who am damned and dead to the world,—they will not kill me! How describe him to you! I can no longer even speak. I am in mourning, I weep, I am afraid. A little coolness, Lord, if you will, if you only will!

"I am a widow. . .—I used to be a widow. . .—ah, yes, I was

really honest once, and I was not born to be a skeleton! . . .—He was hardly more than a child. His mysterious tenderness had seduced me. I forgot all human duty to follow him. What a life! Real life is absent. We are not in the world. I go where he goes, I have to. And often he flies into a rage at me, *me, the poor soul.* The Demon! He is a demon, you know, *he is not a man.*

"He says: 'I do not like women: love must be reinvented, that's obvious. A secure position is all they're capable of desiring now. Security once gained, heart and beauty are set aside: cold disdain alone is left, the food of marriage today. Or else, I see women marked with the signs of happiness, and whom I could have made my comrades, devoured first by brutes with as much feeling as a log. . .'

"I listen to him glorifying infamy, clothing cruelty with charm. I am of a distant race: my ancestors were Norsemen; they used to pierce their sides, drink their blood.—I will cover myself with gashes, tattoo my body. I want to be as ugly as a Mongol: you'll see, I will howl through the streets. I want to become raving mad. Never show me jewels, I should grovel and writhe on the floor. My riches, I want them spattered all over with blood. Never will I work. . .' Many nights his demon would seize me and rolling on the ground I would wrestle with him.—Often at night, drunk, he lies in wait for me, in streets, in houses, to frighten me to death.— 'They will really cut my throat; it will be revolting.' Oh! those days when he goes wrapped in an air of crime!

"Sometimes he speaks in a kind of melting dialect, of death that brings repentance, of all the miserable wretches there must be, of painful toil, of partings that lacerate the heart. In low dives where we would get drunk, he used to weep for those around us, cattle of misery. He would lift up drunkards in the dark streets. He had the pity of a bad mother for little children.—He would depart with the graces of a little girl going to her catechism.—He pretended to have knowledge of everything, business, art, medicine.—I followed him, I had to!

"I saw the whole setting with which in his mind he surrounded himself: clothing, sheets, furniture; I lent him arms, another face.

I saw everything relating to him as he would have liked to create it for himself. When his mind was absent, I followed him, yes I, in strange and complicated actions, very far, good or bad: I was certain of never entering his world. How many hours of the night, beside his dear sleeping body I kept watch, trying to understand why he so longed to escape reality. Never a man had such a wish. I realized,—without any fear for him,—that he could be a serious danger to society. Perhaps he has some secrets for *changing life?* No, I would say to myself, he is only looking for them. In short, his charity is bewitched, and I, its prisoner. No other soul would have enough strength—strength of despair!—to endure it, and to be protected and loved by him. Moreover, I never imagined him with another soul: one sees one's own Angel, never the Angel of someone else—I believe. I was in his soul as in a palace they had emptied, so that no one should see so mean a person as oneself: that was all. Alas! I was really dependent on him. But what could he want with my dull, my craven life? He was making me no better if he wasn't driving me to death! Sometimes, chagrined and sad, I said to him: 'I understand you.' He would shrug his shoulders.

"Thus my sorrow always renewed, and seeming in my eyes more lost than ever,—as in the eyes of all who might have watched me had I not been condemned to be forgotten by all forever!—I hungered for his kindness more and more. With his kisses and his friendly arms, it was really heaven, a sombre heaven into which I entered and where I longed to be left, poor and deaf and dumb and blind. Already it had grown into a habit. I thought of us as two good children, free to wander in the Paradise of sadness. We understood each other. Enraptured, we used to work together. But after a profound caress he would say: 'How queer it will seem to you when I am no longer here—all you have gone through. When you no longer have my arm beneath your head, nor my heart for resting place, nor these lips upon your eyes. For I shall have to go away, very far away, one day. After all I must help others too: it is my duty. Not that it's very appetizing. . . dear heart. . .' Right away I saw myself, with him gone, my senses reeling, hurled into the most horrible darkness: death. I used to make him promise never to leave me. He made it twenty times, that lovers' promise. It was as vain as when I said to him: 'I understand you.'

"Ah! I have never been jealous of him. He will not leave me, I believe. What would become of him? He knows nothing; he will never work. He wants to live a sleep walker. Will his goodness and his charity alone give him the right to live in the real world? There are moments when I forget the abjection to which I have fallen; he will make me strong, we will travel, hunt in the deserts, we will sleep on the pavements of unknown cities, uncared for and without a care. Or else I shall awake, and the laws and customs will have changed,—thanks to his magic power,—or the world, while remaining the same, will leave me to my desires, joys, heedlessness. Oh! the life of adventure in children's books, to recompense me, I have suffered so, will you give me that? He cannot. His ideal is unknown to me. He told me he had regrets, hopes: that should be no concern of mine. Does he talk to God? I should appeal to God, perhaps. I am in the lowest depths, and I can no longer pray.

"If he explained his sadness to me, would I understand it any more than his mockery? He assails me, he spends hours making me ashamed of everything in the world that may have touched me, and is indignant if I weep.

" 'You see that elegant young man going into the beautiful, calm house; his name is Smith, Miller, Maurice, John, or something or other! A woman has devoted her life to loving that wicked idiot: she is dead, she must be a saint in heaven now. You will kill me as he has killed that woman. It is our lot, the lot of us, charitable hearts. . .!' Alas! he had days when all busy men seemed to him grotesque playthings of delirium; he would laugh long and horribly. Then he would revert to his manners of a young mother, a big sister. If he were less untamed we should be saved! But his tenderness too is deadly. I am his slave.—Ah! I am mad!

"One day, perhaps, he will miraculously disappear; but I must know if he is really to ascend into some heaven again, so that I'll not miss the sight of my darling boy's assumption!"

Queer couple!

Delirium (II)

ALCHEMY OF THE WORD

NOW FOR ME! The story of one of my follies.

For a long time I boasted of possessing every possible landscape and held in derision the celebrities of modern painting and poetry.

I loved maudlin paintings, decorative panels, stage-sets, the back-drops of mountebanks, old inn signs, popular prints; old-fashioned literature, church Latin, erotic books innocent of all spelling, the novels of our ancestors, fairytales, children's story-books, antiquated operas, inane refrains and artless rhythms.

I dreamed crusades, unrecorded voyages of discovery, republics without a history, religious wars hushed up, revolutions of customs, the displacements of races and continents: I believed in sorcery of every sort.

I invented the color of vowels!—*A* black, *E* white, *I* red, *O* blue, *U* green.—I regulated the form and the movement of every consonant, and with instinctive rhythms I prided myself on inventing a poetic language accessible some day to all the senses. I reserved all rights of translation.

At first it was an experiment. I wrote silences, I wrote the night. I recorded the inexpressible. I fixed frenzies in their flight.

FAR FROM BIRDS AND FLOCKS and village girls,
What did I drink as I knelt on the heath,
A tender hazel copse around me,
In the warm green mist of the afternoon?

What could I drink in that young Oise,
—Voiceless the trees, flowerless the grass, sky overcast!—
Drink at those yellow gourds far from my cabin
So dear? Liquors of gold that bring heavy sweating.

I seemed a sorry sign for an inn.
—A storm came chasing the sky away. And virgin sands
Drank all the water of the evening woods,
God's wind blew icicles into the ponds;

As I wept I saw gold,—and could not drink.

> MORNING, SUMMER, four o'clock,
> Deep still love's sleep endures.
> While feted evening's odors
> From the green bowers evaporate.
>
> Down in their vast woodyards,
> Under an Hesperian sun,
> The Carpenters—in shirt sleeves—
> Toil already;
>
> Calm in their Deserts of moss,
> Precious canopies preparing,
> Where the city will paint
> Skies fabulous and false.
>
> O, for those charming Workers,
> Subjects of a Babylonian king,
> Venus! a moment leave the Lovers
> Whose souls are wreathed!
>
> O queen of Shepherds, bring
> Spirits of wine to the workers,
> That their powers be appeased
> Awaiting the noon swim in the sea.

POETIC QUAINTNESS PLAYED A LARGE PART in my alchemy of the word.

I became an adept at simple hallucination: in place of a factory I really saw a mosque, a school of drummers composed of angels, carriages on the highways of the sky, a drawing-room at the bottom of a lake; monsters, mysteries; the title of a melodrama would raise horrors before me.

Then I would explain my magic sophisms with the hallucination of words!

Finally I came to regard as sacred the disorder of my mind. I was idle, full of a sluggish fever: I envied the felicity of beasts, caterpillars that represent the innocence of limbo, moles, the sleep of virginity!

My temper soured. In kinds of ballads I said farewell to the world:

SONG OF THE HIGHEST TOWER

O MAY IT COME, the time of love,
The time we'd be enamoured of.

I've been patient too long,
My memory is dead,
All fears and all wrongs
To the heavens have fled.
While all my veins burst
With a sickly thirst.

O may it come, the time of love,
The time we'd be enamoured of.

Like the meadow that is dreaming
Forgetful of cares,
Flourishing and flowering
With incense and tares,
Where fierce buzzings rise
Of the very dirty flies.

O may it come, the time of love,
The time we'd be enamoured of.

I loved the desert, dried orchards, faded shops and tepid drinks. I dragged myself through stinking alleys and, eyes closed, I gave myself to the sun, God of fire.

"General, if on your ruined ramparts an old cannon remains, bombard us with lumps of dried mud.—On the mirrors of magnificent shops! in drawing-rooms! Make the city grovel in its dust. Oxidize the gargoyles. Fill boudoirs with the burning powder of rubies. . ."

Oh! the drunken fly in the inn's privy, enamoured of borage, dissolved by a sunbeam!

HUNGER

IF I'VE A TASTE, it's not alone
For the earth and stones,
Rocks, coal, iron, air,
That's my daily fare.

Roam my hungers, hungers browse
In the field on sound,
Suck up bindweed's gay venom
Along the ground.

Eat the pebbles that one breaks,
Churches' old stones;
Gravel of ancient deluge taste,
And loaves scattered in grey brakes.

HOWLING underneath the leaves
The wolf spits out the lovely plumes
Of his feast of fowls:
Like him I am consumed.

Salads and fruits
Await but the picking;

But violets are the food
Of spiders in the thicket.

Let me sleep! Let me seethe
At the altars of Solomon.
Broth run over the rust
And mix with the Cedron.

At last, O happiness, O reason, I brushed from the sky the
azure that is darkness, and I lived—gold spark of *pure* light. Out
of joy I took on an expression as comical as possible:

IT IS RECOVERED!
What? Eternity.
It is the sea
Mixed with the sun.

My soul eternal,
Redeem your promise,
In spite of the night alone
And the day on fire.

Of human suffrage,
Of common aspirings,
You free yourself then!
You fly according to. . .

Hope never more,
No *orietur*.
Science and patience,
Retribution is sure.

No more tomorrows,
Embers of satin,
Your ardour is now
Your duty only.

It is recovered!
What? Eternity.
It is the sea
Mixed with the sun.

I became a fabulous opera; I saw that all creatures had a fatality for happiness: action is not life, but only a way of spoiling some force, an enervation. Morality is the weakness of the brain.

It seemed to me that to every creature several *other* lives were due. This gentleman knows not what he does: he is an angel. This family is a litter of puppies. With several men I have spoken aloud with a moment of one of their other lives. Thus it was I loved a pig.

Not a single sophistry of madness—madness to confine—was forgotten: I could recite them all again, I know the system.

My health was endangered. Terror came. I would fall into a slumber of days, and getting up would go on with the same sad dreams. I was ripe for death and along a road of perils my weakness led me to the borders of Cimmeria, land of whirlwinds and of darkness.

I had to travel, divert the spells assembled in my brain. Over the sea, that I loved as though it were to cleanse me of a stain, I saw the comforting cross arise. I had been damned by the rainbow. Happiness was my fatality, my remorse, my worm: my life would always be too enormous to be devoted to force and to beauty.

Happiness! Its tooth sweet unto death, warned me at the crowing of the cock,—*ad matutinum*, at the *Christus venit*,—in the darkest cities:

O seasons, O castles!
What soul is without sin!

The magic study I've made,
Of happiness none can evade.

To it each time, good luck,
We hear the Gallic cock.

No more desires for me:
It has taken my life in fee.

Charmed body, soul and brain
Delivered of every strain.

O seasons, O castles!

The hour of flight will be
The hour of death for me!

O seasons, O castles!

That is over. Now I know how to greet beauty.

The Impossible

AH! THAT LIFE OF MY CHILDHOOD, the
highroad in all weathers, supernaturally sober, more disinterested
than the best of beggars, proud to have neither country, nor
friends, what folly it was! And I see it only now!

—I was right to despise those poor saps who would never miss
the chance of a caress, parasites of the cleanliness and health of
our women, now that they are so little in accord with us.

I was right in all my contempts: since I escape.

I escape?

I explain.

Yesterday I was still sighing: "Heavens! aren't there enough
of us damned ones here below! I, myself, have been so long al-
ready in their troupe! I know them all. We recognize each other
always; we disgust each other. Charity is unknown to us. But we
are civil; our relations with the world are most correct." Is it sur-
prising? The world! merchants, simple souls!—We are not dis-
honored.—But the elect, how would they receive us? Now, there
are the surly and joyous ones, the false elect, since we need au-

dacity or humility to approach them. They are the only elect. They are not blessers!

Having recovered two cents' worth of reason,—it is soon gone! —I see that my disquietudes come from having understood too late that we are in the Occident. Occidental swamps! Not that I think light adulterated, form shrunk, motion gone astray. . . Well! here is my spirit insisting on taking upon itself all the cruel developments that the spirit has suffered since the end of the Orient. . . It really insists, my spirit.

. . . My two cents' worth of reason is spent! Spirit is authority, it insists that I be in the Occident. It would have to be silenced to conclude as I wished.

To the devil, I said, with martyrs' crowns, the beams of art, the pride of inventors, the ardor of plunderers; I returned to the Orient and to the first and eternal wisdom.—A dream of vulgar indolence it would seem!

I never thought, however, of the pleasure of escaping modern sufferings. I was not thinking of the bastard wisdom of the Koran. —But is there not real torture in this that, ever since that declaration of science, Christianity, man *fools himself*, proves to himself the obvious, and puffs himself up with the pleasure of reiterating those proofs, and thus only does he live! Subtle, silly torture; source of all my spiritual vagrancies. Nature can be bored, perhaps! Monsieur Prudhomme * was born with Christ.

Is it not because we cultivate fog! We eat fever with our watery vegetables. And drunkenness! and tobacco! and ignorance! and self-sacrifices!—How far all this is from the conception, from the wisdom of the Orient, the original fatherland! Why a modern world if such poisons are invented!

* *Monsieur Prudhomme:* a character created by Henri Monnier (1857) frequently referred to in French literature. Solemnly and ostentatiously banal, he is the prototype of the smug bourgeois who is a reflection of his environment. He has a taste for meaningless grandiloquence, is always pompously "proving the obvious" and unconsciously trying to convince himself and others that he is not a nonentity. The name is a satiric reference to the meaning of the word, *prud'homme*, righteous man. This self-righteous mediocrity, Rimbaud says, "was born with Christ," and for mediocrity Rimbaud reserved his bitterest "contempt" and passionate hatred. [L. V.]

Churchmen will say: Granted. But you mean Eden. Nothing for you in the history of Oriental peoples.—It is true; it is of Eden I was thinking! What has it to do with my dream—that purity of ancient races!

Philosophers: The world has no age. Humanity simply changes place. You are in the Occident, but free to live in your Orient, as ancient as you please, and to live well. Don't be a victim. Philosophers, you are of your Occident.

My spirit, beware. No violent projects of salvation. Bestir yourself!—Ah! for us science is not fast enough!

—But I perceive that my spirit is asleep.

If it were always wide awake from this minute on we should soon reach the truth that may even now surround us with her weeping angels! . . .—If it had been awake up to this very minute, I should never have yielded to my deleterious instincts in an immemorial age! . . .—If it had always been wide awake, I should be under full sail on the high sea of wisdom! . . .

O purity! purity!

It is this moment of awakening that has given me the vision of purity!—Through the spirit we go to God!

Heart-breaking misfortune!

Lightning

HUMAN TOIL! That is the explosion which lights up my abyss from time to time.

"Nothing is vanity; all for science and forward!" cries the modern Ecclesiastes, that is to say *Everybody*. And yet the corpses of the wicked and the sluggards fall on the hearts of others. . . Ah! hurry, do hurry; out there, beyond the night, those future, those eternal rewards. . . shall we escape them? . . .

—What can I do? I know what toil is; and science is too slow. Let prayer gallop and light thunder. . . I see it clearly. It is too simple, and it's too hot; they will get along without me. I have my duty; I shall be proud of it after the fashion of several others by setting it aside.

My life is threadbare. All right! Let's sham and shirk, O pity! And we will go on enjoying ourselves, dreaming monstrous loves, fantastic universes, grumbling, and quarreling with the world's appearances, mountebank, beggar, artist, scoundrel. . . priest! On my hospital bed, the odor of incense came back to me so potent: guardian of the sacred aromatics, confessor, martyr. . .

There I recognize the filthy education of my childhood. What of it? . . . To go my twenty years, if others go their twenty years. . .

No! No! Now I rebel against death! Toil seems too trifling to my pride: my betrayal to the world would be too brief a torture. At the last moment I would strike out, to the right, to the left. . .

Then—oh!—dear, poor soul, would not eternity be lost to us!

Morning

HAD I NOT *once* a lovely youth, heroic, fabulous, to be written on sheets of gold, too much luck! Through what crime, through what fault have I deserved my weakness now? You who declare that beasts sob in their grief, that the sick despair, that the dead have bad dreams, try to relate my fall and my sleep. As for me, I can no more explain myself than the beggar with his endless *Paters* and *Ave Marias. I have forgotten how to speak!*

However, I have finished, I think, the tale of my hell today. It was really hell; the old hell, the one whose doors were opened by the son of man.

From the same desert, in the same night, always my tired eyes awake to the silver star, always, but the Kings of life are not moved, the three magi, mind and heart and soul. When shall we go beyond the mountains and the shores, to greet the birth of new toil, of new wisdom, the flight of tyrants, of demons, the end of superstition, to adore—the first to adore!—Christmas on the earth.

The song of the heavens, the marching of peoples! Slaves! Let us never curse life.

Farewell

AUTUMN ALREADY!—But why regret an eternal sun if we are embarked on the discovery of divine light— far from all those who die with the seasons.

Autumn. Risen through the motionless mists, our boat turns toward the port of misery, the enormous city with fire-and-mud-stained sky. Ah, the putrid rags, the rain-soaked bread, drunkenness, the thousand loves that have crucified me! Will she never have done, then, that ghoul queen of a million dead souls and dead bodies, *and that will be judged!* I see myself again, skin rotten with mud and pest, worms in my armpits and in my hair, and in my heart much bigger worms, lying among strangers without age, without feeling. . . I might have died there. . . Unbearable evocation! I loathe poverty.

And I dread winter because it is the season of comfort!

Sometimes in the sky I see endless beaches covered with white nations full of joy. Above me a great golden ship waves its multi-colored pennants in the breezes of the morning. I created all possible festivities, all triumphs, all dramas. I tried to invent new flowers, new stars, new flesh, new tongues. I thought I was acquiring supernatural powers. Well! I must bury my imagination and my memories! An artist's and storyteller's precious fame flung away!

I! I who called myself angel or seer, exempt from all morality, I am returned to the soil with a duty to seek and rough reality to embrace! Peasant!

Am I mistaken? Would charity be the sister of death for me?

At last, I shall ask forgiveness for having fed on lies And now let's go.

But no friendly hand! And where turn for help!

Yes, the new hour is hard enough.

For I can say that victory is won: the gnashing of teeth, the hissings of fire, the pestilential sighs are abating. All the noisome memories are fading. My last regrets take to their heels,—envy of beggars, thieves, of death's friends, of the backward of all kinds. O damned ones, what if I avenged myself!

One must be absolutely modern.

No hymns! Hold the ground gained. Arduous night! The dried blood smokes on my face, and I have nothing behind me but that horrible bush! . . . Spiritual combat is as brutal as the battle of men: but the vision of justice is the pleasure of God alone.

This, however, is the vigil. Welcome then, all the influx of vigor and real tenderness. And, in the dawn, armed with an ardent patience, we shall enter magnificent cities.

Why talk of a friendly hand! It's all to my advantage that I can laugh at old lying loves and put to shame those deceitful couples, —I saw the hell of women back there;—and I shall be free to *possess truth in one soul and one body.*

Prose Poems

After the Deluge

As soon as the idea of the Deluge was abated,

A hare stopped in the clover and swaying flower-bells, and said a prayer to the rainbow, through the spider's web.

Oh! the precious stones that were hiding,—and the flowers that already looked around.

In the dirty main street, stalls were set up and boats were hauled toward the sea, high-tiered as in old prints.

Blood flowed at Blue-Beard's,—through slaughter houses, in circuses, where windows were blanched by God's seal. Blood and milk flowed.

Beavers built. "Mazagrans" smoked in the little bars.

In the big house with window panes still dripping, children in mourning looked at the marvelous pictures.

A door banged; and in the village square the little boy waved his arms, understood by weather-vanes and cocks on steeples everywhere, in the bursting shower.

Madame —— set up a piano in the Alps. Mass and first communions were celebrated at the hundred thousand altars of the cathedral.

Caravans set out. And Hotel Splendid was built in the chaos of ice and of the polar night.

Ever afterward the moon heard jackals pulling across the deserts of thyme, and eclogues in wooden shoes growling in the orchard. Then, in the violet and budding forest, Eucharis told me it was Spring.

Gush, pond—froth, roll on the bridge and pour over the woods;
198

black palls and organs, lightnings and thunder, rise and roll; waters and sorrows rise and launch the floods again.

For since they have been dissipated—oh, the precious stones being buried and the opened flowers!—it is a shame!—and the Queen, the Witch who lights her embers in the earthen pot, will never tell us what she knows, the thing we do not know.

Genie

HE IS AFFECTION and the present since he has made the house open to foamy winter and to the murmur of summer—he who has purified food and drink—he who is the charm of fleeing places and the superhuman delight of stations.— He is affection and the future, love and force whom we, standing among our rages and our boredoms, see passing in the stormy sky and banners of ecstasy.

He is love, perfect measure re-invented, marvelous and un-looked for reason, and eternity: loved instrument of fatal qual-ities. We all have known the terror of his concession and of ours; O relish of health, the soaring of our faculties, selfish affection and passion for him,—for him who loves us for his infinite life. . .

And we remember him and he has gone on a journey. . . And if Adoration goes, rings, his promise rings: "Away! superstitions, away! those ancient bodies, those couples, and those ages. It is this present epoch that has foundered!"

He will not go away, he will not come down again from any heaven, he will not accomplish the redemption of the angers of women and the gaieties of men and all this Sin: for it is done, he being and being loved.

O his breaths, his heads, his flights: terrible celerity of perfec-tion of forms and of action.

O fecundity of the mind and immensity of the universe!

His body! the dreamed-of release, the shattering of grace crossed by new violence!

His view, his view! all the ancient kneelings and, at his passing, the pains that are lifted.

His day! the abolition of all sonorous and moving afflictions in intenser music.

His step! migrations more vast than the ancient invasions.

O He and we! Pride more compassionate than the lost charities.

O world and the pure song of new evils!

He has known us all and all of us has loved: take heed this winter night, from cape to cape, from the tumultuous pole to the castle, from the crowd to the shore, from look to look, force and feelings weary, to hail him, to see him and to send him away, and under the tides and high in the deserts of snow, to follow his views, —his breaths,—his body,—his day.

Vagabonds

PITIFUL BROTHER! what atrocious vigils I owe him! "I have lacked fervour in this enterprise. I have trifled with his infirmity. My fault should we go back to exile, and to slavery." He thought me unlucky and of a very strange innocence, and would add disquieting reasons.

For reply I would sneer at this Satanic doctor and, in the end, going to the window I would create beyond the countryside crossed by bands of rare music, phantoms of nocturnal luxury to come.

After this vaguely hygienic diversion, I would lie down on my pallet. And almost every night, no sooner asleep than the poor brother would rise, his mouth rotten, eyes starting from his head, —just as he had dreamed he looked!—and would pull me out into the room, howling his dream of imbecilic sorrow.

I had, in truth, taken upon myself in all sincerity, the task of returning him to his primitive state of child of the Sun,—and, nourished by the wine of caverns and the biscuit of the road, we wandered, I impatient to find the place and the formula!

Scenes

ANCIENT COMEDY pursues its harmonies and divides its idylls:

Boulevards of raised platforms.

A long wooden column from one end of the rocky field to the other where the barbarous crowd wanders under the denuded trees.

In the corridors of black gauze, following the promenaders with their lanterns and their leaves,

Bird actors swoop down onto a masonry pontoon swayed by a covered archipelago of spectators' boats.

Lyric scenes with accompaniment of flute and drum, look down from recesses contrived in the ceilings around modern club rooms and halls of Orient.

The fairy spectacle takes place at the summit of the amphitheatre crowned with thickets,—or moves and modulates for the men of Boeotia in the shadow of waving forest trees on the ridge of the cultivated fields.

The *opera-comique* is divided on our stage at the intersection of ten partitions set up between the gallery and the footlights.

Antique (I)

LITHE SON of Pan! Around your forehead crowned with flowrets and with laurel, restlessly roll those precious balls, your eyes. Spotted with brown lee, your cheeks are hollows. Your fangs gleam. Your breast is like a lyre, the tinklings circulate through your blond arms. Your heart beats in that belly where sleeps the double sex. Walk through the night gently moving that thigh, that second thigh, and that left leg.

Antique (*II*)

MONSTROSITIES OF ALL KINDS violate the atrocious gestures of Hortense. Erotic mechanics, her solitude; her lassitude, amorous dynamics. Under a watchful childhood she has been, in numerous epochs, the ardent hygiene of all races. Her door is open to misery. There, the morality of material beings is disembodied in her passion or her action.—O terrible shudder of novice loves on the bloody ground and through the radiant hydrogen!—find Hortense.

Barbarian

LONG AFTER THE DAYS, seasons, beings, and countries,

The banner of raw meat against the silk of seas and arctic flowers; (they do not exist).

Recovered from the old fanfares of heroism,—which still attack the heart and head,—far from the ancient assassins,

—Oh! the banner of raw meat against the silk of seas and arctic flowers; (they do not exist).—

Bliss!

Live embers raining in gusts of white frost.—Bliss!—Those fires in the rain of diamond wind flung out by the earth's heart eternally carbonized for us.—O world!

(Far from the old haunts and the old flames that one hears, that one feels.)

Embers and foam. Music, veerings of chasms and shock of icicles against the stars.

O bliss, O world, O music! And forms, sweat, eyes and long hair floating there. And white tears boiling,—Bliss!—and the feminine voice reaching to the bottom of volcanos and grottos of the arctic seas. . .—The banner. . .

Mystic

ON THE SLOPE OF THE KNOLL angels whirl their woolen robes in pastures of emerald and steel.

From the meadows flames leap up to the summit of the little hill. At the left, the mould is trampled by all the homicides and all the battles, and all the disastrous noises describe their curve. Behind the right-hand ridge the line of Orients and of progress.

And while the band at the top of the picture is formed of the revolving and rushing hum of seashells and of human nights,

The flowering sweetness of the stars, and of the night, and all the rest, descends opposite the knoll like a basket before our face, and makes the abyss perfumed and blue below.

Flowers

FROM GOLDEN STAIRS,—among silk cords, green velvets, gray gauzes, and crystal discs that turn black as bronze in the sun, I see the digitalis opening on a carpet of silver filigree, of eyes and tresses.

Yellow gold-pieces strewn over agate, mahogany columns supporting emerald domes, bouquets of white satin and delicate sprays of rubies, surround the water-rose.

Like a god with huge blue eyes and limbs of snow, the sea and sky attract to the marble terraces the throng of roses, young and strong.

Ruts

TO THE RIGHT the summer dawn wakes the leaves, the mists, and the noises in this corner of the park, and the left hand knolls hold in their violet shadows the thousand rapid ruts of the damp road. Wonderland procession! To be sure:

floats covered with animals of gilded wood, poles and awnings in motley stripes, to the furious galloping of twenty dappled circus horses, and children and men on their perfectly fantastic beasts; —twenty vehicles, embossed and decorated with flags and flowers, like Fairy-tale or ancient Coaches, full of children all dressed up for a suburban pastoral. Even coffins under their black canopies lifting aloft their ebon plumes, to the trot of huge mares, blue and black.

To a Reason

A RAP OF YOUR FINGER on the drum fires all the sounds and starts a new harmony.

A step of yours: the levy of new men and their marching on.

The head turns away: O the new love! The head turns around: O the new love!

"Change our lots, confound the plagues beginning with time," to you these children sing. "Raise, no matter where, the substance of our fortunes and our desires," they beg you.

Forever arriving, you will go everywhere.

Morning of Drunkenness

O MY GOOD! O my Beautiful! Atrocious fanfare where I never falter. Rack of enchantments! Hurrah for the unbelievable work and for the marvelous body, for the first time! It began in the midst of children's laughter, with their laughter it will end. This poison will stay in all our veins even when, the fanfares shifting, we shall return to the old inharmony. O now let us, who are so worthy of these tortures! redeem that superhuman promise made to our body and our soul created: that promise, that madness! Elegance, science, violence! They have promised us to bury in darkness the tree of good and evil, to deport tyrannic respectabilities so that we may bring hither our very pure love. It began with a certain disgust—and it ends—unable instantly to grasp this eternity,—it ends with a riot of perfumes.

Laughter of children, discretion of slaves, austerity of virgins, loathing of faces and objects here, holy be all of you in memory of this vigil. It began with every sort of boorishness, behold, it ends with angels of flame and of ice!

Little drunken vigil, holy! if only because of the mask you have bestowed on us. We pronounce you, method! We shall not forget that yesterday you glorified each one of our ages. We have faith in the poison. We know how to give our whole life every day.

The time of the Assassins is here.

Vigils

I   IT IS REPOSE IN THE LIGHT, neither fever nor languor, on a bed or on a meadow.

It is the friend neither violent nor weak. The friend.

It is the beloved neither tormenting nor tormented. The beloved.

Air and the world not sought. Life.

—Was it really this?

—And the dream fades.

II   THE LIGHTING COMES ROUND to the roof-tree again. From the two extremities of the hall—quite ordinary scenery—harmonic elevations join. The wall opposite the watcher is a psychological succession of atmospheric sections, friezes, bands, and of geological accidents. Intense, quick dream of sentimental groups of beings with all possible characters among all possible appearances.

III   THE LAMPS AND THE RUGS of my vigil make the noise of waves in the night along the hull and around the steerage.

The sea of the vigil, like Emily's breasts.

The hangings half way up, undergrowth of emerald tinted lace, where dart the vigil doves.

The metal plaque of the black hearth, real suns of seashores: ah! magic wells; only sight of the dawn this time.

IV   YOU ARE STILL at the temptation of St. Anthony. Capers of clipped zeal, grimacings of puerile pride, collapse and terror.

But you will set yourself this task: all harmonic and architectural possibilities will be aroused around your seat. Perfect beings, never dreamed of, will present themselves for your experiments. The curiosity of ancient multitudes and idle luxuries will pensively throng in your vicinity. Your memory and your senses will be simply the nourishment of your creative impulse. As for the world, when you emerge, what will it have become? In any case nothing of what it seems at present.

Anguish

IS IT POSSIBLE that She will get us forgiven for ambitions continually crushed,—that an affluent end will make up for the ages of indigence,—that one day of success will lull us to sleep on the shame of our fatal incompetence?

(O palms! diamond!—Love, force!—higher than all joys and all fame!—in every respect,—everywhere, demon, god,—youth of this being here: myself!)

And may the accidents of scientific wonders and the movements of social brotherhood be cherished as the progressive restitution of our primitive franchise.

But the Vampire who makes us agreeable, commands us to enjoy ourselves with what she leaves us, or, in other words, that we should be more amusing.

Wounds from the tossings of the wearing air and the sea; torments from the silence of the waters and murderous air; tortures that laugh in their silence abominably rough.

Common Nocturne

A BREATH OPENS OPERAESQUE BREACHES in the walls,—blurs the pivoting of crumbling roofs,—disperses the boundaries of hearths,—eclipses window-frames.

Along a grape vine, having steadied my foot on a gargoyle,—I descended into this coach, its period indicated clearly enough by the convex panes of glass, the bulging panels, the bulbous sofas. Hearse of my sleep, isolated, shepherd's house of my inanity, the vehicle veers on the grass of the obliterated highway: and in a defect at the top of the right hand window pane revolved pale lunar figures, leaves, and breasts.

—A very deep green and blue invade the picture.

A scampering off along a stretch of gravel.

Here will they whistle for the storm, Sodoms and Solymas, wild beasts, and armies,—

(Postilion and animals of dream, will they begin again in the stifling forests, to plunge me, up to my eyes in the silken spring?)—

And send us whipped through the splashing of waters and spilled drinks, to be tossed on the barking of bulldogs. . .

—A breath disperses the boundaries of hearths.

Dawn

I HAVE EMBRACED the summer dawn.

Nothing yet stirred in front of the palaces. The water was dead. The shadows still camped in the woodland road. I walked. waking quick warm breaths; and gems looked on, and wings rose without a sound.

The first venture was, in a path already filled with fresh. pale glints, a flower who told me her name.

I laughed at the waterfall that tousled through the pines: on the silver summit I recognized the goddess.

Then, one by one, I lifted up her veils. In the lane, waving my arms. Across the plain, where I denounced her to the cock. To the city she fled among the steeples and the domes; running like a beggar on the marble quays, I chased her.

Far up the road near a laurel wood, I wrapped her round with her gathered veils, and I felt a little her immense form. Dawn and the child sank down at the border of the wood.

Waking, it was noon.

Phrases

WHEN THE WORLD shall have shrunk to a single dark woods for our four eyes' astonishment,—a beach for two faithful children,—a musical house for our pure sympathy,— I shall find you.

Should there be here below but a solitary old man, handsome and calm in the midst of incredible luxury, I'll be at your feet.

Should I realize every one of your memories,—should I be the one who can bind you hand and foot,—I will strangle you.

WHEN WE ARE VERY STRONG,—who draws back? very gay,—who cares for ridicule? When we are very bad,—what would they do to us?

Deck yourself, dance, laugh. I could never send Love out of the window.

MY COMRADE, beggar-girl, monster-child! O it's all one to you, these unhappy women, these wiles and my discomfiture. Bind yourself to us with your impossible voice, your voice! Sole soother of our vile despair.

A COVERED MORNING IN JULY. A taste of ashes flies through the air; —an odour of sweating wood on the hearth,—stale flowers,— devastation along the promenades,—mists over the canals through the fields,—why not incense and toys already?

I HAVE STRETCHED ROPES from steeple to steeple; garlands from window to window; golden chains from star to star, and I dance.

THE UPLAND POND smokes continuously. What witch will rise against the white West sky? What violet frondescence fall?

WHILE PUBLIC FUNDS EVAPORATE in feasts of fraternity, a bell of rosy fire rings in the clouds.

REVIVING A PLEASANT TASTE of India ink, a black powder rains on my vigil, I lower the jets of the chandelier, I throw myself on my bed, and turning my face toward the darkness, I see you O my daughter, O my Queens!

THE CASCADE RESOUNDS behind light-opera huts. Candelabra extend out through the orchards and alleys of the neighboring labyrinth,—the greens and reds of the setting sun. Horace nymphs with First Empire coiffures. Siberian rounds, and Boucher's Chinese ladies.

Childhood

I   THAT IDOL, black eyes and yellow shag, without parents or court, nobler than the fable, Mexican and Flemish; his domain, insolent azure and verdure, runs on the beaches called by the shipless waves, names ferociously Greek, Slav, Celt

On the border of the forest,—dream flowers tinkle, flash and flare,—the girl with lips like oranges, knees crossed in the clear flood that gushes from the fields, nakedness shaded, traversed, dressed, by rainbow, flora, sea.

Ladies who stroll on terraces adjacent to the sea; infanta and giantess, superb blacks in the verdegris moss, jewels upright on the rich ground of groves and little thawed gardens,—young mothers and big sisters with eyes full of pilgrimages, sultanas, and princesses tyrannic of costume and carriage, little foreigners and persons gently unhappy.

What boredom the hour of the "dear body" and "dear heart"!

II   IT IS SHE, the little girl, dead behind the rose-bushes.—The young mama, lifeless, comes down the stoop.—The cousin's carriage creaks on the sand.—The little brother (he is in India!) there, in the setting sun in the meadow of pinks. The old men who have been buried straight up in the rampart of gilly-flowers.

Swarms of golden leaves surround the general's house. They are in the south.—You follow the red road to reach the empty inn. The chateau is for sale; the shutters hang on their hinges. The priests must have taken away the keys of the church. In the park the keeper's cottages are uninhabited. The enclosures are so high that nothing can be seen but the rustling tree tops. Besides, there is nothing to be seen inside.

The meadows go up to hamlets without anvils or cocks. The

sluice is open. O the calvaries and the mills of the desert, islands and haystacks.

III   MAGIC FLOWERS DRONED. The slopes cradled him. Beasts of a fabulous elegance moved about. The clouds gathered over the high seas formed of an eternity of hot tears.

IV   IN THE WOODS there is a bird; his song stops you and makes you blush.

There is a clock that never strikes.

There is a swamp with a nest of white beasts.

There is a cathedral that goes down and a lake that comes up.

There is a little carriage abandoned in the copse or that goes running down the road be-ribboned.

There is a troupe of strolling players in costume, glimpsed on the road through the border of the woods.

And then, when you are hungry and thirsty there is someone who chases you away.

V   I AM THE SAINT at prayer on the terrace like beasts grazing down to the sea of Palestine.

I am the scholar of the dark armchair. Branches and rain beat against the casements of the library.

I am the pedestrian of the highroad by way of the dwarf woods; the roar of the sluices covers my steps. I see for a long time the melancholy golden wash of the setting sun.

I might well be the child abandoned on the jetty gone out to the high sea, the little farm-boy following the lane whose forehead touches the sky.

The paths are rough. The hillocks are covered with broom. The air is motionless. How far the birds and the springs are! This can only be the end of the world, going forward.

VI   LET THEM RENT ME this whitewashed tomb, at last, with the cement lines in relief,—far down under the earth.

I lean my elbow on the table, the lamp shines brightly on these newspapers I am fool enough to read again, these uninteresting books.

At an enormous distance above my underground drawing room, houses root themselves, fogs gather. The mud is red or black. Monstrous City, night without end!

Less high are the sewers. At the sides, nothing but the thickness of the globe. Chasms of azure perhaps, wells of fire? It is on these planes perhaps that moons and comets meet, fables and seas.

In hours of bitterness, I imagine balls of sapphire, of metal. I am master of silence. Why should the semblance of a vent pale in the corner of the vault?

Cities (I)

WHAT CITIES! This is a people for whom these Alleghenies and these Lebanons of dream were staged! Chalets of crystal and of wood move along invisible rails and pulleys. Old craters, encircled by colossuses and copper palms, redden melodiously in the fires. Amorous revels ring over the canals pendant behind the chalets. The chase of the chimes clamours in the gorges. Guilds of giant singers hurry along in robes and oriflammes as dazzling as the light of summits. On platforms among precipices Rolands trumpet their valour. On the footbridges of the abyss and on the roofs of inns, the conflagration of the sky decks the staffs with flags. The collapse of apotheoses rejoins the upland fields where seraphic centauresses wander among the avalanches. Above the level of the highest peaks, a sea, troubled by the eternal birth of Venus, covered with *Orpheonic* fleets and the murmur of precious conches and of precious pearls, the sea darkens at times with deathly gleams. On the slopes harvests of flowers, large as your arms and goblets, bellow. Processions of Mabs in russet dresses and opaline, climb the ravines. High up, with feet in waterfall and brambles, stags suckle at Diana's breast. Bacchantes of the suburbs sob, and the moon burns and bays. Venus enters the caverns of iron-smiths and hermits. Groups of belfries ring out the ideas of the peoples. Out of castles built of bone comes undreamed-of music. All the legends wander, and impulses surge through the town. The paradise of storms collapses. Savages dance ceaselessly the Revels of the Night. And, one hour, I went down into the bustle of a boulevard in Bagdad where companies sang the joy of new toil, in a dense breeze, constantly moving about but unable to elude the fabulous phantoms of the heights where they were to have met again.

What good arms, what lovely hour will give me back that region whence come my sleeps and slightest movements.

Fairy

For HELEN IN VIRGIN SHADOWS and impassible radiance in the astral silence, ornamental saps conspired. Summer's ardour was confided to silent birds and indispensable indolence to a priceless mourning boat through gulfs of dead loves and fallen perfumes.

—After the moment of the woodswomen's song to the rumble of the torrent in the ruin of the wood, from the bells of the cattle to the echo of the vales, and the cries of the steppes.—

For Helen's childhood shadows and thickets shuddered, and the breast of the poor and the legends of the sky.

And her eyes and her dance superior, even to the precious glitterings, cold influences, or the pleasure of the unique setting and the unique hour.

Being Beauteous

AGAINST THE SNOW a Being of high-statured beauty. Whistlings of death and circles of muffled music make the adored body, like a spectre, rise, expand and quiver; wounds of black and scarlet burst in the superb flesh.— Life's own colors darken, dance and stand forth around the vision in the yards.—Shudders rise and whirr and the wild mad savor of these effects being charged with the deadly whistlings and the hoarse music that the world, far behind us, hurls at our mother of beauty,—she recoils, she straightens. Oh, our bones are clothed with a new and amorous body.

O ashy face, horsehair escutcheon, crystal arms! the canon on which I am to fall in the melee of trees and light air!

Cities (II)

THE OFFICIAL ACROPOLIS among the most colossal conceptions of modern barbarity: impossible to describe the opaque light produced by the immutably gray sky, by the glitter of the imperial buildings, and the eternal snow of the ground. With a singular taste for atrocities, all the classical marvels of architecture have been reproduced, and I attend exhibitions of painting in premises twenty times as immense as Hampton Court. What painting! A Norwegian Nebuchadnezzar has built the stairways of the government buildings; even the subordinates I have seen are already as proud as Brennuses, and I trembled at the aspect of the guardians of the colossi and the officials in charge of construction. With their grouping of the buildings around squares, courts and closed terraces, they have inebriated the cabbies. The parks represent primitive nature cultivated with supreme art, there are parts of the upper town that are inexplicable: an arm of the sea without boats rolls its sleet blue waters between quays covered with giant candelabra. A short bridge leads to a postern right under the dome of the

Sainte-Chapelle. This dome is an armature of artistic steel about fifteen thousand feet in diameter.

From certain points on the copper foot-bridges, on the platforms, on the stairways that wind around markets and pillars, I thought I would be able to judge the depth of the city! This is the prodigy I was unable to discover: what are the levels of other districts above or below the acropolis? For the stranger of our day verification is impossible. The business district is a circus in a uniform style with galleries under arcades. No shops are to be seen, but the snow of the roadway is trampled; some nabobs, as rare as pedestrians on Sunday mornings in London, make their way toward a diligence of diamonds. A few red velvet sofas: polar drinks are served whose price varies from eight hundred to eight thousand rupees. At the thought of looking for theatres on this circus, I say to myself that the shops must contain dramas quite dismal enough. I suppose that there is a police force; but the law must be so strange that I give up trying to imagine what adventurers can be like here.

The suburb, as elegant as a beautiful street of Paris, is favoured with air like light, the democratic element counts some hundred souls. There, too, the houses are detached; the suburb loses itself queerly in the country, the "County," that fills the eternal West with forests and prodigious plantations where gentlemen savages hunt their news items by light that has been invented.

Youth

I *Sunday*   PROBLEMS PUT BY, the inevitable descent of heaven and the visit of memories and the assembly of rhythms occupy the house, the head and the world of the spirit.

—A horse scampers off on the suburban track and along tilled fields and woodlands, pierced by the carbonic pest. A miserable woman of drama, somewhere in the world, sighs for improbable desertions. Desperados pine for strife, drunkenness and wounds. —Along the rivers little children stifle their maledictions.

Let us resume our study to the noise of the devouring work that is assembling and rising in the masses.

II   *Sonnet*   Man OF ORDINARY CONSTITUTION, was not the flesh a fruit hung in the orchard;—O child days; the body, a treasure to squander;—O to love the peril or the power of Psyche? The earth had slopes fertile in princes and artists, and lineage and race incited you to crimes and mournings: the world, your fortune and your peril. But at present, that labour crowned, you and your calculations,—you and your impatiences—are nothing but your dance and your voice, not fixed and never forced, although of a double consequence of invention and achievement, a cause,—in a fraternal and discreet humanity through an image-less universe;—might and right reflect your dance and your voice, only appreciated at present.

III   *Twenty Years Old*   INSTRUCTIVE VOICES EXILED. . . Physical candour bitterly quelled. . .—Adagio.—Ah! the infinite egoism of adolescence, the studious optimism: how the world was full of flowers that summer! Airs and forms dying. . .—A choir to calm impotence and absence! A choir of glasses, of nocturnal melodies. . . Quickly, indeed, the nerves take up the chase.

IV   *War*   WHEN A CHILD, certain skies refined my vision: all the signs modified my physiognomy. The Phenomena were aroused.—At present, the eternal inflection of moments and the infinity of mathematics drives me through the world, where I endure every civil success, respected by strange childhood and enormous affections.—I dream of a war of right and of might, of a quite unforeseen logic.

It is as simple as a musical phrase.

Promontory

GOLDEN DAWN AND SHIVERING EVENING find our brig standing out to sea off this villa and its dependencies that form a promontory as extensive as Epirus and the Peloponnesus, or as the large island of Japan, or as Arabia! Fanes lighted up by the returning embassies; immense views of the fortifications of modern coasts; dunes illustrated with ardent flowers and Bacchanals; grand canals of Carthage and embankments of a dubious Venice; languid eruptions of Etnas and crevasses of flowers and of waters. Glaciers, wash-houses surrounded by German poplars, slopes of extraordinary parks; and circular facades of the "Grands" and the "Royals" of some Brooklyn; and their railways flank, go under, and overhang the hotel premises, selected from the history of the most elegant and the most colossal constructions of Italy, America, and Asia, whose windows and terraces, at present full of expensive illumination, drinks and breezes, are open to the fancy of travelers and nobles, and during daylight hours allow all the illustrious tarantellas of art marvelously to decorate the façades of Promontory Palace.

Historic Evening

ANY EVENING, for example, where the naive tourist happens to be, retired from our economic horrors, a master's hand awakes the meadows' harpsichord; they are playing cards at the bottom of the pond, mirror evoking favourites and queens; there are women-saints, veils, threads of harmony, and legendary chromatisms in the setting sun.

He shudders as the hunts and hordes go by. The comedy drips on the grass platforms. And the distress of the poor and the weak on these stupid planes!

To his slave's vision Germany goes scaffolding to moons; Tartar deserts are lighted up; ancient revolts ferment in the center of the Celestial Empire; along stairways and armchairs cut in the rock, a little world pale and flat, Africa and Occidents, will be erected. Then a ballet of familiar seas and lights, worthless chemistry and impossible melodies.

The same bourgeois magic wherever the mail-train sets you down. Even the most elementary physicist feels that it is no longer possible to submit to this personal atmosphere, fog of physical regrets, whose mere constatation is an affliction in itself.

No! The moment of the burning cauldron, of risen seas, of subterranean conflagrations, of the planet swept away, and the consequent exterminations, certitudes indicated with so little malignity in the Bible and by the Norms, and that it is for the serious-minded to observe. It will be no effect of legend, however.

Side-Show

VERY STURDY ROGUES. Several of them have exploited your worlds. With no needs, and in no hurry to make use of their brilliant faculties and their knowledge of your consciences. O such mature men! Eyes vacant after the manner of the summer night, red and black, tricoloured, steel studded with gold stars; faces distorted, leaden, wan, on fire; burlesque hoarsenesses! The cruel strut of gaudy trumperies. Some are young,—how would they look on Cherubin?—endowed with terrifying voices and some dangerous resources. They are sent to take the back road in town, tricked out with nauseating *luxury*.

O most violent Paradise of the unbridled grimace! Not to be compared with your Fakirs and other theatrical buffooneries. In improvised costumes like something out of a bad dream, they play laments, tragedies of scoundrels and demi-gods, spiritual as history or religions have never been. Chinese, Hottentots, Bohemians, nitwits, hyenas, Molochs, old dementias, sinister demons, they combine popular, maternal tricks with bestial poses and caresses. They would interpret new plays or "girlish" ditties. Master jugglers, they transform place and persons and have recourse to magnetic comedy. Eyes aflame, blood sings, bones swell, tears and red filaments stream down. Their mockery or their terror lasts a minute or entire months.

I alone have the key to this savage side-show.

Devotions

To Sister Louise Vanaen de Voringhem:—With her blue cornet turned toward the North Sea.—For the ship-wrecked.

To Sister Léone Aubois d'Ashby. Baou!—the buzzing, stinking summer grass.—For the fever of mothers and children.

To Lulu.—demon—who has kept a taste for the oratories of the time of *Best-Friends* and her unfinished education.—For men.

To Madame—

To the adolescent that I was. To that holy old man, hermitage or mission.

To the spirit of the poor. And to a very exalted clergy.

As well as to all cults, in a certain memorial place of cults, or among certain events that one succumbs to according to the aspirations of the moment or one's own serious vice.

This evening to Circeto of the icy heights, fat as a fish, and coloured like the ten months of the red night—(her heart amber and *spunsk*).—For my prayer alone, silent as those nocturnal regions, and preceding feats more violent than the chaos of the poles.

At any price and with every air, even in metaphysical journeys.—But even more *then*.

Royalty

ONE FINE MORNING in a land of very gentle people, a superb man and woman shouted in the public square: "Friends, I want her to be queen!" "I want to be queen!" She laughed and trembled. He spoke to his friends of revelations, of trials terminated. They leaned on each other in ecstasies.

And, in fact, they were rulers for a whole morning, while tapestries were hung up on all the houses, and for the entire afternoon, while they strolled toward the palm gardens.

Metropolitan

FROM THE INDIGO STRAITS to Ossian's seas, on pink and orange sands washed by the vinous sky, crystal boulevards have just arisen and crossed, immoderately inhabited by poor young families who get their food at the green grocers. Nothing rich.—The city.

Straight from the bituminous desert flee in confusion, with sheets of fog spaced in horrible bands across the sky that curves, recedes, descends, formed by the most sinister black smoke that Ocean in mourning can produce, helmets, wheels, boats, rumps.
—The battle.

Lift your head: that arched wooden bridge; those last truck gardens; those faces reddened by the lantern lashed by the cold night; silly Undine in her noisy dress down by the river; those luminous skulls among the peas,—and all the other phantasmagoria.—The country.

Those roads bordered by walls and iron fences that with difficulty hold back their groves, and lousy flowers that might be called loves and doves, damask damning drowsily,—the possessions of wonderful aristocracies, ultra-Rhenish, Japanese, Guaranian, still qualified to receive ancestral music,—and there are inns that already never open any more forever,—there are princesses, and if you are not completely overcome, the study of the stars. The sky.

The morning when with Her you struggled among those bursts of snow, those green lips, those blocks of ice, black banners and blue beams, and those purple perfumes of the polar sun.—Your strength.

Lives

I   O THE ENORMOUS AVENUES of the Holy Land, the temple terraces! What has become of the Brahman who explained the proverbs to me? Of that time, of that place, I can still see even the old women! I remember silver hours and sunlight by the rivers, the hand of the girl on my shoulder, and our caresses standing in the spicy plains.—A flight of pigeons thunders round my thoughts. An exile here, I once had a stage on which to play all the masterpieces of literature. I would show you unheard of riches. I observe the history of the treasures that you found. I see the sequel. My wisdom is as scorned as chaos. What is my nothingness to the stupefaction that awaits you?

II   I AM AN INVENTOR more deserving far than all those who have preceded me; a musician, moreover, who has discovered something like the key of love. At present, a country gentleman of a lean land with a sober sky, I try to arouse myself with the memory of my beggar childhood, my apprenticeship or my arrival in wooden shoes, of polemics, of five or six widowings, and of certain convivialities when my level head kept me from rising to the diapason of my comrades. I do not regret my old portion of divine gaiety: the sober air of this acrid country feeds vigorously my atrocious scepticism. But since this scepticism can not, henceforth, be put to use, and since, moreover, I am consecrated to a new anxiety,—I expect to become a very dangerous madman!

III   IN A LOFT where I was shut up when I was twelve I got to know the world, I illustrated the human comedy. In a wine cellar I learned history. In a northern city, at some nocturnal revel, I met all the women of the old masters. In an ancient arcade of Paris I was taught the classical sciences. In a magnificent dwelling encircled by the entire Orient, I accomplished my prodigious work and spent my illustrious retreat. I have brewed my blood. My duty has been remitted. That is not even to be thought of any longer. I am really from beyond the tomb, and no messages.

Tale

A PRINCE WAS VEXED at having devoted himself only to the perfection of ordinary generosities. He foresaw astonishing revolutions of love, and suspected his women of being able to do better than that affable acquiescence set off by heaven and luxuries. He wanted to see the truth, the hour of essential desire and satisfaction. Whether it was an aberration of piety or not, that is what he wanted. Enough worldly power, at least, he had.

All the women who had known him were assassinated: what havoc in the garden of Beauty! At the point of the sword they blessed him. He did not order new ones.—Women re-appeared.

He killed everyone who followed him after the hunt or after the libations.—Everyone followed him.

He amused himself cutting the throats of rare animals. He set pálaces in flames. He would rush upon people and hack them to pieces.—Throngs, gilded roofs, beautiful animals still remained.

Can one be in ecstasies over destruction, and through cruelty grow younger! The people did not complain. None opposed him.

One evening he was proudly galloping. A Genie appeared, of an ineffable beauty, unavowable even. In his face and in his bearing shone the promise of a complex and multiple love! of an indescribable happiness, unendurable even! The Prince and the Genie probably annihilated each other in essential health. How could they possibly have helped dying of it? Together then they died.

But the Prince died in his palace at an ordinary age, the Prince was the Genie, the Genie was the Prince.—Skilled music is lacking to our desire.

Working People

O THAT WARM FEBRUARY MORNING! The inopportune South came to stir up our absurd paupers' memories, our young distress.

Henrika had on a brown-and-white-check cotton skirt which must have been worn in the last century, a bonnet with ribbons, and a silk scarf. It was much sadder than any mourning. We were taking a stroll in the suburbs. The weather was overcast and that wind from the South excited all the evil odours of the desolate gardens and dried fields.

It could hardly have irked my wife to the extent it did me. In a puddle left by the rains of the preceding month on a path fairly high up, she called my attention to some very little fishes.

The city with its smoke and its noises followed us far out along the roads. O other world, habitation blessed by sky and shade! The South reminded me of miserable incidents of my childhood, my summer despairs, the horrible quantity of force and knowledge that fate has always kept from me. No! we will not spend the summer in this avaricious country where we shall never be anything but affianced orphans. I want this arm no longer to drag along a cherished image.

Skies

SKIES THE GRAY OF CRYSTAL. A strange design of bridges, some straight, some arching, others descending at oblique angles to the first; and these figures repeated in other lighted circuits of the canal, but all so long and light that the banks, laden with domes, are lowered and diminished. A few of these bridges are still covered with hovels, others support poles, signals, frail parapets. Minor chords cross each other and disappear; ropes ascend from the shore. One can make out a red coat, perhaps other costumes and musical instruments. Are they popular tunes, snatches of seignorial concerts, remnants of public hymns? The water is gray and blue, wide as an arm of the sea.

A white ray falling from high up in the sky destroys this comedy.

City

I AM AN EPHEMERAL and a not too discontented citizen of a metropolis considered modern, because all known taste has been avoided in the furnishings and the exterior of the houses, as well as in the lay out of the city. Here you would find no trace of any monument of superstition. Morals and language are reduced to their simplest expression, at last! These millions of people, who do not even know each other, conduct education, business, and old age so similarly, that the course of their lives must be several times less long than that which a mad statistics finds for the peoples of the Continent. Moreover, while from my window I see new spectres rolling through the thick and eternal city smoke—our woodland shade our summer night!— new Eumenides in front of my cottage, which is my country and all my heart since everything here resembles it,—Death without tears, our diligent daughter and servant, a desperate Love, and a pretty Crime howl in the mud of the street.

Departure

SEEN ENOUGH: The vision has been met with in every air.

Had enough. Tumult of cities, in the evening, and in the sun and always.

Known enough. Life's halts.—O Tumults and Visions!

Departure in new affection and new noise.

Sale

FOR SALE what the Jews have not sold, what neither nobility nor crime have tasted, what is unknown to execrable love and to the infernal probity of the masses! what neither time nor science need recognize:

Reconstituted Voices; fraternal awakening of all choral and orchestral energies and their instantaneous application; the opportunity, the only one, for the deliverance of our senses!

For sale Bodies without price, outside any race, any world, any sex, any lineage! Riches gushing at every step! Uncontrolled sale of diamonds!

For sale anarchy for the masses; irresistible satisfaction for rare connoisseurs; atrocious death for the faithful and for lovers!

For sale habitations and migrations, sports, enchantments and unparalleled comforts, and the noise and the movement and the future that they make!

For sale the fruits of calculation and the incredible soarings of harmony. Amazing discoveries, and terms never dreamed of,—immediate possession.

Insensate and infinite flight toward invisible splendours, toward immaterial delights—and its maddening secrets for every vice—and its gaiety, terrifying to the mob.

For sale, the bodies, the voices, the enormous and incontestable wealth—that which will never be sold. Salesmen are not at the end of their bargains! No danger that travelers will be called to account in a hurry.

Democracy

"THE FLAG goes with the foul landscape, and our jargon muffles the drum.

"In great centers we shall aliment the most cynical prostitution, and massacre logical revolts.

"In spicy and drenched lands!—at the service of monstrous exploitations, either industrial or military.

"Farewell here, no matter where. Conscripts of good will, ours will be a ferocious philosophy, ignorant as to science, rabid for comfort; and let the rest of the world croak."

That's the system. Let's get going!

Bottom

REALITY BEING TOO THORNY for my great personality,—I found myself, nevertheless, at my lady's, an enormous gray-blue bird, soaring toward the cornices of the ceiling and trailing my wings through the shadows of the evening.

I was at the foot of the canopy supporting her adored gems and her physical masterpieces, a great bear with violet gums, fur hoary with sorrow, eyes on the silver and crystal of the consoles.

Everything became shadow and ardent aquarium.

In the morning,—battling dawn of June,—a donkey, I rushed into the fields, braying and brandishing my grievance until the Sabine women of the suburbs came and threw themselves at my breast.

Illuminations

A Feeling

ON SUMMER EVENINGS I shall take the bridle-ways,
Wheat pecking at my wrists, slim grass beneath my tread;
I'll feel its coolness penetrate my dreamy haze
And let the wind wash over my uncovered head.

I shall not speak, I shall not think of anything.
But through my soul will surge all love's infinity;
Far, far away I'll go, a gipsy wandering
Content in Nature as in woman's company.

The Gallows Ball

ON THE BLACK GALLOWS, one-armed, bland,
They dance and dance, the paladins,
Thin paladins, the devil's band,
The skeletons of Saladins.

Messire Beelzebub controls by their cravats
His little jumping-jacks grimacing at the sky;
With an old slipper on their bobbing heads he pats,
And makes them dance and dance to Christmas minstrelry.

The jumping-jacks entwine frail arms in wincing throes.
Like sombre organ-pipes, frames open to the weather,
On which in other days fair maidens sought repose,
Time after time are locked in grim embrace together.

Hurrah, you jolly dancers whose abdomens rattle!
There's room enough to caper on this lengthy stage.
Hop, till one knows not if it be a dance or battle!
Beelzebub claws at his fiddles in a rage.

O hard, smooth heels that never shall wear out a sandal!
Their shirts of skin were shed, most of them, long ago.
All that remains need rouse no nausea or scandal.
Each skull's surmounted by a stately hat of snow.

On these cracked heads the crows stand out like baleful crests.
From their thin jaws, perchance, pieces of dry flesh hang.
One thinks of them as knights wheeling with rigid breasts
In some dim clash of arms raising a cardboard clang.

Hurrah, winds whistle at the skeletons' grand ball!
Hear the black gallows roaring like a steely organ!
From purple forests comes the wolves' responsive call
The red horizon glares, as hellish as a Gorgon . . .

These captains of the tomb, come rouse them up for me.
Who with their mighty, broken fingers slyly thread
A rosary of love on their pale vertebrae.
This is no monastery here, I say, you dead.

But see how, in the midst of these macabre dances,
Through the red sky a big, mad skeleton bounds loose,
Like an uprearing horse in quickened spirits prances,
And, feeling still about his neck the tightened noose,

With all ten fingers grips his bony thighs, which crack
Derisively and with a cachinnating sound;
Then, like a mountebank re-entering his shack,
Bounds back into the ball, while the bones sing all round.

On the black gallows, one-armed, bland,
They dance and dance, the paladins.
Thin paladins, the devil's band,
The skeletons of Saladins.

Sonnet

("... Frenchmen of '70, Bonapartists or Republicans, remember your forefathers of '92 ..."—PAUL DE CASSAGNAC, *in* LE PAYS.)

DEAD MEN OF 'NINETY-TWO, also of 'ninety-three,
Pale at the lusty kiss of liberty, who broke
Resolvedly beneath your clogs the tyrants' yoke
That bows the soul and head of all humanity;

Men who enjoyed ecstatic glory in your pain,
Whose hearts beneath your tatters leapt with love alone,
O soldiers whom your noble lover Death has sown
That in the ancient furrows you may rise again;

Whose blood washed greatness clean of all impurity,
Dead of Valmy, Fleurus, dead men of Italy,
You million murdered Christs, your eyes sombre and true;

You and the French Republic we consigned to sleep,
We whom the blows of Kings in prostrate bondage keep—
And these de Cassagnacs speak to us now of you!

The Rooks

LORD, WHEN THE MEADOW has gone cold
And in the shell-torn villages
The angelus is no more tolled
And Nature shows her ravages,
Make them descend from the great heights,
The rooks, my darlings and delights!

Strange army with such austere cries,
The bitter winds attack your nests.
Along the river's yellow crests,

On roads with ancient Calvaries,
Over the trenched and pitted ground
Scatter and wheel and rally round!

By thousands over the French plain,
Where sleep the dead of two days back,
In winter won't you wheel and clack
To make each passer think again?
Be crier, then, of duty's word,
Our funeral and sable bird.

But, saints of heaven, at oak's high top,
Mast on which magic eve doth close,
Forsake May's warblers, turn to those
Who in the wood's deep places stop,
In grass from which there's no retreat,
Chained by a futureless defeat!

My Gipsy Days

OFF I WOULD GO, with fists into torn pockets pressed.
My overcoat became a wrap of mystery.
Under the great sky, Muse, I was your devotee.
Eh, what fine dreams I had, each one an amorous gest!

My only trousers gaped behind; and thus I went
Tom Thumb the dreamer, husking out some lyric line.
My nightly inn had always the Great Bear for sign.
My stars moved with a silken rustle of content.

And often, sitting by the roadside, I would listen,
On calm September evenings, with fine dew a-glisten
Upon my brow, like drops of cordial, sweet yet tart;

Where, rhyming in these shadowy, fantastic places,
As if I played a lyre, I'd gently pluck the laces
Of my burst boots, one foot hugged tight against my heart!

Evil

WHILST THE RED SPITTLE of the grape-shot sings
All day across the endless sky, and whilst entire
Battalions, green or scarlet, rallied by their kings,
Disintegrate in crumpled masses under fire;

Whilst an abominable madness seeks to pound
A hundred thousand men into a smoking mess—
Pitiful dead in summer grass, on the rich ground
Out of which Nature wrought these men in holiness;

He is a God who sees it all, and laughs aloud
At damask altar-cloths, incense and chalices,
Who falls asleep lulled by adoring liturgies

And wakens when some mother, in her anguish bowed
And weeping till her old black bonnet shakes with grief
Offers him a big sou wrapped in her handkerchief.

The Sedentaries

THEIR FACES BLACK WITH WENS, pock-marked, green rings of age
Around their eyes, puffed fingers clenched against their bones,
The sincipita embossed with horny bumps of rage,
Like leprous efflorescences upon old stones:

They've grafted in long, epileptic love-embrace
Their weird bone-structures to the big, black skeleton
Of every chair; their feet endlessly interlace
With the rachitic bars, while days go on and on.

These ancients have been always woven with their seats;
They feel how in the sun their skins are calico'd,
Or, gazing at the panes on which the snow retreats,
They tremble with the agued sorrow of the toad.

The seats have used them well: the straw, brownly imbued,
Yields kindly to the angular and awkward flesh;
So is the soul of ancient suns dimly renewed,
Swathed in those wheaten ears, where once the grain was fresh.

The Sitters, knees to teeth, green pianists obsessed,
Drumming beneath their seats with all ten fingertips,
Follow their choppy barcarolles with gloomy zest;
Their pates in doting frenzy pitch and roll like ships.

Oh, do not make them stir! For them, that is shipwreck . . .
Scolding like outraged cats, they gradually rise,
Stretching their shoulder-blades, oh fury without check!
Hate puffs their pantaloons around their bloated thighs.

You hear them knocking their bald heads about the room,
Bobbing and bumping on warped feet across the floor.
The buttons on their coats like fulvous eyeballs loom
And pierce you from the far end of a corridor!

These creatures also have an unseen hand that kills.
When they turn round, their look discharges a black poison
Such as the sore eye of a punished bitch distils;
And then you sweat with fear, caught in a gruesome prison.

Reseated, with their fists in dirty sleeves concealed,
They brood upon the people who disturbed their doze;
And from sunrise to dark clusters of gland congealed
Beneath their puny chins tremble in angry throes.

When austere sleep has drawn its visor on their faces,
Heads propped, they dream of seats lavishly multiplied,
Of darling little pets of chairs all in their places,
Aligned by writing-desks beaming paternal pride;

Black flowers of ink, that spill a pollen-punctuation,
Become their cradles; on the calices they perch,
As dragon-flies in rows of irises take station,
—And then the straw grows prickly, and they give a lurch.

Quatrain

THE STAR HAS WEPT DOWN rose into thy ears' deep nests,
The infinite rolled white along thy nape and back;
The sea pearled russet at thy crimson-nippled breasts,
And on thy sovereign flank has Man himself bled black . . .

The Entranced

SEEN BLACK against the fog and snow,
Close by the big vent-hole, whose glow
    Is warm and red,

With rounded bottoms crouch—heart-breaking!—
Five children, eyes on the man baking
    Pale, heavy bread.

They watch the strong white arm that plies
The greyish dough, till soon it lies
    In its bright lair.

They hear the good bread hissing, while
The baker with a cozy smile
    Hums an old air.

They huddle near, and not one stirs
As the red vent-hole breathes and purrs,
    Warm as a breast.

When, ordered for some midnight rout,
In crescent shapes the bread comes out,
    How keen their zest!

And when, beneath the smoky beams,
The perfumed crust so sweetly screams,
    And crickets chatter,

What breath of life comes through the hole!
It penetrates them to the soul
    Through every tatter.

They're having such a lovely time,
Poor little Christs all stiff with rime,
    Just to be there,

Nuzzling the bars, with mutterings
Of wonder at these lovely things
    In the oven's glare;

Quite stupid, bent in adoration
Before this brilliant revelation
    Of heaven grown kind,

Bent down so low, their breeches crack
And shirts fly loose from each small back
    In the cold wind.

Seven-Year-Old Poet

AND SO THE MOTHER, shutting up the duty-book,
Went, proud and satisfied. She did not see the look
In the blue eyes, or how with secret loathing wild,
Beneath the prominent brow, a soul raged in her child.

All the day long he sweated with obedient zeal;
A clever boy; and yet appearing to reveal,
By various dark kinks, a sour hypocrisy.
In corridors bedecked with musty tapestry
He would stick out his tongue, clenching his two fists tight
Against his groin, and with closed eyes see specks of light.
A door stood open on the evening; when, aloof,
Under a gulf of brightness hanging from the roof,
High on the banisters they saw him crowing.

In summer, cowed and stupid, he'd insist on going
Off to the cool latrines, for that was where he chose
To sit in peace and think, breathing deep through his nose.

In winter-time, when, washed by all the smells of noon,
The garden plot behind the house shone in the moon;
Lying beneath a wall, in lumpy earth concealed
And straining long for visions, till his eyesight reeled,
He listened to the creak of mangy trellises.
Soft heart! He chose out as his sole accomplices
Those wretched, blank-browed children, of slurred eye and cheek
And grubby, thin, sick fingers plunged in clothes that reek
Of excrement: already old, whose conversation
Is held with gentle, imbecilic hesitation.
And if his mother, catching him at some foul act
Of pity, showed alarm, the child must face a fact
That to his earnest, tender mind brought grave surprise:
That's how it was. She had the blue-eyed stare—which lies!

At seven years he wrote romances about lives
In the great desert, where an exiled Freedom thrives,
Savannahs, forests, shores and suns! He had some aid
From illustrated magazines, whose gay parade
Of Spanish and Italian ladies made him blush.
When, brown-eyed, bold, in printed cotton, in would rush
The eight-year daughter of the working-folk next door,
And when the little savage down upon him bore,
Cornered him, leaping on his back, and tossed her hair,
He from beneath would bite her thighs, for they were bare
—She never put on drawers. Then, though she grappled fast,
Pounding with fists and heels, he'd shake her off at last
And bring the odours of her skin back to his room.

He feared December Sundays, with their pallid gloom,
When, with pommaded hair, from a mahogany ledge
He read a Bible with a gold, green-tarnished edge.
Dreams pressed upon him in the alcove every night.

Not God he loved, but men whom by the sallow light
Of evening he would see return, begrimed and bloused,
To suburbs where the crier's triple roll aroused
A jostling crowd to laugh and scold at the decrees.
He dreamed of the rapt prairie, where long brilliancies
Like waves and wholesome scents and golden spurts of force
Persist in their calm stir and take their airy course.

And, as he relished most all things of sombre hue,
He'd sit in the bare, shuttered chamber, high and blue,
Gripped in an acrid, piercing dampness, and would read
The novel that was always running in his head
Of heavy, ochre skies and forests under floods
And flowers of living flesh scattered through starry woods.
—Then vertigo, collapse, confusion, ruin, woe!—
While noises of the neighbourhood rose from below,
He'd brood alone, stretched out upon a canvas bale,
Raw canvas, prophesying strongly of the sail! . . .

Poor People in Church

BETWEEN OAK BENCHES, in mean corners stowed away,
Warming the air with fetid breath, fixing their vision
On the gilt-dripping chancel's twenty mouths, which bray
The pious canticles with meaningless precision;

Sniffing the wax like fragrant bread, and revelling,
Like dogs that have been whipped, in their humiliation,
The Poor unto dear God, the master and the king,
Offer their laughable and stubborn supplication.

The women are well pleased to wear the benches smooth
After the six black days that God has just bestowed!
Tangled in curious swaddling-clothes, they rock and soothe
Their hardly-human babes, a weeping, fatal load.

Their grimy bosoms bared, these feeders upon soup,
With a prayer in their eyes, though they have never prayed,
Are watching the unseemly movements of a group
Of pert young girls, who in their battered hats parade.

Outside are cold and hunger, husbands on the booze.
Well, there's this hour; then come the evils without names.
Meanwhile, all round them, whining, snuffling, whispering news,
Sits a whole gathering of ancient, dewlapped dames.

The timid ones, the epileptic ones, from whom
Yesterday at the cross-roads people turned aside,
The blind ones, nosing at old missels in the gloom,
Who creep into the court-yards with a dog for guide;

All, slavering their stupid beggars' creed, recite
Their endless plaint to Jesus, while he dreams on high
Beyond the murky window, in its yellowed light,
Far from thin evil ones, far from the fat and sly,

Far from the smells of meat, the smells of musty serge,
Prostrate and sombre farce in loathsome pantomime.
And now the worship blossoms with a keener urge,
The mysticalities become still more sublime,

When, coming from the naves through which no sunlight files,
Banal in silk, the Ladies of the town's best quarter
—O Christ!—the ones with liver-trouble and green smiles,
Offer bleached fingers to the kiss of holy-water.

Vowels

A BLACK, E WHITE, I red, U green, O blue—I'll tell
One day, you vowels, how you come to be and whence.
A, black, the glittering of flies that form a dense,
Velvety corset round some foul and cruel smell,

Gulf of dark shadow; E, the glaciers' insolence,
Steams, tents, white kings, the quiver of a flowery bell;
I, crimsons, blood expectorated, laughs that well
From lovely lips in wrath or drunken penitence;

U, cycles, the divine vibrations of the seas,
Peace of herd-dotted pastures or the wrinkled ease
That alchemy imprints upon the scholar's brow;

O, the last trumpet, loud with strangely strident brass,
The silences through which the Worlds and Angels pass:
—O stands for Omega, His Eyes' deep violet glow!

The Hands of Jeanne-Marie

THE HANDS OF JEANNE-MARIE are strong,
Dark as the hands of a Sultana,
Yet pale as dead men's hands: 'twere wrong,
Perhaps, to call them hands of Juana?

Have they collected the brown creams
That float on tides of luxury?
Or have they dabbled in moon-beams
Upon pools of serenity?

Have they absorbed barbarian climes,
Laid calmly on a charming knee?
Can they have rolled cigars at times,
Or been engaged in I.D.B.?

At the bright feet of the Madonnas
Fading gold flowers did they once heap?
It's the black blood of belladonnas
That in their palms flashes asleep.

Hands that have chased the flying things
That buzz within your dawny blues

Towards the nectared home of wings?
Hands that decanted poison-brews?

Oh, what the dream or necromancy
That makes them stretch and yearn afar?
Some abstruse Asiatic fancy
Of Zion or of Kangavar?

Not orange-seller's hands, and not
Upon the feet of gods made brown;
They've never washed the clothes of squat,
Small babies with an eyeless frown.

No dainty cousin's hands are these,
Nor hands of working-girls, who run
Through woods that reek of factories,
Scorched by a tarry, drunken sun.

The sort of hands to bend a spine,
Hands guilty of no hurtful deed,
More murderous than a machine
And stronger than a whole great steed!

Fluttering like a fiery blaze
And rippling warmly on and on,
Their flesh sings out a Marseillaise
And never an Eleison!

They'd break your necks, you evil dames,
You noble ladies, they would crush
Those hands of yours, hands rife with shames,
Full of white sheen and carmine flush.

These hands have such a tender brilliance
That drowsy flocks turn round to stare!
The fine joints have such glowing fragrance,
The sun puts secret rubies there.

A stain of common populace
Has browned them like an ancient breast.

The back of these hands is the place
Where each proud rebel's kisses rest!

They have shone pale in the great sun's
Love-loaded rays, that somersault
Along the barrels of the guns
All across Paris in revolt!

Ah, sometimes, hands of holiness,
On those wrists where, in trembling pain,
Our lips intoxicated press
Jangle the bright links of a chain!

And strangely something goes awry
Within us, when we feel a need,
Angelic hands, to suck you dry,
Bruising the fingers till they bleed.

The Lice-Pickers

WHEN THE CHILD'S FOREHEAD, racked by torments hot and red,
Begs the white benison of some vague, swarming dream,
Two tall and charming sisters come close to his bed,
Their fragile hands with silver finger-nails agleam.

Beside a widely open window, where the blue
Air bathes a tangled bunch of flowers, they set the child,
And in his heavy hair besprinkled with the dew
Their delicate fingers travel, terrible and mild.

He hears the singing of their breaths sharp with suspense.
Flower-sweet with herbal, rosy honeys, that a kiss
Interrupts now and then, saliva on the tense
Lip suddenly caught back, or longing for a kiss.

Amid the perfumed silence he can hear their black
Eyelashes beat; he lolls in drunken paradise,

While 'neath their royal nails, with soft, electric crack,
Their gentle fingers spell death to the little lice.

And now there mounts in him the wine of idleness,
A concertina-sighing that is close to raving;
And, while he palpitates beneath each slow caress,
There falls and rises endlessly a tearful craving.

Golden Age

FROM THE REST, one voice
—What angelic strains!—
Biddeth me rejoice;
Sharply it explains:

Questions multiplied
Through a thousand twists
In the end betide
Dreams and drunken mists.

*Terque
quaterque:* Well you know this mood,
Gay and quick to win;
'Tis all flower and flood,
And it is thy kin!

Now another voice—
What angelic strains!—
Biddeth me rejoice;
Sharply it explains,

And goes chanting on,
Sister to the breath,
In a German tone,
But ardent and fresh:

'All the world's to blame.'
Does that cause thee wonder?

Live! Cast on the flame
Every dismal blunder.

Pluries: Ah, palace transparent
In brilliance of splendour,
What Age was thy parent,
Great prince and defender,
Great brother so tender?

Indesin-
enter: I too shall aspire!
You sisterly choir
Proclaimed in no story,
Grant your bashful glory
To be my attire.

Bliss

SEASONS and palaces,
What soul's transgressionless?

Seasons and palaces,

Bliss has been my occult school;
Even zero owns its rule.

Three times three I'll give it cheer
With the Gallic Chantecleer.

But I've nothing more to crave;
All my life is now its slave,

Spell that took me flesh and soul,
Dissipated every goal.

How to give these words a sense?
Bliss has set them flying hence.

Seasons and palaces!

Paris Repopulated

COWARDS, YONDER SHE LIES! Out through the termini!
The sun's breath swept the avenues, down which one night
The victor hordes of the barbarians swept by.
There lies the holy City, on her Western site!

Forward: forestall the ebbing tide of conflagration!
There lies the quays, there lie the avenues, and there
The houses stand, against the mild illumination
Of skies that one night shook above the red bombs' glare!

Hide the dead palaces in darkened lairs of planks!
Scared, ancient daylight wakes your glances to new zest.
Here comes the ruddy crew of trulls with writhing flanks:
Be mad, your haggard looks shall but enhance the jest.

Bitches on heat that nuzzle poultices, a call
From gilded houses breaks and summons you to eat.
Eat, then! The swollen joys and spasms of night now fall
Upon the weary town: poor drinkers of the street,

Drink, then! For when the rays, intense and frantic, come
Delving into the streaming luxuries that rise
All round you, surely you won't sit, bemused and dumb,
Dribbling into your glass, with distance-ravished eyes?

Swallow, then, for the Queen with loins in streaming dance!
Listen and hear the noise of stupid, rending retches;
On through the glaring night hear the mad rabble prance,
Clowns, dotards, lackeys, idiots with deathly screeches!

O you with filthy hearts, you mouths abominable,
You mouths that, opening, stink, emit still louder roars!
Set wine for these ignoble sloths upon the table!
Your stomachs are dissolved in shame, O Conquerors!

Distend your nostrils wide in nausea of disdain,
Steep the fine tendons of your neck in poison-brew;

Upon your childish napes the poet's hands are lain:
"Cowards, dare to be mad!" the poet says to you.

Is it because you rummage in the Woman's womb
That you now fear from her a new convulsion, lest
She seize you with a shriek and the embrace of doom,
Asphyxiating your foul brood upon her breast?

Ventriloquists, kings, madmen, syphilitics, wags,
How can the harlot Paris care for your distress,
Your bodies and your souls, your poison and your rags?
She'll shake you off, with all your spleen and rottenness.

When you are lying low, your sorry entrails spilled
And loins exhausted, whining for your money back,
Then the red courtesan, her breasts with battles filled,
Far from your squalid swoon, her toiler's fists shall rack.

After your feet have danced at such a raging pace,
Paris! Sprawling prostrate, stabbed by so many knives,
And while in your clear eyes, though fugitive the trace,
Some lingering sweetness of the fallow spring survives.

O city of much sorrow, city like to dead,
So pale, yet head and breasts towards the bright Future cast,
Which stands with all its myriad gates before you spread,
City that might be blessed fitly by the dark Past.

Body remagnetized for new enormous pains,
You drink appalling life again, once more you feel
The flood of livid worms uprising through your veins;
Over your clear desire the icy fingers steal.

And though we shrink to see you mired with such disgrace,
And though men never yet had made of any city
A more empested ulcer on green Nature's face,
The poet's words to you are: splendid is your beauty!

By the storm's highest poetry you are anointed;
The elements in huge commotion take your part;

Your work boils up, death mutters round. City appointed,
Gather the stridence at the muffled bugle's heart.

The poet shall take for his own the outcast's sob,
The convict's hatred, the despairing madman's cries.
His scourging rays of love shall make the women throb,
His stanzas bound and sing: Look, bandits, there she lies!

Society, all's as before: old orgies start
In the old lupanars their epileptic seizure;
Along the crimson'd walls the raving gasses dart
Sinister jets of flame towards the lurid azure.

Brussels

JULY, BOULEVARD DU RÉGENT

FLOWER-BEDS OF AMARANTHUS stretching to
The charming palace that belongs to Jove.
—I know it's You who in this ivied grove
Mingle your almost-of-Sahara blue.

Then see how sunlight's pine, creeper and rose
Have stowed away in hiding here their toys,
Cage of the little widow! . . .
                                   Ah, the noise
Of troops of birds, O ya, yaiyo, aiyo! . . .

Calm houses, passions faded long ago;
Kiosk of Her whom fondness robbed of wit.
Next, the round buttocks of the rose-trees, low
And shady balcony for Juliet.

Juliet calls to memory Henriette,
Dear railway-station in a mountain's heart,
As if deep in an orchard, where blue hosts
Of levitating devils pirouette.

Green bench where the white Irishwoman stoops
To a guitar and serenades the storm.
Then, the Guiana dining-room, its swarm
Of babbling children and its chicken-coops.

You ducal window, making me recall
The poison of the snails, and of yon row
Of sleeping box-trees in the sun.
                                        Ah, no,
It is too beautiful! Let silence fall.

Boulevard with no movement and no commerce,
Dumb witness of all comedy and drama,
Reunion of the infinite panorama,
I know you and I gaze at you in silence.

The Stolen Heart

My sad heart drivels at the poop,
My heart that's overlaid with shag;
They spatter it with squirts of soup,
My sad heart drivels at the poop,
Under the gibes of the whole troop
That howls with laughter at each wag,
My sad heart drivels at the poop,
My heart that's overlaid with shag.

The sturdy-tooled, footslogging chaps,
Their gibes have made it turn obscene.
The rudder's carved with witty scraps
By sturdy-tooled, footslogging chaps.
O waves, you mystical claptraps,
Seize on my heart and wash it clean.
The sturdy-tooled, footslogging chaps,
Their gibes have made it turn obscene.

When they have chewed up all their quid.
What to do then, O stolen heart?
The bacchic belches fly unhid
When they have chewed up all their quid,
My stomach queasily shall skid
If they take you for counterpart:
When they have chewed up all their quid.
What to do then, O stolen heart?

Sister of Charity

THE YOUNG MAN with the brilliant eyes and swarthy skin,
Whose handsome, twenty-year-old body should go bare—
In Persia, 'neath the moon, he'd have born to wear
A copper circulet, and worship unknown Jinn—

Impetuous with virginal, obscure delights,
Elated by his first ambitions and beliefs,
Like the young seas, impassioned tears of summer nights
That proudly toss and turn on diamond beds and reefs;

The young man, fronted by a world of ugliness
Quakes in his heart with widely-flung antipathy,
And, wounded by an everlasting, deep distress
Falls to desiring her—sister of charity.

But, Woman, mass of entrails, shape of soft compassion,
Sister of Charity is not your name, O never!
Not that dark look, nor breasts formed in such splendid fashion,
Belly where russet shadows brood, nor fingers clever.

O unawakened one, with eyes wide but unseeing,
When we embrace you 'tis an answer that we crave;
'Tis you who hang on us, you udder-laden being,
We nurse and rock you, rather, Passion sweet and grave.

Your hates, your stubborn torpors, quick abandonments.
And the brutalities endured long since, you wreak
Them all on us, O Night, yet with no ill intents,
Like an excess of blood discharged at each fourth week.

When from her ecstasy an instant he recoils,
Love and the song of life and the loud song of action,
Then the green Muse and ardent Justice set their toils,
To tear him cruelly with their august attraction.

Ah! Ever thirsty for high splendours and repose,
Forsaken by those two insatiate Sisters now,
Imploring science its kind arms round him to close,
He brings to nature's flowering prime his bleeding brow.

But sacred studies and black alchemy repel
The wounded man, this fervid scholar of proud gloom.
He feels appalling solitudes above him swell.
Still stalwart, then, and never shrinking from the tomb,

May he pursue vast ends, those Dreams or Promenades
That reach across the nights of Truth's immensity,
And in his soul and ailing limbs call on thy shades,
O thou mysterious Death, Sister of Charity!

Tear-Drop

FAR AWAY FROM BIRDS and herds and village maidens
I was drinking, crouched among a patch of heather
Girdled by nut-trees with barks all soft and wet.
On a green warm afternoon of hazy weather.

What had I to drink from Oise, that youthful river,
Voiceless elms and flowerless turf, sky heavy laden?
In that gourd of coco-root what draught was hidden?
Some insipid, gold liqueur that makes you sweat.

So I crouched there like a clumsy tavern-sign.
Then the storm till evening altered the whole sky.
Lo! black countries, lakes where perches leap and shine.
Colonnades beneath blue night, and termini.

Forest water lost itself in virgin sand, and hail
Drove before the wind upon the pools . . . To think
How, obsessed as fishers up of gold or shell,
I, the fool, had not a thought to pause and drink!

The Drunken Boat

As I PROCEEDED down along impassive rivers,
I lost my crew of haulers; they'd been seized by hosts
Of whooping Redskins, who had emptied out their quivers
Against these naked targets, nailed to coloured posts.

Little I cared for any crew I bore, a rover
With Flemish wheat or English cottons in my hold.
When once the tribulations of my crew were over,
The rivers let me go where my own fancy told.

Amid the fury of the loudly chopping tide,
I, just last winter, with a child's insensate brain,
Ah, how I raced! And no Peninsulas untied
Were ever tossed in more triumphant hurricane.

The blessing of the storm on my sea-watch was shed.
More buoyant than a cork I darted for ten nights
Over the waves, those famed old trundlers of the dead,
Nor missed the foolish blink of homely warning lights.

The wash of the green water on my shell of pine,
Sweeter than apples to a child its pungent edge;
It cleansed me of the stains of vomits and blue wine
And carried off with it the rudder and the kedge.

And afterwards down through the poem of the sea,
A milky foam infused with stars, frantic I dive
Down through green heavens where, descending pensively,
Sometimes the pallid remnants of the drowned arrive;

Where suddenly the bluish tracts dissolve, desires
And rhythmic languors stir beneath the day's full glow.
Stronger than alcohol and vaster than your lyres,
The bitter humours of fermenting passion flow!

I know how lightning splits the skies, the current roves;
I know the surf and waterspouts and evening's fall;
I've seen the dawn arisen like a flock of doves;
Sometimes I've seen what men believe they can recall.

I've seen the low sun blotched with blasphemies sublime,
Projecting vividly long, violet formations
Which, like tragedians in very ancient mime
Bestride the latticed waves, that speed remote vibrations.

My dreams were of green night and its bedazzled snow,
Of kisses slowly mounting up to the sea's eyes,
Of winding courses where unheard-of fluids go,
Flares blue and yellow that from singing phosphors rise.

For whole months at a time I've ridden with the surge
That like mad byres a-toss keeps battering the reefs,
Nor thought that the bright touch of Mary's feet could urge
A muzzle on the seas, muting their wheezy griefs.

And, yes, on Florida's beyond belief I've fetched,
Where flowers and eyes of panthers mingle in confusion,
Panthers with human skin, rainbows like bridles stretched
Controlling glaucous herds beneath the sea's horizon.

I've seen fermenting marshes like huge lobster-traps
Where in the rushes rots a whole Leviathan,
Or in the midst of calm the water's face collapse
And cataracts pour in from all the distant span.

Glaciers, silver suns, pearl waves and skies afire,
Brown gulfs with loathsome strands in whose profundities
Huge serpents, vermin-plagued, drop down into the mire
With black effluvium from the contorted trees!

I longed to show the children how the dolphins sport
In the blue waves, these fish of gold, these fish that sing.
Flowers of foam have blessed my puttings-out from port,
Winds from I know not where at times have lent me wing.

And often, weary martyr of the poles and zones,
Dark blooms with yellow mouths reached towards me from the
    seas
On which I gently rocked, in time to their soft moans;
And I was left there like a woman on her knees.

Trembling peninsula, upon my decks I tossed
The dung of pale-eyed birds and clacking, angry sound;
And on I sailed while down through my frail cordage crossed
The sleeping, backwards falling bodies of the drowned.

I, lost boat in the hair of estuaries caught,
Hurled by the cyclone to a birdless apogee,
I, whom the Monitors and Hansamen had thought
Nor worth the fishing up—a carcase drunk with sea;

Free, smoking, touched with mists of violet above,
I, who the lurid heavens breached like some rare wall
Which boasts—confection that the goodly poets love—
Lichens of sunlight on a mucoid azure pall;

Who, with electric moons bedaubed, sped on my way,
A plank gone wild, black hippocamps my retinue,
When in July, beneath the cudgels of the day
Down fell the heavens and the craters of the blue;

I, trembling at the mutter, fifty leagues from me,
Of rutting Behemoths, the turbid Maelstrom's threats,
Spinning a motionless and blue eternity
I long for Europe, land of ancient parapets.

Such starry archipelagoes! Many an isle
With heavens fiercely to the wanderer wide-thrown;
Is it these depthless nights that your lone sleep beguile,
A million golden birds, O Vigour not yet known?

And yet, I've wept too much. The dawns are sharp distress,
All moons are baleful and all sunlight harsh to me
Swollen by acrid love, sagging with drunkenness—
Oh, that my keel might rend and give me to the sea!

If there's a water in all Europe that I crave,
It is the cold, black pond where 'neath the scented sky
Of eve a crouching infant, sorrowfully grave,
Launches a boat as frail as a May butterfly.

Soaked in your languors, waves, I can no more go hunting
The cotton-clippers' wake, no more can enterprise
Amid the proud displays of lofty flags and bunting,
Nor swim beneath the convict-hulks' appalling eyes!

Listen to It Bell

LISTEN TO IT BELL
near the thorny bush,
in April, the lush
green branch in the dell.

In its clear-cut steam,
moon-wards! you behold
their moving heads teem,
holy men of old . . .

Far from the bright ricks,
capes, roofs on the sky,
each dear Ancient sticks
to this philtre sly . . .

Nothing festive here
nor celestial—
only the mist's drear
and nocturnal pall.

Nonetheless they stay,
Sicily, Germany—
in this fog so grey
and sad: that is why!

Pleasant Morning Thought

AT FOUR A.M. in summer's light
the sleep of love is heavy still
in thickets; from the dawn distil
        the smells of festive night.

Then down in the huge work-shop, faced
towards the Hesperidean sun,
the carpenters, with shirt-sleeves braced,
        already run.

Placidly in their foaming waste
they make the precious canopies
where soon the city's wealth and taste
        shall laugh beneath false skies

Venus! For these dear labourers,
slaves whom a cruel Pharaoh sweats,
quit briefly your philanderers
        with souls in coronets.

        O Queen of Shepherds, bring
the workers brandy, so that soon
their muscles may stop quivering
while they wait for their bathe down on the beach at noon.

Comedy of Thirst

I FAMILY

WE ARE YOUR PARENTS Grand and Great,
In state!
Covered in the frosty sweats
Of the moon, the green forests.
Our dry wines were full of heart.
In the sun, without deceit,
What should man do? Drink is best.

Drown in the barbarous rivers.

We are your parents Grand and Great,
The estate!
Water's at the withy's root;
See the current in the moat
Round the mouldy castle float.
In our still-rooms come and dote;
Set the milk and cider out.

Go where cows are drinking.

We are your parents Grand and Great;
Come, take
Our liqueurs, in cupboards stored.
Tea and coffee, which we hoard,
Bubbling in the urns are heard.
See the statues, flowers . . . regard,
We are back from the church-yard.

Ah! to drain dry all the urns.

II THE SPIRIT

ETERNAL OCEAN NYMPHS,
Cleave the delicate lymphs.

Venus, sister of the azure,
    Set the waves a measure.

Jews that from Norway come and go,
    Tell me of the snow.

Old exiles dear to me,
    Tell me of the sea.

No more these pure oases:
These bubble-cups are burst.
Neither fables nor faces
Can appease my thirst.

Songster, my crazy drouth
For thy daughter craves—
Hydra without a mouth
That saps and enslaves.

III FRIENDS

COME, the Wines beat the shore
And the waves without a stop.
See the Bitters roar
Down from the mountain-top.

Good pilgrims, let us seek
Absinthe's green-pillared hall . . .

These landscapes are too weak;
Friends, what is drunkenness?

Better, it would seem,
To rot in the pond,
Under frightful cream,
Branches floating round.

IV THE POOR MAN'S REVERIE

AN EVENING may be near
When in peace I'll sit down

To drink in some old Town
And die with better cheer,
Because I'm patient here.

If my distress declines,
If ever I grow rich,
I'll choose, I wonder which,
North, or the Land of Vines? . . .
—Give up all these designs.

Such dreams are waste and sin.
And if once more I were
The old-time traveller,
Never could the green inn
Open to let me in.

V   CONCLUSION

The pigeons fluttering in the long grass,
The running game that's wakeful all night through,
The water-animals, the burdened ass
And the last butterflies! . . . are thirsty, too.

But how to melt away where melts yon straying cloud,
To be the darling love of all that's cool and lush,
To die with these damp violets for shroud,
Whose dawns have charged the forest with their flush?

Michael and Christine

WHY, WHAT MATTER if the sun should quit these parts?
Flee, bright deluge! Shadow swarms along the road.
On the willows, on the ancient princely court
Now the first big drops of storm have overflowed.

Hundred lambs, the idyll's fair-haired warriors,
From the aqueducts and from the scanty heather

Flee away! Horizons, deserts, plains and moors
Are attending at the tempest's red leveé.

Black dog and brown shepherd with wind-swollen cloak,
Flee the hour of lightning-flashes from on high;
Gleaming flock, when hither shade and sulphur soak,
See that you descend to safer sanctuary.

But, for my part, Lord! see how my spirit flies
Chasing red-iced heavens, skimming underneath
Banks of great celestial clouds, that run and fly
Through a hundred railroad-bare, deserted heaths.

Lo! a thousand wolves and savage seeds flit by,
Borne on this religious afternoon of storm
(With a special love for the convolvuli)
Through old Europe, where a hundred hordes shall swarm.

Afterwards, the moonlight! Everywhere waste land;
Facing the black skies with ruddy foreheads go
Men-at-arms on ghostly chargers riding slow,
While the pebbles crackle under this proud band.

Shall I see the yellow wood and the bright vale,
See the blue-eyed Spouse, the red-faced man, O Gaul,
And the Paschal Lamb at their dear feet extend,
Michael and Christine—and Christ! the idyll's end.

Time Without End

WE HAVE FOUND IT again.
What? Time without end.
'Tis the ocean gone
For a walk with the sun.

Soul, you sentinel,
Murmur and confess,

Day is fiery hell,
Night is nothingness.

From the common urges,
From the human highest
Far thy path diverges:
Following thou fliest . . .

No expectancy,
No *orietur*.
Science patiently;
Punishment is sure.

From your blaze alone,
Satin flames of force,
Duty's breath is blown;
No-one says: of course.

We have found it again.
What? Time without end.
'Tis the ocean gone
For a walk with the sun.

Festival of Hunger

I AM HUNGRY, lass, lass;
  Be off on your ass.

Nigh the only taste I feel
Is for earth and stone. So peal
Dinn-din! Dinn-din! Make your meal
Air and rock and coal and steel.

Hungers, pasture greedily
  On the sounds' common!
Suck from the convolvuli
  Their gaudy venom.

Eat the poor road-mender's bits of stone,
    Slabs from ancient churches hewn,
Boulders by the deluge thrown,
    Loaves in the grey valley strewn!

Hungers, 'tis the black air's tips,
    The ringing blue;
'Tis my stomach's eager grips,
    It is pure woe.

On the earth the leaves are thick:
On soft flesh of fruit I sup.
At the furrow's breast I pick
The kingcup and buttercup.

I am hungry, lass, lass;
    Be off on your ass.

What Do They Mean to Us?

WHAT DO THEY MEAN TO US, my heart, the sheets of fire
And blood, a thousand murders, the long caterwauls
Of rage, sobs from all hell that bring to pass entire
Confusion; Boreas still on the broken walls;

And all such vengeance? Nothing . . . Yet if, just the same,
We wish it! Princes, senates, lords of industry,
Perish! Down with all power, justice and history!
That is our due. Cry blood! blood and the golden flame!

Give over everything to vengeance, terrors, wars.
Come, spirit, let us twist inside the wound. Begone,
Republics of this world! To all you emperors,
Regiments, peoples, colonists, we say: have done!

Who should stir up these raging, fiery vortices
But we and those of our imagined brotherhood?

Help us, you storied friends: here is a task will please.
Never, ah never shall we work, O fiery flood!

Europe, America and Asia, you are doomed.
Before our march of vengeance everything must yield,
City and countryside! We all shall be consumed!
Volcanoes will leap upward! And the seas congealed . . .

Ah, friends! 'Tis sure, O heart, these are our kin by birth.
Strange Negro folk, when once we start! Quick, quick, begin!
Alas, a trembling takes me, and the ancient earth—
Round me who more and more am yours—the earth caves in.
(*That's nonsense: I'm still there, and always shall be.*)

Song from the Highest Tower

YOUTH SO FULL OF LEISURE,
Slave to each new taste,
In fine choice of pleasure
My life went to waste.

Ah, may the time come
When hearts are as one!

I bethought me: Go,
Hide thee from men's sight.
Never shalt thou know
Loftier delight.

Let no hindrance meet
Thy august retreat.

Ah, the soul is lonely.
Thousand times bereft
Widow, she has only
Mary's image left.

Are prayers truly said
To the Virgin Maid?

I have suffered so,
Memory is dead.
All my fear and woe
To the skies are fled.

Morbid thirst remains
Darkening my veins.

So oblivion looming
From the meadow stares,
Meadow wide and blooming
With incense and tares;

Crazy dronings rise
From the filthy flies.

Youth so full of leisure,
Slave to each new taste,
In fine choice of pleasure
My life went to waste.

Ah, may the time come
When hearts are as one!

Disgrace

WHILE THE FATAL BLADE not yet
Shall have cleft this brain in two,
White and greenish lump, whose sweat
Gives off steam that's never new . . .

(Ah, what he should do's to slice
Off his nose, his lip, his ears—
Belly, too!—and sacrifice
Both his legs. Oh, hearty cheers!)

No, a better plan, I think:
Till the blade upon his brain,
Till the flints upon his flank,
Till upon his guts the flame

Shall have done their work, the boy,
Troublesome and stupid creature,
Ought to make his one employ
To deceive and be a traitor,

Like a Rocky Mountain cat
To empest surrounding air
—Granted though, sweet heaven, that
At his death may rise a prayer . . .

Memory

BRIGHT WATER: like the salty tears of infancy;
assault upon the sun of women's brilliant flesh;
the lily oriflammes that spread their silken mesh
by walls to whose defence some Joan possessed the key;

the sport of angels; no . . . see the gold current march.
moving its arms of grass, thick, black and cool. Meanwhile
the grass, sky-canopied and with a darkling smile,
insists on curtains, for her shade, from hill and arch.

II

Ho! the wet pavement stretches its transparent soup.
The water loads the beds with bottomless, pale stocks
of gold. The little girls' green and discoloured frocks
make willows out of which birds without bridles swoop.

Yellower than a guinea, eyelid warm and clear,
the water's vigil—Spouse, thy plighted loyalty!—

at quick mid-day with tarnished mirror jealously
espies in hot, grey sky the pink, beloved Sphere.

III

Madam in the next meadow hold herself too straight,
where threads of toil are snowing down; sunshade in hand,
she tramples down (they're far too grand!) the clusters bland;
some children in the flowering greenery prostrate,

reading their book of red morocco. He, alack,
as if a thousand angels parted company,
takes himself off afar beyond the mountain. She,
all dark and bleak, pursues the man's receding track.

IV

Regrets for young, strong arms of the clean grass. The gold
of April moons deep in the holy bed. Hurray
for river wharves long since abandoned as a prey
to August evenings, that begot this sprouting mould.

Let her weep by the ramparts for the present. Breath
of poplars from above acts as the only wind.
Then there's the stream, reflectionless and sourceless, blind;
an old man dredging in his barge as still as death.

V

Puppet of this drab water-eye, in vain I ache—
ah, motionless canoe and arms too short!—to choose
this or the other flower: the yellow one that woos
yonder; or else the blue, upon the ash-grey lake.

Ah, powder from the willows that a wing has blown!
the roses of the reeds devoured for so long time!
My fixed canoe, its chain eternally drawn down
deep in this edgeless eye of water—to what slime?

Paul Verlaine

Selected Verse

Moonlight

YOUR SOUL is as a moonlit landscape fair,
  Peopled with maskers delicate and dim,
That play on lutes and dance and have an air
  Of being sad in their fantastic trim.

The while they celebrate in minor strain
  Triumphant love, effective enterprise,
They have an air of knowing all is vain,—
  And through the quiet moonlight their songs rise,

The melancholy moonlight, sweet and lone,
  That makes to dream the birds upon the tree,
And in their polished basins of white stone
  The fountains tall to sob with ecstasy.

The Alley

POWDERED AND ROUGED as in the sheepcotes' day,
Fragile 'mid her enormous ribbon bows,
Along the shaded alley, where green grows
The moss on the old seats, she wends her way
With mincing graces and affected airs,
Such as more oft a petted parrot wears.
Her long gown with the train is blue; the fan
She spreads between her jewelled fingers slim

267

Is merry with a love-scene, of so dim
Suggestion, her eyes smile the while they scan.
Blonde; dainty nose; plump, cherry lips, divine
With pride unconscious.—Subtler, certainly,
Than is the *mouche* there set to underline
The rather foolish brightness of the eye.

On the Grass

THE ABBÉ RAMBLES."—"You, marquis,
  Have put your wig on all awry."—
"This wine of Cyprus kindles me
  Less, my Camargo, than your eye!"

"My passion"—"Do, mi, sol, la, si."—
  "Abbé, your villany lies bare."—
"Mesdames, I climb up yonder tree
  And fetch a star down, I declare."

"Let each kiss his own lady, then
  The others."—"Would that I were, too
A lap-dog!"—"Softly, gentlemen!"
  "Do, mi."—"The moon!—Hey, how d'ye do?"

On the Promenade

THE MILKY SKY, the hazy, slender trees,
  Seem smiling on the light costumes we wear,—
  Our gauzy floating veils that have an air
Of wings, our satins fluttering in the breeze.

And in the marble bowl the ripples gleam,
  And through the lindens of the avenue

The sifted golden sun comes to us blue
And dying, like the sunshine of a dream.

Exquisite triflers and deceivers rare,
    Tender of heart, but little tied by vows,
    Deliciously we dally 'neath the boughs,
And playfully the lovers plague the fair.

Receiving, should they overstep a point,
    A buffet from a hand absurdly small,
    At which upon a gallant knee they fáll
To kiss the little finger's littlest joint.

And as this is a shocking liberty,
    A frigid glance rewards the daring swain,—
    Not quite o'erbalancing with its disdain
The red mouth's reassuring clemency.

The Faun

An ANCIENT terra-cotta Faun,
    A laughing note in 'mid the green,
Grins at us from the central lawn,
    With secret and sarcastic mien.

It is that he foresees, perchance,
    A bad end to the moments dear
That with gay music and light dance
    Have led us, pensive pilgrims, here.

Mandolin

THE COURTLY SERENADERS,
    The beauteous listeners,
Sit idling 'neath the branches
    A balmy zephyr stirs.

It's Tircis and Aminta,
  Clitandre,—ever there!—
Damïs, of melting sonnets
  To many a frosty fair.

Their trailing flowery dresses,
  Their fine beflowered coats,
Their elegance and lightness,
  And shadows blue,—all floats

And mingles,—circling, wreathing,
  In moonlight opaline,
While through the zephyr's harping
  Tinkles the mandoline.

Love on the Ground

THE WIND THE OTHER NIGHT blew down the Love
  That in the dimmest corner of the park
  So subtly used to smile, bending his arc,
And sight of whom did us so deeply move

One day! The other night's wind blew him down!
  The marble dust whirls in the morning breeze,
  Oh, sad to view, o'erblotted by the trees,
There on the base, the name of great renown!

Oh, sad to view the empty pedestal!
  And melancholy fancies come and go
  Across my dream, whereon a day of woe
Foreshadowed is—I know what will befall!

Oh, sad!—And you are saddened also, Sweet,
  Are not you, by this scene? although your eye
  Pursues the gold and purple butterfly
That flutters o'er the wreck strewn at our feet.

Muted

TRANQUIL in the twilight dense
 By the spreading branches made,
Let us breathe the influence
 Of the silence and the shade.

Let your heart melt into mine,
 And your soul reach out to me,
'Mid the languors of the pine
 And the sighing arbute-tree.

Close your eyes, your hands let be
 Folded on your slumbering heart.
From whose hold all treachery
 Drive forever, and all art.

Let us with the hour accord!
 Let us let the gentle wind,
Rippling in the sunburnt sward,
 Bring us to a patient mind!

And when Night across the air
 Shall her solemn shadow fling,
Touching voice of our despair,
 Long the nightingale shall sing.

Sentimental Colloquy

IN THE DESERTED PARK, silent and vast,
Erewhile two shadowy glimmering figures passed.

Their lips were colourless, and dead their eyes;
Their words were scarce more audible than sighs.

In the deserted park, silent and vast,
Two spectres conjured up the buried past.

"Our ancient ecstasy, do you recall?"
"Why, pray, should I remember it at all?"

"Does still your heart at mention of me glow?
Do still you see my soul in slumber?" "No!"

"Ah, blessed, blissful days when our lips met!
You loved me so!" "Quite likely,—I forget."

"How sweet was hope, the sky how blue and fair!"
"The sky grew black, the hope became despair."

Thus walked they 'mid the frozen weeds, these dead,
And Night alone o'erheard the things they said.

From THE GOOD SONG

Since Shade Relents

SINCE SHADE RELENTS, since 't is indeed the day,
    Since hope I long had deemed forever flown,
Wings back to me that call on her and pray,
    Since so much joy consents to be my own,—

The dark designs all I relinquish here,
    And all the evil dreams. Ah, done am I
Above all with the narrowed lips, the sneer,
    The heartless wit that laughed where one should sigh.

Away, clenched fist and bosom's angry swell,
    That knave and fool at every turn abound.
Away, hard unforgivingness! Farewell,
    Oblivion in a hated brewage found!

For I mean, now a Being of the Morn
    Has shed across my night excelling rays
Of love at once immortal and newborn,—
    By favour of her smile, her glance, her grace,—

I mean by you upheld, O gentle hand,
  Wherein mine trembles,—led, sweet eyes, by you,
To walk straight, lie the path o'er mossy land
  Or barren waste that rocks and pebbles strew.

Yes, calm I mean to walk through life, and straight,
  Patient of all, unanxious of the goal,
Void of all envy, violence, or hate:
  It shall be duty done with cheerful soul.

And as I may, to lighten the long way,
  Go singing airs ingenuous and brave,
She'll listen to me graciously, I say,—
  And, verily, no other heaven I crave.

O'er the Wood's Brow

O'ER THE WOOD'S BROW,
    Pale, the moon stares;
In every bough
    Wandering airs
Faintly suspire. . . .
O heart's-desire!

Two willow-trees
    Waver and weep,
One in the breeze,
    One in the deep
Glass of the stream. . . .
Dream we our dream!

An infinite
    Resignedness
Rains where the white
    Mists opalesce
In the moon-shower. . . .
Stay, perfect hour!

The Scene

THE SCENE behind the carriage window-panes
Goes flitting past in furious flight; whole plains
With streams and harvest-fields and trees and blue
Are swallowed by the whirlpool, whereinto
The telegraph's slim pillars topple o'er,
Whose wires look strangely like a music-score.

A smell of smoke and steam, a horrid din
As of a thousand clanking chains that pin
A thousand giants that are whipped and howl,—
And, suddenly, long hoots as of an owl.

What is it all to me? Since in mine eyes
The vision lingers that beatifies,
Since still the soft voice murmurs in mine ear,
And since the Name, so sweet, so high, so dear,
Pure pivot of this madding whirl, prevails
Above the brutal clangor of the rails?

Before Your Light Quite Fail

BEFORE YOUR LIGHT QUITE FAIL,
Already paling star,
        (The quail
Sings in the thyme afar!)

Turn on the poet's eyes
That love makes overrun—
        (See rise
The lark to meet the sun!)

Your glance, that presently
Must drown in the blue morn;

                    (What glee
          Amid the rustling corn!)

          Then flash my message true
          Down yonder,—far away!—
                    (The dew
          Lies sparkling on the hay.)

          Across what visions seek
          The Dear One slumbering still.
                    (Quick, quick!
          The sun has reached the hill!)

The Rosy Hearth

THE ROSY HEARTH, the lamplight's narrow beam,
The meditation that is rather dream,
With looks that lose themselves in cherished looks;
The hour of steaming tea and banished books;
The sweetness of the evening at an end,
The dear fatigue, and right to rest attained,
And worshipped expectation of the night,—
Oh, all these things, in unrelenting flight,
My dream pursues through all the vain delays,
Impatient of the weeks, mad at the days!

It Shall Be, Then

IT SHALL BE, THEN, upon a summer's day:
    The sun, my joy's accomplice, bright shall shine,
    And add, amid your silk and satin fine,
To your dear radiance still another ray;

The heavens, like a sumptuous canopy,
    Shall shake out their blue folds to droop and trail

About our happy brows, that shall be pale
With so much gladness, such expectancy;

And when day closes, soft shall be the air
  That in your snowy veils, caressing, plays,
  And with soft-smiling eyes the stars shall gaze
Benignantly upon the wedded pair.

From ROMANCES WITHOUT WORDS

The Trees' Reflection

*The nightingale who looks down into the river from the top of a branch,
thinks that it has fallen in. It is high up in the oak tree, yet is afraid of
drowning*—CYRANO DE BERGERAC.

THE TREES' REFLECTION in the misty stream
  Dies off in livid steam;
Whilst up among the actual boughs, forlorn,
  The tender wood-doves mourn.

How wan the face, O traveller, this wan
  Gray landscape looked upon;
And how forlornly in the high tree-tops
  Lamented thy drowned hopes!

The Keyboard

The joyous, importunate sound of a resonant harpsichord.
                                —PÉTRUS BOREL.

THE KEYBOARD, over which two slim hands float,
Shines vaguely in the twilight pink and gray,
Whilst with a sound like wings, note after note
Takes flight to form a pensive little lay

That strays, discreet and charming, faint, remote,
About the room where perfumes of Her stray.

What is this sudden quiet cradling me
To that dim ditty's dreamy rise and fall?
What do you want with me, pale melody?
What is it that you want, ghost musical
That fade toward the window waveringly
A little open on the garden small?

Brussels

HILLS AND FENCES hurry by
Blent in greenish-rosy flight,
And the yellow carriage-light
Blurs all to the half-shut eye.

Slowly turns the gold to red
O'er the humble darkening vales;
Little trees that flatly spread,
Where some feeble birdling wails.

Scarcely sad, so mild and fair
This enfolding Autumn seems;
All my moody languor dreams,
Cradled by the gentle air.

It Weeps in My Heart

It rains softly on the city—ARTHUR RIMBAUD.

IT WEEPS IN MY HEART
As it rains on the town.
What is this dull smart
Possessing my heart?

Soft sound of the rain
On the ground and the roofs!

To a heart in pain,
O the song of the rain!

It weeps without cause
In my heart-sick heart.
In her faith, what? no flaws?
This grief has no cause.

'T is sure the worst woe
To know not wherefore
My heart suffers so
Without joy or woe.

Streets

LET'S DANCE THE JIG!

Above all I loved her eyes,
More clear than stars of cloudless skies,
And arch and mischievous and wise.

Let's dance the jig!

So skilfully would she proceed
To make a lover's bare heart bleed,
That it was beautiful indeed!

Let's dance the jig!

But keenlier have I relished
The kisses of her mouth so red
Since to my heart she has been dead.

Let's dance the jig!

The circumstances great and small,—
Words, moments . . . I recall, recall!
It is my treasure among all.

Let's dance the jig!

Spleen

THE ROSES WERE SO RED, so red,
    The ivies altogether black.

If you but merely turn your head,
    Beloved, all my despairs come back!

The sky was over-sweet and blue,
    Too melting green the sea did show.

I always fear,—if you but knew!—
    From your dear hand some killing blow.

Weary am I of holly-tree
    And shining box and waving grass

Upon the tame unending lea,—
    And all and all but you, alas!

Birds in the Night

I

YOU WERE NOT OVER-PATIENT with me, dear;
    This want of patience one must rightly rate:
You are so young! Youth ever was severe
    And variable and inconsiderate!

You had not all the needful kindness, no;
    Nor should one be amazed, unhappily:
You're very young, cold sister mine, and so
    'T is natural you should unfeeling be!

Behold me therefore ready to forgive;
    Not gay, of course! but doing what I can
To bear up bravely,—deeply though I grieve
    To be, through you, the most unhappy man.

II

But you will own that I was in the right
    When in my downcast moods I used to say
That your sweet eyes, my hope, once, and delight!
    Were come to look like eyes that will betray.

It was an evil lie, you used to swear,
    And your glance, which was lying, dear, would flame,—
Poor fire, near out, one stirs to make it flare!—
    And in your soft voice you would say, *"Je t'aime!"*

Alas! that one should clutch at happiness
    In sense's, season's, everything's despite!—
But 't was an hour of gleeful bitterness
    When I became convinced that I was right!

III

And wherefore should I lay my heart-wounds bare?
    You love me not,—an end there, lady mine;
And as I do not choose that one shall dare
    To pity,—I must suffer without sign.

Yes, suffer! For I loved you well, did I,—
    But like a loyal soldier will I stand
Till, hurt to death, he staggers off to die,
    Still filled with love for an ungrateful land.

O you that were my Beauty and my Own,
    Although from you derive all my mischance,
Are not you still my Home, then, you alone,
    As young and mad and beautiful as France?

IV

Now I do not intend—what were the gain?—
    To dwell with streaming eyes upon the past;
But yet my love which you may think lies slain,
    Perhaps is only wide awake at last.

My love, perhaps,—which now is memory!—
    Although beneath your blows it cringe and cry
And bleed to will, and must, as I foresee,
    Still suffer long and much before it die,—

Judges you justly when it seems aware
    Of some not all banal compunction,
And of your memory in its despair
    Reproaching you, "Ah, *fi!* it was ill done!"

V

I SEE YOU STILL. I softly pushed the door—
    As one o'erwhelmed with weariness you lay;
But O light body love should soon restore,
    You bounded up, tearful at once and gay.

O what embraces, kisses sweet and wild!
    Myself, from brimming eyes I laughed to you:
Those moments, among all, O lovely child,
    Shall be my saddest, but my sweetest, too.

I will remember your smile, your caress,
    Your eyes, so kind that day,—exquisite snare!—
Yourself, in fine, whom else I might not bless,
    Only as they appeared, not as they were.

VI

I SEE YOU STILL! Dressed in a summer dress,
    Yellow and white, bestrewn with curtain-flowers;
But you had lost the glistening laughingness
    Of our delirious former loving hours.

The eldest daughter and the little wife
    Spoke plainly in your bearing's least detail,—
Already 't was, alas! our altered life
    That stared me from behind your dotted veil.

Forgiven be! And with no little pride
    I treasure up,—and you, no doubt, see why,—

Remembrance of the lightning to one side
    That used to flash from your indignant eye!

VII

SOME MOMENTS, I'm the tempest-driven bark
    That runs dismasted mid the hissing spray,
And seeing not Our Lady through the dark
    Makes ready to be drowned, and kneels to pray.

Some moments, I'm the sinner at his end,
    That knows his doom if he unshriven go,
And losing hope of any ghostly friend,
    Sees Hell already gape, and feels it glow.

Oh, but! Some moments, I've the spirit stout
    Of early Christians in the lion's care,
That smile to Jesus witnessing, without
    A nerve's revolt, the turning of a hair!

Green

SEE, BLOSSOMS, BRANCHES, fruit, leaves I have brought,
    And then my heart that for you only sighs;
With those white hands of yours, oh, tear it not,
    But let the poor gift prosper in your eyes.

The dew upon my hair is still undried,—
    The morning wind strikes chilly where it fell.
Suffer my weariness here at your side
    To dream the hour that shall it quite dispel.

Allow my head, that rings and echoes still
    With your last kiss, to lie upon your breast,
Till it recover from the stormy thrill,—
    And let me sleep a little, since you rest.

Oh, Heavy, Heavy

OH, HEAVY, HEAVY my despair,
Because, because of One so fair.

My misery knows no allay,
Although my heart has come away.

Although my heart, although my soul,
Have fled the fatal One's control.

My misery knows no allay,
Although my heart has come away.

My heart, the too, too feeling one,
Says to my soul, "Can it be done,

"Can it be done, too feeling heart,
That we from her shall live apart?"

My soul says to my heart, "Know I
What this strange pitfall should imply,

"That we, though far from her, are near.
Yea, present, though in exile here?"

From WISDOM

Sleep

SLEEP, darksome, deep,
Doth on me fall:
Vain hopes all, sleep,
Sleep, yearnings all!

Lo, I grow blind!
Lo, right and wrong
Fade to my mind. . . .
O sorry song!

> A cradle, I,
>   Rocked in a grave:
> Speak low, pass by,
>   Silence I crave!

What Say'st Thou, Traveller

WHAT SAY'ST THOU, TRAVELLER, of all thou saw'st afar?
    On every tree hangs boredom, ripening to its fall,
Didst gather it, thou smoking yon thy sad cigar,
    Black, casting an incongruous shadow on the wall?

Thine eyes are just as dead as ever they have been,
    Unchanged is thy grimace, thy dolefulness is one,
Thou mind'st one of the wan moon through the rigging seen,
    The wrinkled sea beneath the golden morning sun,

The ancient graveyard with new gravestones every day,—
    But, come, regale us with appropriate detail,
Those disillusions weeping at the fountains, say,
    Those new disgusts, just like their brothers, littered stale,—

Those women! Say the glare, the identical dismay
    Of ugliness and evil, always, in all lands,
And say Love, too,—and Politics, moreover, say,
    With ink-dishonoured blood upon their shameless hands.

And then, above all else, neglect not to recite
    Thy proper feats, thou dragging thy simplicity
Wherever people love, wherever people fight,
    In such a sad and foolish kind, in verity!

Has that dull innocence been punished as it should?
    What say'st thou? Man is hard,—but woman? And thy tears,
Who has been drinking? And into what ear so good
    Dost pour thy woes for it to pour in other ears?

Ah, others! ah, thyself! Gulled with such curious ease,
    That used to dream (Doth not the soul with laughter fill?)
One knows not what poetic, delicate decease,—
    Thou sort of angel with the paralytic will!

But now what are thy plans, thine aims? Art thou of might?
    Or has long shedding tears disqualified thy heart?
The tree is scarcely hardy, judging it at sight,
    And by thy looks no topping conqueror thou art.

So awkward, too! With the additional offence
    Of being now a sort of dazed idyllic bard
That poses in a window, contemplating thence
    The silly noon-day sky with an impressed regard.

So totally the same in this extreme decay!
    But in thy place a being with some sense, pardy,
Would wish at least to lead the dance, since he must pay
    The fiddlers,—at some risk of flutt'ring passers-by!

Canst not, by rummaging within thy consciousness,
    Find some bright vice to bare, as 't were a flashing sword?
Some gay, audacious vice, which wield with dexterousness,
    And make to shine, and shoot red lightnings Heavenward!

Hast one, or more? If more, the better! And plunge in,
    And bravely lay about thee, indiscriminate,
And wear that face of indolence that masks the grin
    Of hate at once full-feasted and insatiate.

Not well to be a dupe in this good universe,
    Where there is nothing to allure in happiness
Save in it wriggle aught of shameful and perverse,—
    And not to be a dupe, one must be merciless!

—Ah, human wisdom, ah, new things have claimed mine eyes,
    And of that past—of weary recollection!—
Thy voice described, for still more sinister advice,
    All I remember is the evil I have done.

In all the curious movements of my sad career,
  Of others and myself, the chequered road I trod,
Of my accounted sorrows, good and evil cheer,
  I nothing have retained except the grace of God!

If I am punished, 't is most fit I should be so;
  Played to its end is mortal man's and woman's rôle,—
But steadfastly I hope I too one day shall know
  The peace and pardon promised every Christian soul.

Well not to be a dupe in this world of a day,
  But not to be one in the world that hath no end,
That which it doth behoove the soul to be and stay
  Is merciful, not merciless,—deluded friend.

The Sky-Blue

THE SKY-BLUE smiles above the roof
      Its tenderest;
A green tree rears above the roof
      Its waving crest.

The church-bell in the windless sky
      Peaceably rings,
A skylark soaring in the sky
      Endlessly sings.

My God, my God, all life is there,
      Simple and sweet;
The soothing bee-hive murmur there
      Comes from the street!

What have you done, O you that weep
      In the glad sun,—
Say, with your youth, you man that weep,
      What have you done?

The False Fair Days

THE FALSE FAIR DAYS have flamed the livelong day,
And still they flicker in the brazen West.
Cast down thine eyes, poor soul, shut out the unblest:
A deadliest temptation. Come away.

All day they flashed in flakes of fire, that lay
The vintage low upon the hill's green breast,
The harvest low,—and o'er that faithfullest,
The blue sky ever beckoning, shed dismay.

Oh, clasp thy hands, grow pale, and turn again!
If all the future savoured of the past?
If the old insanity were on its way?

Those memories, must each anew be slain?
One fierce assault, the best, no doubt, the last!
Go pray against the gathering storm, go pray!

I've Seen Again the One Child

I'VE SEEN AGAIN THE ONE child: verily,
I felt the last wound open in my breast,
The last, whose perfect torture doth attest
That on some happy day I too shall die!

Good icy arrow, piercing thoroughly!
Most timely came it from their dreams to wrest
The sluggish scruples laid too long to rest,—
And all my Christian blood hymned fervently.

I still hear, still I see! O worshipped rule
Of God! I know at last how comfortful
To hear and see! I see, I hear alway!

O innocence, O hope! Lowly and mild,
How I shall love you, sweet hands of my child,
Whose task shall be to close our eyes one day!

Son, Thou Must Love Me

"SON, THOU MUST LOVE ME! See—" my Saviour said,
"My heart that glows and bleeds, my wounded side,
My hurt feet that the Magdalene, wet-eyed,
Clasps kneeling, and my tortured arms outspread

"To bear thy sins. Look on the cross, stained red!
The nails, the sponge, that, all, thy soul shall guide
To love on earth where flesh thrones in its pride,
My Body and Blood alone, thy Wine and Bread.

"Have I not loved thee even unto death,
O brother mine, son in the Holy Ghost?
Have I not suffered, as was writ I must,

"And with thine agony sobbed out my breath?
Hath not thy nightly sweat bedewed my brow,
O lamentable friend that seek'st me now?"

Give Ear Unto the Gentle Lay

GIVE EAR UNTO THE GENTLE LAY
That's only sad that it may please;
It is discreet, and light it is:
A whiff of wind o'er buds in May.

The voice was known to you (and dear?),
But it is muffled latterly
As is a widow,—still, as she
It doth its sorrow proudly bear,

And through the sweeping mourning veil
That in the gusts of Autumn blows,
Unto the heart that wonders, shows
Truth like a star now flash, now fail.

It says,—the voice you knew again!—
That kindness, goodness is our life,
And that of envy, hatred, strife,
When death is come, shall naught remain.

It says how glorious to be
Like children, without more delay,
The tender gladness it doth say
Of peace not bought with victory.

Accept the voice,—ah, hear the whole
Of its persistent, artless strain:
Naught so can soothe a soul's own pain,
As making glad another soul!

It pines in bonds but for a day,
The soul that without murmur bears. . .
How unperplexed, how free it fares!
Oh, listen to the gentle lay!

It Is You, It Is You

IT IS YOU, IT IS YOU, poor better thoughts!
The needful hope, shame for the ancient blots,
Heart's gentleness with mind's severity,
And vigilance, and calm, and constancy,
And all!—But slow as yet, though well awake;
Though sturdy, shy; scarce able yet to break
The spell of stifling night and heavy dreams.
One comes after the other, and each seems
Uncouther, and all fear the moonlight cold.

"Thus, sheep when first they issue from the fold,
Come,—one, then two, then three. The rest delay,
With lowered heads, in stupid, wondering way,
Waiting to do as does the one that leads.
He stops, they stop in turn, and lay their heads
Across his back, simply, not knowing why." *
Your shepherd, O my fair flock, is not I,—
It is a better, better far, who knows
The reasons, He that so long kept you close,
But timely with His own hand set you free.
Him follow,—light His staff.
                          And I shall be,
Beneath his voice still raised to comfort you,
I shall be, I, His faithful dog, and true.

Hope Shines

HOPE SHINES—as in a stable a wisp of straw.
Fear not the wasp drunk with his crazy flight!
Through some chink always, see, the moted light!
Propped on your hand, you dozed— But let me draw

Cool water from the well for you, at least,
Poor soul! There, drink! Then sleep. See, I remain,
And I will sing a slumberous refrain,
And you shall murmur like a child appeased.

Noon strikes. Approach not, Madam, pray, or call. . . .
He sleeps. Strange how a woman's light footfall
Re-echoes through the brains of grief-worn men!

Noon strikes. I bade them sprinkle in the room.
Sleep on! Hope shines—a pebble in the gloom.
—When shall the Autumn rose re-blossom,—when?

* Dante, *Purgatorio.*

'Tis the Feast of Corn

'TIS THE FEAST OF CORN, 'tis the feast of bread,
    On the dear scene returned to, witnessed again!
So white is the light o'er the reapers shed
    Their shadows fall pink on the level grain.

The stalkèd gold drops to the whistling flight
    Of the scythes, whose lightning dives deep, leaps clear;
The plain, labour-strewn to the confines of sight,
    Changes face at each instant, gay and severe.

All pants, all is effort and toil 'neath the sun,
    The stolid old sun, tranquil ripener of wheat,
Who works o'er our haste imperturbably on
    To swell the green grape yon, turning it sweet.

Work on, faithful sun, for the bread and the wine,
    Feed man with the milk of the earth, and bestow
The frank glass wherein unconcern laughs divine,—
    Ye harvesters, vintagers, work on, aglow!

For from the flour's fairest, and from the vine's best,
    Fruit of man's strength spread to earth's uttermost,
God gathers and reaps, to His purposes blest,
    The Flesh and the Blood for the chalice and host!

From LONG AGO AND NOT SO LONG AGO

Prologue

    GLIMM'RING TWILIGHT THINGS are these,
    Visions of the end of night.
    Truth, thou lightest them, I wis,
    Only with a distant light,

Whitening through the hated shade
In such grudging dim degrees,
One must doubt if they be made
By the moon among the trees,

Or if these uncertain ghosts
Shall take body bye and bye,
And uniting with the hosts
Tented by the azure sky,

Framed by Nature's setting meet,—
Offer up in one accord
From the heart's ecstatic heat,
Incense to the living Lord!

Prologue

OFF, BE OFF, NOW, graceless pack:
Get you gone, lost children mine:
Your release is earned in fine:
The Chimaera lends her back.

Huddling on her, go, God-sped,
As a dream-horde crowds and cowers
Mid the shadowy curtain-flowers
Round a sick man's haunted bed.

Hold! My hand, unfit before,
Feeble still, but feverless,
And which palpitates no more
Save with a desire to bless,

Blesses you, O little flies
Of my black suns and white nights.
Spread your rustling wings, arise,
Little griefs, little delights,

Hopes, despairs, dreams foul and fair,
All!—renounced since yesterday

By my heart that quests elsewhere. **. . .**
Ite, aegri somnia!

Melancholy

I AM THE EMPIRE in the last of its decline,
That sees the tall, fair-haired Barbarians pass,—the while
Composing indolent acrostics, in a style
Of gold, with languid sunshine dancing in each line.

The solitary soul is heart-sick with a vile
Ennui. Down yon, they say, War's torches bloody shine.
Alas, to be so faint of will, one must resign
The chance of brave adventure in the splendid file,—

Of death, perchance! Alas, so lagging in desire!
Ah, all is drunk! Bathyllus, hast done laughing, pray?
Ah, all is drunk,—all eaten! Nothing more to say!

Alone, a vapid verse one tosses in the fire;
Alone, a somewhat thievish slave neglecting one;
Alone, a vague disgust of all beneath the sun!

From SATURNINE POEMS

Prologue

THE SAGES OF OLD TIME, well worth our own,
Believed—and it has been disproved by none—
That destinies in Heaven written are,
And every soul depends upon a star.
(Many have mocked, without remembering
That laughter oft is a misguiding thing,
This explanation of night's mystery.)
Now all that born beneath SATURNUS be,—

Red planet, to the necromancer dear,—
Inherit, ancient magic-books make clear,
Good share of spleen, good share of wretchedness.
Imagination, wakeful, vigourless,
In them makes the resolves of reason vain.
The blood within them, subtle as a bane,
Burning as lava, scarce, flows ever fraught
With sad ideals that ever come to naught.
Such must Saturnians suffer, such must die,—
If so that death destruction doth imply,—
Their lives being ordered in this dismal sense
By logic of a malign Influence.

Song of Autumn

LEAF-STREWING GALES
Utter low wails
    Like violins,—
Till on my soul
Their creeping dole
    Stealthily wins. . . .

Days long gone by!
In such hour, I,
    Choking and pale,
Call you to mind,—
Then like the wind
    Weep I and wail.

And, as by wind
Harsh and unkind,
    Driven by grief,
Go I, here, there,
Recking not where,
    Like the dead leaf.

Nevermore

REMEMBRANCE, what wilt thou with me? The year
Declined; in the still air the thrush piped clear,
The languid sunshine did incurious peer
Among the thinned leaves of the forest sere.

We were alone, and pensively we strolled,
With straying locks and fancies, when, behold
Her turn to let her thrilling gaze enfold,
And ask me in her voice of living gold,

Her fresh young voice, "What was thy happiest day?"
I smiled discreetly for all answer, and
Devotedly I kissed her fair white hand.

—Ah, me! The earliest flowers, how sweet are they!
And in how exquisite a whisper slips
The earliest "Yes" from well-beloved lips!

After Three Years

WHEN I HAD PUSHED the narrow garden-door,
Once more I stood within the green retreat;
Softly the morning sunshine lighted it,
And every flow'r a humid spangle wore.

Nothing is changed. I see it all once more:
The vine-clad arbor with its rustic seat. . . .
The waterjet still plashes silver sweet,
The ancient aspen rustles as of yore.

The roses throb as in a bygone day,
As they were wont, the tall proud lilies sway.
Each bird that lights and twitters is a friend.

I even found the Flora standing yet,
Whose plaster crumbles at the alley's end,
—Slim, 'mid the foolish scent of mignonette.

The Nightingale

LIKE TO A SWARM OF BIRDS, with jarring cries
Descend on me my swarming memories;
Light mid the yellow leaves, that shake and sigh,
Of the bowed alder—that is even I!—
Brooding its shadow in the violet
Unprofitable river of Regret.
They settle screaming— Then the evil sound,
By the moist wind's impatient hushing drowned,
Dies by degrees, till nothing more is heard
Save the lone singing of a single bird,
Save the clear voice— O singer, sweetly done!—
Warbling the praises of the Absent One. . . .
And in the silence of a summer night
Sultry and splendid, by a late moon's light
That sad and sallow peers above the hill,
That humid hushing wind that ranges still
Rocks to a whispered sleepsong languidly
The bird lamenting and the shivering tree.

The Kiss

KISS! HOLLYHOCK in Love's luxuriant close!
   Brisk music played on pearly little keys,
   In tempo with the witching melodies
Love in the ardent heart repeating goes.

Sonorous, graceful Kiss, hail! Kiss divine!
   Unequalled boon, unutterable bliss!
   Man, bent o'er thine enthralling chalice, Kiss,
Grows drunken with a rapture only thine!

Thou comfortest as music does, and wine,
   And grief dies smothered in thy purple fold.
   Let one greater than I, Kiss, and more bold,
Rear thee a classic, monumental line.

Humble Parisian bard, this infantile
   Bouquet of rhymes I tender half in fear. . . .
   Be gracious, and in guerdon, on the dear
Red lips of One I know, alight and smile!

My Familiar Dream

OFT DO I DREAM this strange and penetrating dream:
An unknown woman, whom I love, who loves me well,
Who does not every time quite change, nor yet quite dwell
The same,—and loves me well, and knows me as I am.

For she knows me! My heart, clear as a crystal beam
To her alone, ceases to be inscrutable
To her alone, and she alone knows to dispel
My grief, cooling my brow with her tears' gentle stream.

Is she of favour dark or fair?—I do not know.
Her name? All I remember is that it doth flow
Softly, as do the names of them we loved and lost.

Her eyes are like the statues',—mild and grave and wide;
And for her voice she has as if it were the ghost
Of other voices,—well-loved voices that have died.

To a Woman

To YOU THESE LINES for the consoling grace
Of your great eyes wherein a soft dream shines,
For your pure soul, all-kind!—to you these lines
From the black deeps of mine unmatched distress.

'T is that the hideous dream that doth oppress
My soul, alas! its sad prey ne'er resigns,
But like a pack of wolves down mad inclines
Goes gathering heat upon my reddened trace!

I suffer, oh, I suffer cruelly!
So that the first man's cry at Eden lost
Was but an eclogue surely to my cry!

And that the sorrows, Dear, that may have crossed
Your life, are but as swallows light that fly
—Dear!—in a golden warm September sky.

Epilogue

I

THE SUN, LESS HOT, looks from a sky more clear;
The roses in their sleepy loveliness
Nod to the cradling wind. The atmosphere
Enfolds us with a sister's tenderness.

For once hath Nature left the splendid throne
Of her indifference, and through the mild
Sun-gilded air of Autumn, clement grown,
Descends to man, her proud, revolted child.

She takes, to wipe the tears upon our face,
Her azure mantle sown with many a star;

And her eternal soul, her deathless grace,
Strengthen and calm the weak heart that we are.

The waving of the boughs, the lengthened line
Of the horizon, full of dreamy hues
And scattered songs, all,—sing it, sail, or shine!—
To-day consoles, delivers!—Let us muse.

II

So, THEN, THIS BOOK IS CLOSED. Dear Fancies mine,
That streaked my grey sky with your wings of light,
And passing fanned my burning brow, benign,—
Return, return, to your blue Infinite!

Thou, ringing Rhyme, thou, Verse that smooth didst glide,
Ye, throbbing Rhythms, ye, musical Refrains,
And Memories, and Dreams, and ye beside
Fair Figures called to life with anxious pains,

We needs must part. Until the happier day
When Art, our Lord, his thralls shall re-unite,
Companions sweet, Farewell and Wellaway,
Fly home, ye may, to your blue Infinite!

And true it is, we spared not breath or force,
And our good pleasure, like a foaming steed
Blind with the madness of his earliest course,
Of rest within the quiet shade hath need.

—For always have we held thee, Poesy,
To be our Goddess, mighty and august,
Our only passion,— Mother calling thee,
And holding Inspiration in mistrust.

III

AH, INSPIRATION, splendid, dominant,
Egeria with the lightsome eyes profound,
Sudden Erato, Genius quick to grant,
Old picture Angel of the gilt background,

Muse,—ay, whose voice is powerful indeed,
Since in the first come brain it makes to grow
Thick as some dusty yellow roadside weed,
A gardenful of poems none did sow,—

Dove, Holy Ghost, Delirium, Sacred Fire,
Transporting Passion,—seasonable queen!—
Gabriel and lute, Latona's son and lyre,—
Ah, Inspiration, summoned at sixteen!

What we have need of, we, the Poets True,
That not believe in Gods, and yet revere,
That have no halo, hold no golden clue,
For whom no Beatrix leaves her radiant sphere,

We, that do chisel words like chalices,
And moving verses shape with unmoved mind,
Whom wandering in groups by evening seas,
In musical converse ye scarce shall find,—

What we need is, in midnight hours dim-lit,
Sleep daunted, knowledge earned,—more knowledge still!
Is Faust's brow, of the wood-cuts, sternly knit,
Is stubborn Perseverance, and is Will!

Is Will eternal, holy, absolute,
That grasps—as doth a noble bird of prey
The steaming flanks of the foredoomèd brute,—
Its project, and with it,—skyward, away!

What we need, we, is fixedness intense,
Unequalled effort, strife that shall not cease,
Is night, the bitter night of labour, whence
Arises, sun-like, slow, the Master-piece!

Let our Inspired, hearts by an eye-shot tined,
Sway with the birch-tree to all winds that blow,
Poor things! Art knows not the divided mind—
Speak, Milo's Venus, is she stone or no?

We therefore, carve we with the chisel Thought
The pure block of the Beautiful, and gain
From out the marble cold where it was not,
Some starry-chitoned statue without stain,

That one far day, Posterity, new Morn,
Enkindling with a golden-rosy flame
Our Work, new Memnon, shall to ears unborn
Make quiver in the singing air our name!

From IN PARALLEL FASHION

Dedication

Do YOU REMEMBER, you a gay young woman,
Who indulged your faults when younger—that's no matter
In the jolly times when, being both inhuman,
You heard me, green-horn, when I used to chatter?

Do you keep now, in your obscurity
That worn spun silk, the horror of the Muses,
Thoughts of my conjuring-book and my futurity,
And certain written things, that no one chooses?

Have you forgotten, now you are a gammer,
Not even in your worst stupidities,
My faults of taste, certainly not of grammar,
On the wrong side of your bitter cupidities?

And when sounded the hour of our nuptials, atrocious,
An Ariadne mourning for her Bacchus,
My gluttonous eyes, and to my kisses ferocious,
Your negations, when there's nothing now to rack us?

Do you recall, if this were ever feasible,
In your hard heart that had no sense of passion,
This I always ready, terrible, horrible, seizable,
This you, dear, taking taste in your own fashion,

And all the bitteration of a marriage
Which by misfortune was not right for my age?
Have you forgot what used to be my carriage
And all the wrongs of your age and of my age?

This is most odious! See me, lamentable
Derelict scattered on all the floods of Vices,
That see you, you, you jade detestable,
And the need I have to write to you of—my spices!

Allegory

A VERY ANCIENT TEMPLE ruinous
High on a yellow hill its splendour keeps,
As a discrowned King for his lost throne weeps
And has no end of Sorrows sorcerous.
With sleepy grace and sad eyes slumbrous,
A wicked girl up to a young Faun creeps
With subtle agitations as he leaps
Away from her with laughter furious.

A very banal subject that saddens me,
Say, what poet of all poets maddens me,
What morose workman wove for Giulia
A very wonderful woven Tapestry,
Banal as the scenery of an opera,
Factitious, alas, as my own Destiny?

On the Balcony

THEY SAW THE SWALLOWS flying rapidly:
One pale with black hair and the other's face
Fair and rose red, in subtle grace old lace

Serpentined around them, clouds, luxuriously.
And both breathed the hot air passionately,
As in the sky a mad moon rose in space,
Savoured the night's passion as the fire-fledged race
Of hearts with hearts in one strange Tragedy.

Such, their arms clasped, moist, round each other's waist,
Strange creatures of a chastity unchaste.
Such dreamed these women in their souls, alone.

Behind them, in the sombreness of the shade,
Emphatic as a melodramatic throne
And full of odours, their scented Bed, unmade.

Pierrot the Gamin

IT IS NOT PIERROT in the grasses,
Nor Pierrot when the wild wind passes,
It is Pierrot, Pierrot, Pierrot,
Pierrot rascal and infernal,
As a lass out of a kernel,
It is Pierrot, Pierrot, Pierrot!

Not as near high as Demeter,
The dear droll knows how in metre
From their eyes to shoot forth thunder
That his subtle genius vicious
Makes more infinitely malicious
Than the grimacing Poet's wonder.

Lips red wounded with Insanity
Where slumbers lulling Luxury.
Pale faces all in agitation,
Long and very accentuated,
One might say habituated
To no serious contemplation.

Body slender and not thinner
Than a girl's who is a sinner,
Youth beyond all youth's surprising.
Voice in the head, festal feature
Of this singular mad creature
Made for sensual appetizing.

Go, beyond all Good and Evil,
Beat your feet and make the Devil
In your dream and over Paris,
That's the world, and be the soul there,
Infamous as any hole there
Where no fallen spirit marries!

Yet the custom is to greaten
To the huge height of our Satan
In an immense exaggeration,
Caricature and saintless faces,
Soulless symbols and Disgraces
Of our feverish agitation!

Per Amica Silentia

THE LONG CURTAINS of white muslin serpentine
Over the vague light in the room tenebrous
As in the wind floats a wild opaline
In the shadow sombrely mysterious.

The great curtains of the bed of Adeline
Have heard, Claire, thy voice made amorous,
Thy caressing voice with cadences divine
That another voice enlaces furious.

"Let us love, love!" said your mixed voices in one tone,
Claire, Adeline, adorable as the hearts we rhyme
In passionate praises of your souls sublime.

Love and be loved! Dear beings left alone
Since in these days of woe, for evil and good
The glorious stigmata is stained with your pure blood.

Young Girls at School

ONE HAD SIXTEEN YEARS and the other less:
Both of them slept in the same scented room.
It was a September night, the room hid gloom,
And both were equal in their wantonness.
Each has quitted, to show her nakedness,
The fine nightdress that keeps its flesh perfume.
The younger bends, so women bend their womb,
And her sister kisses her breasts that rise to the caress,
Then falls on her knees, then becomes mad and wild,
And all her mouth exultant of that child
Plunges in the grey shadows, that held the night's
Treasures; and the child, beyond all beguiling,
Counts her dene tune as the sense in her invites
The tragedy that is destroyed by sin's defiling.

Spring

THE RED-HAIRED SLENDER GIRL divines
    That such innocence irritates.
    Words to excite the girl she hates
To drink of deeper draughts than wines:

—Sap that rises and declines,
    Childhood has but changing fates!
    Foam like breasts my touch awaits
Where the red rose petal shines.

Let me, where the grass is denser,
Drink the drops of dew that twinkled
Where the dew the flower besprinkled,
So that pleasure be intenser
In thine arms where all the Spring is
As the dawn where the bird's wing is.

Summer

AND THE CHILD REPLIES, one swoon
Under the formidable caresses
Of this mistress she possesses
—Beloved, I am dying soon!

I am dying: what consumes me
Is thy throat where drunkennesses
Sting the flesh and drink my tresses
In thy odour that perfumes me;

It has, thy flesh, no charm of maids
But the heat that gives no wonder,
It has the amber, it has the shades;

The gusty winds make thy voice thunder,
And thy tresses, stained and bloody,
The night whirls around thy body.

In the Manner of Paul Verlaine

IT IS BECAUSE OF THE MIDNIGHT MOON
That I assume this mask nocturnal
And of Saturn's urn and his power infernal
And of moon after moon in the hot mid-noon.

Songs without words have these romances,
That clash in discordant chords together
And hurt my sad soul in dusty weather.
O the shiver and sound of the dancer's dances!

Pardoned are these with their sins acquainted,
Thanks to the fiery sword in the garden:
As for myself I pardon
Not without grace returning painted.

I pardon this lie for its banality
In favour of an immensity of pleasure
Absurd enough in its lack of leisure
And not as sorrowful as Insanity.

To Princess Roukhine

SHE HAD THE SALT OF SIN within her,
    She had no powder in her tresses
    O loved of Venus, one confesses
The stingless beauty of this sinner!

But I believe her mine, she named me
    So, for her tresses and grimaces
    Her heats erotic and her graces
That by all its ends inflamed me.

She is to me more than a rapture
    As a flamboyant pregnant creature
    Before the sacred door, each feature
And all that burning bush my capture!

Who could swear on her salvation
    If not I her priest, whose song surpassed her,
    And her humble slave and her master
Who would endure for her damnation.

This body rare that has no virtue,
    As white as are the reddest roses
    And whiter still than any roses,
Like purple lilies, that can hurt you.

Fair thighs, ripe breasts and what intense is
    In the back, the reins, the belly, none rests there
    Feast for the eyes and the hand that quests there,
And for the mouth and all the senses?

Dear, let us see if still thy bed
    Has under the curtains for my vizard
    The moving pillows of the wizard
And the mad bed clothes—towards thy bed.

False Impression

        LITTLE LADY MOUSE,
        Black upon the grey of light;
        Little lady mouse,
        Grey upon the night.

        Now they ring the bell,
        All good prisoners slumber deep;
        Now they ring the bell,
        Nothing now but sleep.

        Only pleasant dreams,
        Love's enough for thinking of;
        Only pleasant dreams,
        Long live love!

        Moonlight over all,
        Someone snoring heavily;
        Moonlight over all,
        In reality.

Now there comes a cloud,
It is dark as midnight here;
Now there comes a cloud,
Dawn begins to peer.

Little lady mouse,
Rosy in a ray of blue,
Little lady mouse,
Up now, all of you!

The Last Gallant Festival

LET US BE SEPARATED and eternally,
Dear damsels and dear knights after your fashions
Enough of all the tragedy of our passions.
Of our comic pleasures passed infernally.

Let there be no regret and no disaster!
It is so awful to feel our own affinity
With wicked little elves' divinity
Ridiculous as this ridiculous poetaster.

Let us be separated, who knew not what the dark meant.
O that our hearts that for our sins were yearning
After sad Sodom cry for Gomorrah burning
As Sodom did and for our last embarkment!

Explanation

THE LUXURY OF BLEEDING on a heart not mine,
The need of somehow weeping on his breast,
The desire of speaking to him, of our unrest,
The dream of remaining together without design

The woe of hating women furiously,
The satiety of being a machine obscene,
The impure cries of a succubus unclean,
The nightmare of shifting oneself incessantly!

To die for God's sake, leap in hell's abysses,
To die and live on someone's savoury kisses,
And kiss the mouth that lies, that heavens misses!
To live beyond one's torments furious
Of ripe hearts and eyes of mistresses incurious,
And, for the rest, toward what deaths infamous!

Other

THE COURT IS FLOWERING with Cares
That make no sound
On any stairs
Of those who round
As shadows on their thin thigh-bones
The uncircled night
Where walls and stones
Are made with light.

Turn, Samsons without Delila,
No Philistine,
The wheel that, ah!
Grinds Fate and Sin
Thou that art lawless, laughable,
Change turn by turn
Thine hearts, thy hell,
Thy loves that burn!

They go! and their poor slippers' creak
Humiliated,
The pipe in beak,
With sluggish tread.

The cell, if even a word's forgot,
Not even a sigh,
The air's so hot,
One seems to die.

I am one of this Circus scared
Submitted besides
But unprepared
For turns of tides.
Yet have I not failed fatally
That do not know,
Society,
Which way to go?

Come, good old thieves, here none are slaves,
Dear Vagabond,
And dearer knaves,
Our aims beyond
Our very philosophic smoke·
Walk two by two,
Like honest folk:
Nothing to do.

Reversibility

I HEAR THE PUMPS that make
The cry of cats
And other sounds that shake
Like shrieking rats.
Ah, when sadness distils
The alreadys are the stills!

O the vague angelus!
(Whence comes the soul?)
Salvation shines for us
Out of a hole!

Ah, in these dull delays
The nevers are the always!

What dreams that make one throb,
Walls perilous!
And what repeated sob,
Mad, dolorous!
Ah, in those piteous evers,
The Always are the Nevers!

Thou diest suddenly,
In obscurity,
Loving not ardently
Loves that shall come to thee!
Ah, when one's nerve one steadies
The Stills are the Alreadys!

Casta Piana

Thy blue hair mixed with red gives heat,
Thine eyes too hard that are too sweet,
Thy beauty in which beauties swoon
Thy breasts demented, thy breaths scented,
A cruel devil in hell invented,
Thy pallor stolen from the moon.

We have put in all our states,
Notre-Dame of the garrets and gates,
Lighted with candles all surrounding
Thee unblest, and the Aves said
And the angelus for the dead,
Hours unvirginal always sounding.

Certainly thou dost scent the faggot:
Can turn a man into a maggot,
A cypher, a symbol, and a breath,

The time to say or to make yes,
The time of astonished nakedness,
The time to kiss thy shoes to death.

A terrible place, thine own attic:
One takes thee on the heap dramatic
To demolish a certain hideous fellow,
And make decamp the way of scents,
Furnished with all the Sacraments,
Those that think that thy slipper's yellow!

Love me better, thou hast reason,
Than the younger men whose treason
Know not of thy several passions,
I as thou a malefactor,
I who jest as any actor
With a heart full of thy fashions!

Do not frown, no need of frowning,
Casta, when my heart is drowning.
Let me suck in all thy balms,
Piane, peppered, sugared, salted,
And let me drink in thine exalted
Salted, sacred, scented balms.

Prologue of a Book

I AM ONE OF THE THUNDERSTRUCK GODS,
    Certainly not for me a misfortune
    Certainly poetic as one's evil fortune,
Certainly worth the luck of the odds!

One knows woe's price might be an obsession
    One might lose in the act of squandering.
    You shall never know my age, my wandering,
Nor the evil secrets of my heart's confession.

And these sad verses right in their scansion
    Made in prison, for all one's saying,
    Are neither better nor worse than flaying.
May good God keep you from all expansion!

One gives you a book for admonishment.
    Take it for what it is worth, nor number
    My *aegri somnium* nor my bad slumber
Who finds himself here in astonishment.

One puts here, for one's satisfaction,
    All the handwriting that one possesses
    For oneself as oneself confesses
Oneself and one's absolute fascination.

You shall read these verses of no venality,
    As you might read those of another,
    Never oneself is one's own mother,
Nor am I framed for criminality.

One word more, and this an illusion,
    A certain light on eventuality,
    One's luckless luck's actuality:
I am the Slave of my Delusion.

I have lost my life, I have wandered far,
    As for blame and shame, you might ask **a dancer:**
    To all I have said I can give one answer:
I was really born under Saturn's star.

    I would, to slay thee, devastating Time,
    Return again to royal realms of Rhyme,
    And lull to slumber Luxury and Shame
    Lest they should give me the wind's endless **Fame.**
    This hour being fatal I as Tiberius
    Shake with forced laughter, let the imperious
    Sleep if he likes! I dream of some strange jewel
    Worn by a woman as Faustina cruel,
    I dance with in the balls—there let **none delve—**
    At midnight on the sudden stroke of twelve.

Sappho

WITH HOLLOW EYES and breasts rigid, furious,
Sappho, irritated by her supreme desire,
As a she-wolf by the sea runs ravenous.

Dreaming of Phaon, not of her own heart's fire,
She, seeing to this point disdained her caresses
Tears with angry hands at her tragic tresses.

Then unrepentant for herself she evokes
Her passionate desires to satiety,
Where lust turns lust and dies as ardently
In sleeping virgins spirits she invokes:
She lowers her weary eyelids where hill smokes
And leaps into the depths of the Red Sea:
Pale in the sky Silene intolerably
Avenges the Virgins that her madness strokes.

Saturnine Poem

THIS WAS BIZARRE and Satan had laughed at it.
The day's heat had given me intoxication.
What impossible street-singer—none had chaffed at it—
And all she vomited to my vexation!

The very sound had been too much for me
And for no special reason uniquely!
I believe that it might have been a touch for me
As I heard my words change their sense obliquely.

Oblique were certainly my sensations
And I was a prey to fantastic visions.
Refrains of the café-concerte damnations
Falsified by masques and sung in divisions.

To what had the vision in me reverted
As I went wandering in stupid spaces?
Three evil creatures with eyes perverted
Grimaced without end on my grimaces.

I was hooted, there was no joking,
By these urchins, not far from the station,
And I was so gluttonously provoking
That I never thought of my own damnation.

I return: one touches me, one mazes me,
A ghost-like step. Is there none, my Folly?
All night in my ear a voice that crazes me
Ah! the hour that sounds for you, my jolly!

The Unrepenting One

WANDERER JADED, thine eyes faded
Satanic desires desiring, degraded,
Not in any sense a rascal's,
When at passing something gentle,
Hurl a lightning not like Pascal's.

Thy slang hangs, not elemental,
Sharp as spears, not detrimental,
All fruit, all flower, all Galilean,
And thy man's tongue in two fended
Licks thy lips, Epicurean.

Old Faun, spying things intended
Hast thou heightened thine amended
Feature of the four dimensions?
Art thou mad enough to be hated
For thy wicked words' extensions?

What, despite reins dissipated,
This thrashed heart, thine irritated

Sense of luxury's devotion,
Heart and reins and nothing sunny
In thy gizzard's mute emotion?

Sweet as any salted honey,
Diamonds than hell's fires less funny,
Blue as flower, and black with wonder,
Passionate eyes, thine eyes pernicious,
Of all kinds despite of Thunder.

Thy nose pleases thee, O Vicious,
Or else singularly malicious,
Having the force of indications,
Having also, as Ulysses,
Presages and explanations.

Kisses bigger than abysses,
More astringent little kisses
That suck the soul that has no answers,
Fuller kisses much more heating,
Than a flame, than kissing dancers.

Kisses eaten, kisses eating,
Kisses drinking, wines completing,
Kisses languid, kisses frantic,
Thou lovest best, and this admitting
Is it not? Such kisses antic.

Bodies are of thy taste, submitting,
Better upright perhaps than sitting.
Moving where one has to march,
And no matter in what climate,
Pont Saint-Esprit or Pont de-l'Arche.

So that this taste makes them to rhyme at
Verses, perverse, pale, not to climb at,
One must have both youth and passion:
Small strong feet, and no adversity,
Muscular and hairy in the fashion.

Of hair falling, no conversity
So intensely wicked in perversity
As those are, little enough decency,
At least, to make one say: "I'll save her!"
What shadow of indecency?

No, no! You, witness in our favour,
Knowing gods that cannot savour,
That these matters, just for one sense,
Are to make no more illusion
Nor to wander into nonsense.

So things go in some confusion
As the jesters make delusion.
Thou canst laugh at our incenses—
Such as one whose need is pressing
Passes beyond mural defenses.

Thou canst answer, not in blessing,
Weary of the least confessing,
With thy voice by thirst degraded
And that certainly is not seedy:
"What's to do, when one's invaded,

If we are not even needy?"

SELECTED BIBLIOGRAPHY
OF BOOKS IN ENGLISH
ON BAUDELAIRE, RIMBAUD AND VERLAINE

Baudelaire

BAUDELAIRE, CHARLES: *The Letters of Baudelaire,* translated by Arthur Symons; Albert and Charles Boni, New York, 1927.

BENNETT, JOSEPH D.: *Baudelaire: A Criticism;* Princeton University Press, Princeton, N.J., 1944.

ELIOT, T. S.: *For Lancelot Andrewes;* Doubleday, Doran and Co., New York, 1929.

FORD, CHARLES HENRY, editor: *The Mirror of Baudelaire;* New Directions, Norfolk, Conn., 1942.

GILMAN, MARGARET: *Baudelaire, the Critic;* Columbia University Press, New York, 1943.

HUNEKER, JAMES GIBBONS: *Egoists: a book of Supermen;* Charles Scribner's Sons, New York, 1925.

LOVING, PIERRE: *Gardener of Evil;* Brewer and Warren, New York, 1931.

MORGAN, EDWARD: *Flower of Evil, a life of Charles Baudelaire;* Sheed and Ward, New York, 1943.

PORCHÉ, FRANCOIS: *Charles Baudelaire,* translated by John Mavin; H. Liveright, New York, 1928.

QUENNELL, PETER: *Baudelaire and the Symbolists;* Chatto and Windus, London, 1929.

RHODES, S. A.: *The Cult of Beauty in Charles Baudelaire,* 2 vols.; Columbia University, New York, 1929.

SHANKS, LEWIS PIAGET: *Baudelaire: Flesh and Spirit;* Little, Brown and Co., Boston, 1930.

STARKIE, ENID: *Baudelaire;* G. P. Putnam's Sons, New York, 1933.

SYMONS, ARTHUR: *Charles Baudelaire; a study;* E. Mathews, London, 1920.

VALÉRY, PAUL: *Variety: second series,* translated by William Aspenwall Bradley; Harcourt, Brace and Co., New York, 1938.

Rimbaud

CARRÉ, JEAN MARIE: *A Season in Hell: the life of Arthur Rimbaud,* translated by Hannah and Matthew Josephson; The Citadel Press, New York, 1931.

FOWLIE, WALLACE: *Rimbaud;* New Directions, New York, 1946.

RICKWORD, EDGELL: *Rimbaud: the Boy and the Poet;* W. Heinemann Ltd., London, 1924.

STARKIE, ENID: *Arthur Rimbaud;* Faber and Faber, London, 1938.

WILSON, EDMUND: *Axel's Castle;* Charles Scribner's Sons, New York, 1931.

Verlaine

BERTHON, HENRY EDWARD, editor: *Nine French Poets 1820–1880;* Macmillan and Co., London, 1930.

COULON, MARCEL: *Poet under Saturn: the tragedy of Verlaine,* translated by Edgell Rickword; H. Toulmin, London, 1932.

NICOLSON, HAROLD: *Paul Verlaine;* Constable and Co., London, 1921.

ROBERTS, CARL ERIC BECHHOFER: *Paul Verlaine;* Jarrolds, London, 1937.

A Complete Listing of Citadel Underground Books
Published by Carol Publishing Group

Citadel Underground T-Shirt $15.00 Adult
Size Large: (#59900) Extra-Large: (#59901)

Aquarius Revisited: Seven Who Created the Sixties Counterculture That Changed America by Peter O. Whitmer, with Bruce van Wyngarden $10.95 paperback (#51222)

Baudelaire, Rimbaud, Verlaine: Selected Verse and Prose Poems, edited by Joseph M. Bernstein $11.95 paperback (#50196)

Bob Dylan: Portraits From the Singer's Early Years by Daniel Kramer $16.95 paperback (#51224)

Conversations With The Dead: The Grateful Dead Interview Book by David Gans $14.95 paperback (#51223)

Conversations With The Dead Poster by Rick Griffin $8.00 (#59992)

The Crazy Green of Second Avenue, a novel by Erje Ayden $12.95 paperback (#51292)

Famous Long Ago: My Life and Hard Times with the Liberation News Service, at Total Loss Farm and on the Dharma Trail by Ray Mungo $14.95 paperback (#51204)

Growing Up Underground by Jane Alpert $12.95 paperback (#51196)

Gulcher: Post-Rock Cultural Pluralism in America (1649-1993) by Richard Meltzer $9.95 paperback (#51197)

Jambeaux, a novel by Laurence Gonzales $10.95 paperback (#51200)

Johnny Got His Gun, a novel by Dalton Trumbo $9.95 paperback (#51281)

Moving Through Here by Don McNeill $9.95 paperback (#51165)

Negrophobia: An Urban Parable by Darius James $19.95 hardcover (#51293)

The Psychedelic Reader: Classic selections from The Psychedelic Review, the revolutionary 1960s forum of psychopharmalogical substances, edited by Timothy Leary, Ralph Metzner & Gunther M. Weil $12.95 paperback (#51451)

Really The Blues by Mezz Mezzrow & Bernard Wolfe $12.95 paperback (#51205)

Red-Dirt Marijuana and Other Tastes by Terry Southern $9.95 paperback (#51167)

Ringolevio: A Life Played for Keeps by Emmett Grogan $12.95 paperback (#51168)

Rock Folk: Portraits From the Rock 'n' Roll Pantheon by Michael Lydon $9.95 paperback (#51206)

The Second Greatest Story Ever Told, a novel by Gorman Bechard $17.95 hardcover (#51263)

Street Fighting Years: An Autobiography of the Sixties by Tariq Ali $10.95 paperback (#51282)

Tales of Beatnik Glory by Ed Sanders $12.95 paperback (#51172)

Turn It Up (I Can't Hear the Words): The Best of the Singer/Songwriters by Bob Sarlin $12.95 paperback (#51315)

Uncovering the Sixties: The Life and Times of the Underground Press by Abe Peck $12.95 paperback (#51225)

Wanted Man: In Search of Bob Dylan, edited by John Bauldie $9.95 paperback (#51266)

Look for these books at your bookstore. Or to order, call 1-800-447-BOOK (MasterCard or Visa) or send a check or money order for the books purchased, plus $3 shipping and handling for the first book and $.50 for each additional book, to: Citadel Underground, Dept. 196, 120 Enterprise Avenue, Secaucus, NJ 07094.

...or for a free Citadel Underground brochure, write to the address above.